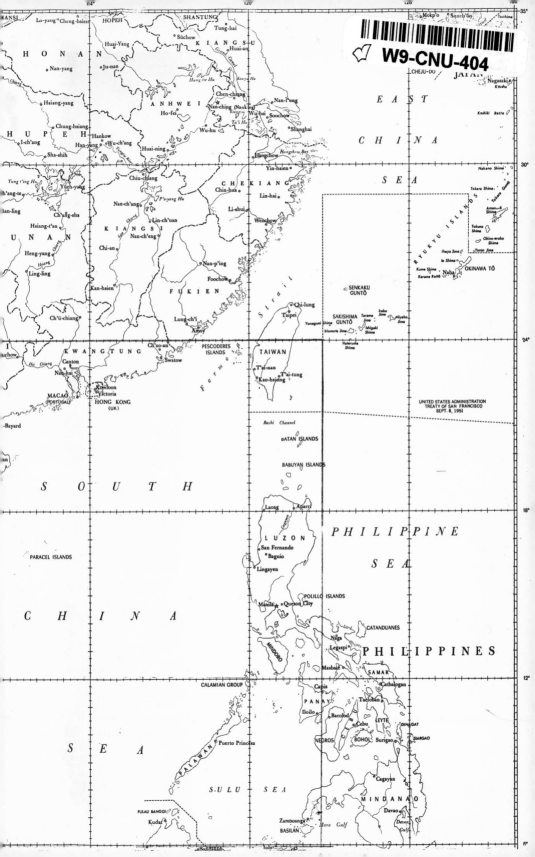

AMERICA ON TRIAL

The War for Vietnam

★ ★ ★

AMERICA ON TRIAL

The War for Vietnam

by GEN. THOMAS A. LANE, USA (Ret.)

Foreword by GEN. A. C. WEDEMEYER, USA (Ret.)

ARLINGTON HOUSE   New Rochelle, N.Y.

Library of Congress Catalog Card Number 73-139889

ISBN 0-87000-103-5

MANUFACTURED IN THE UNITED STATES OF AMERICA

TO JEAN

Contents

★ ★ ★

Foreword

★ ★ ★

America on Trial: The War in Vietnam is certain to create controversy and serious discussion, for it is a hard-hitting, no-holds-barred exposé of the futility of U.S. foreign policies. Without acrimony or bitterness, General Lane portrays his findings with wit and clarity in revealing the sham and political nonsense that have characterized U. S. policies in the Far East throughout the past twenty years. With carefully marshalled and solidly buttressed facts, he tells the inside and outside story of the tragic events that have been so costly in American lives and treasure.

Few people are better qualified to do this, for he served most of his mature life in the United States Army and filled positions of great responsibility in various parts of the world, including Asia. Recently on a trip to the Far East, he held meaningful conversations with local political leaders and foreign diplomats and representatives. On numerous occasions he personally visited active combat areas in Vietnam. This book presents the observations and the considered judgments of a responsible professional military man—not of a newspaper correspondent who, understandably, seeks the dramatic but, not understandably, often distorts the issues.

Why do our so-called friends and former allies continue to provide equipment for the Communists who are now killing our men in Vietnam? What were our missed opportunities and miscalculations concerning developments in the Far East? What happened to the concerted efforts and shared responsibilities for peace clearly stipulated in the charters of the highly touted international organizations—the UN, NATO and SEATO? What contributions have they really made to peace? Why are our American boys called upon to fight, to sacrifice, and even to die under severe handicaps, imposed not by the enemy but as the direct result of past political policies and decisions made on the highest levels? The answers to these vital questions are wholly or in part to be found in this comprehensive analysis of U. S. strategy in the Far East.

It is generally accepted today that a nation should never resort to military force unless and until all other available measures have failed. However, it should be emphasized that when President Kennedy decided to employ strong military pressure, including ground forces, in Southeast Asia, there should have been no vacillation—no halfway measures in the commitment to achieve victory. We would not be experiencing the impasse in which we find ourselves today and from which our present political leaders are courageously attempting to extricate us. The current scheduled withdrawal of U. S. ground forces on a carefully determined basis and the neutralization of the Cambodian sanctuary give promise of an honorable solution in the American tradition.

A. C. WEDEMEYER
General, U. S. Army *(Ret.)*

AUTHOR'S PREFACE

★　　★　　★

The course of national policy may be obscured by propaganda but its direction cannot be hidden from the public view. Cause and effect still prevail. If we reap disaster today, it is because bad leadership set our course yesterday. If a country flourishes, it is because the country has had good leadership.

The action which follows tells us of the policy decision which went before. Policy choices made in 1960 and 1961 ordained the course of the war in Vietnam. Toleration of the North Vietnamese invasion of Laos by President Eisenhower, refusal to oppose that aggression by President Kennedy, denial of South Vietnam's right to counterattack North Vietnamese aggression waged from Laos, limitation of the battlefield to South Vietnam —all these critical errors were known at the time the decisions were taken.

The decisions were said to promote peace and limit the war. They had, predictably, the opposite effect. But neither the opposition party nor the press exposed and condemned the policy errors. The people had no advocate of sound policy to sound the alarm. Our political system had broken down.

We have had some revelation by advisers of Presidents Kennedy and Johnson of the Presidential decisions which thrust us into the catastrophe of war in Vietnam. What stands revealed is not some insuperable obstacle to the maintenance of peace but the inadequacy of individuals in the highest policy-making ranks of government. The political structure of the country brings to positions of power individuals ill-prepared for the responsibilities of world leadership. The prevailing utopianism of American political thought is a barrier to realistic perception of the national interest.

Nowhere is this inadequacy of personal competence more striking than in United States relations with Great Britain. In diplomacy, in military affairs, in economic analysis—in every facet of foreign policy, British representatives have shown a capacity to bend American policy to serve British interests. The illusion of partnership, the premise of a common interest where none exists, the mythology of superior British experience all combine to render American leaders incapable of sustaining any policy which Britain opposes. Among our Secretaries of State since World War II, only John Foster Dulles was capable of maintaining an American foreign policy.

We cannot reach responsible relationships with other allies because these commitments are subordinated to conflicting British interests. British influence reduces our treaties to scraps of paper. Our power is expended in futile gesturing which neither friend nor enemy can respect.

We reap in this relationship that harvest of disaster of which President George Washington warned in his Farewell Address:

"Observe good faith and justice toward all nations. Cultivate peace and harmony with all. Religion and morality enjoin this conduct. And can it be that good policy does not equally enjoin it? It will be worthy of a free, enlightened, and at no distant period a great nation to give mankind the magnanimous and too novel example of a people always guided by an exalted justice and benevolence. Who can doubt that in the course of time and things the fruits of such a plan would richly repay any temporary advantages which might be lost by a steady adherence to it? Can it be that Providence has not connected the permanent felicity of a nation to its virtue? The experiment, at least, is recommended by every sentiment which ennobles human nature. Alas! is it rendered impossible by its vices?

"In the execution of such a plan nothing is more essential than that permanent, inveterate antipathies against particular nations and passionate attachments for others should be excluded, and that in place of them just and amicable feelings toward all should be cultivated. The nation which indulges toward another an habitual hatred or an habitual fondness is in some degree a slave. It is a slave to its animosity or to its affection, either of which is sufficient to lead it astray from its duty and its interest. Antipathy in one nation against another disposes each more readily to offer insult and injury, to lay hold of slight causes of umbrage, and to be haughty and intractable when accidental or trifling occasions of dispute occur.

"So, likewise, a passionate attachment of one nation for another produces a variety of evils. Sympathy for the favorite nation, facilitating the illusion of an imaginary common interest in cases where no real common interest exists, and infusing into one the enmity of the other, betrays the former into a participation in the quarrels and wars of the latter without adequate inducement or justification. It leads also to concessions to the favorite nation of privileges denied to others, which is apt doubly to injure the nation making the concessions by unnecessarily parting with what ought to have been retained, and by exciting jealousy, ill will, and a disposition to retaliate in the parties from whom equal privileges are withheld; and it gives to ambitious, corrupted, or deluded citizens (who devote themselves to the favorite nation) facility to betray or sacrifice the interests of their own country without odium, sometimes even with popularity, gilding with the appearances of a virtuous sense of obligation, a commendable deference for public opinion, or a laudable zeal for public good the base or foolish compliances of ambition, corruption, or infatuation. . . .

"Against the insidious wiles of foreign influence (I conjure you to believe me, fellow-citizens) the jealousy of a free people ought to be constantly awake, since history and experience prove that foreign influence is one of the most baneful foes of republican government. But that jealousy, to be useful, must be impartial, else it becomes the instrument of the very influence to be avoided, instead of a defense against it. Excessive partiality for one foreign nation and excessive dislike of another cause those whom they actuate to see danger only on one side, and serve to veil and even second the arts of influence on the other. Real patriots who may resist the intrigues of the favorite are liable to become suspected and odious, while its tools and dupes usurp the applause and confidence of the people to surrender their interests.

"The great rule of conduct for us in regard to foreign nations is, in extending our commercial relations to have with them as little political connection as possible. So far as we have already formed engagements let them be fulfilled with perfect good faith. Here let us stop."

Our first President foresaw the mistakes which we make today. Our favorite ally has been decisive in shaping American war policy in Korea and in Vietnam. That policy has served British interests but it cannot be reconciled with any rational concept of the United States interest.

America is on trial. It stands indicted for giving inept leadership to its own people and to the Free World.

THOMAS A. LANE
McLean, Va.
January 5, 1971

ABBREVIATIONS USED

★　　　★　　　★

ARVN——Army of Vietnam
DMZ——Demilitarized Zone
GVN——Government of Vietnam
JCS——Joint Chiefs of Staff
MACV——Military Assistance Command, Vietnam
NVA——North Vietnamese Army
NVN——North Vietnam
ROK——Republic of Korea
RVN——Republic of Vietnam
SVN——South Vietnam
TET——Chinese New Year

AMERICA ON TRIAL

The War for Vietnam

I
THE CURIOUS WAR

★ ★ ★

THE WAR FOR VIETNAM HAS ITS ROOTS IN THE SUCCESS-
ful Bolshevik counter-revolution of 1918. That triumph of Lenin gave new strength and hope to other revolutionary movements throughout the world. It also established a powerful base
with vast resources from which to wage the Communist war
for the world.

Lenin's success sparked a rash of subversive and revolutionary operations around the world. In Hungary, Bela Kun had a
short-lived success. In China, Sun Yat-sen was momentarily
influenced by the Bolshevik philosophy. In other countries of
the West, Communist thrusts for power were suppressed. The
world revolution settled down to its task of subversion, guided
and supported by the Kremlin.

In the ordinary course of history, it could have been an-
ticipated that Vietnam would recover its independence by mid-
century. The western empires of the nineteenth century had a
role to play in spreading modern technology into the remote
areas of a world loosed from the grasp of static cultures. But the
colonial masters had, in their concepts of personal worth and
liberty, the seeds of the colonial dissolution. It was inevitable
that the subject nations would, in absorbing Western ideas of

freedom, insist upon their own independence.

Because the Vietnamese people are highly intelligent and cultured, they needed only exposure to modern science to master it. Their early independence was assured.

But then, unhappily, Vietnam was caught up in the world Communist revolution. Through the political skill and shrewd initiatives of Nguyen Ai Quoc, creator of the Indochinese Communist Party, through the absence of responsible authority following the defeat of Japan in 1945, and through the ineptitude of French administration following World War II, the independence movement of Vietnam was divided. Some Vietnamese dedicated to the goal of liberation from French rule remained in the Viet Minh front even after Ho Chi Minh (his new name) liquidated the non-Communist leadership. Other Vietnamese recognized that a Viet Minh success would saddle the country with a Communist imperialism more hateful and oppressive than the French rule. These Vietnamese fought against the Viet Minh with a purpose of achieving independence in freedom.

Through the years, the war for Vietnam has drawn into its orbit the major powers of the world. Stalin directed and supported the Communist effort from the beginning. After his triumph in China in 1949, Mao Tse-tung gave new support to the Viet Minh. Harry Truman gave military aid to France and Vietnam. Dwight Eisenhower assumed the primary support role for the new government of South Vietnam after the partition of the country in 1954 and the expulsion of the French military mission.

At first the American support produced favorable results. South Vietnam enjoyed some years of peace and growing prosperity before the Communist program of village assassinations was mounted in 1957. Even then, governmental authority was firmly administered and widely respected in South Vietnam until the assault on the country was mounted from Laos in 1961.

President Kennedy faced a steadily eroding situation. His illusions about peace-making cracked up on the hard rock of Nikita Khrushchev's realism.

President Johnson inherited a condition of chaos in which the Communists were rapidly extending their control of the countryside. He fought a deepening war of attrition with diminishing popular support until he accepted defeat after the Tet Offensive of 1968 and sued for peace.

Hanoi was not granting peace: it was demanding surrender. But American public opinion would not support surrender, so Lyndon Johnson hobbled along with bombing pauses to create an illusion of progress. His party lost the 1968 election despite these initiatives.

President Nixon embarked on a squeeze play. With peace negotiations producing nothing, he had to have another program. He embraced the "Vietnamization" inaugurated by Clark Clifford, President Johnson's Secretary of Defense. The plan was to arm and equip South Vietnamese forces to replace American combat troops. It was expected that the reduction of U. S. combat casualties would reduce domestic dissent about the war to politically tolerable levels and would concurrently soften the world image of the powerful United States waging war against little North Vietnam. It might allay public concern until after the 1970 congressional elections.

That a reduction of U. S. combat participation in the war would probably produce the cited effects was credible. That the substitution of South Vietnamese for U. S. combat forces would of itself enable the South to defeat the aggression was not credible. So the problem of defending free countries against Communist aggression remained unsolved.

Through the tragic years of its continuance, the war for Vietnam has become a focus of the confrontation between communism and freedom. Its prosecution has illustrated the strengths and weaknesses, the ambitions and illusions, the methods and stratagems of both sides. In this war, the full gamut of human error has had its play, carefully concealed by political propaganda.

The United States marched into the new decade of the Seventies in a state of shock enduring from the psychotic decade of the Sixties. It was not Vietnam alone but the continuing tension of the Communist confrontation which had undermined its ethic and its self-confidence, and left it blundering along in an epic war hardly comprehended.

Picture the spectacle of the most powerful nation in the world frustrated by tiny North Vietnam! The United States had set out to protect its ally, South Vietnam, from Communist aggression. It had failed and had withdrawn from the battlefield, leaving the task to its ally, South Vietnam. As Hamish Fraser wrote from Scotland in *Approaches:* "And now Richard Nixon . . . valiantly summons the mightiest nation in the world to steel itself for a rout which makes even Caporetto seem an epic of military prowess."

War is primarily an intellectual struggle. Power can do only what the mind can conceive. If fear or illusion closes off the avenues of effective action for peace, leaders are left with only the alternatives which lead to endless, desultory war and eventual defeat.

In broad perspective, this was the course taken by the United States in the Sixties. Its leaders refused to face up to the reality of Communist goals and strategy. They rejected the alternative of honest confrontation and resolute adherence to their own principles. They ascribed to the Communist leadership an interest in world peace and security which did not in fact exist. Then they plotted a course of action founded on these illusory premises. How could such denial of reason produce anything but the disasters of the Sixties!

We saw American cities burned by their own residents. Our public officials restrained the police while criminals plundered urban stores and shops, and thereby encouraged revolutionary cadres to foment the destructive riots. The American mind had first been paralyzed by the rationalization of crime as a product of poverty before it abandoned long-established principles of law enforcement. This was one phase of the war.

In a time of unprecedented economic prosperity and full employment, the country exhibited a pathological concern about its poverty. Of course there was food and shelter for all. But politicians reaching for power recruited a formidable following by drawing the poverty line at a $3,000 annual income for a family of four. They didn't then have the nerve to set the line at $5,500.

American industry continued its powerful strides, performing in this decade the miracle of the moon landings. Were these and other magnificent achievements hailed as works of the most productive economic organization the world has ever known? No, indeed. Our youth were alienated from American industry, taught the lies of socialist philosophy by know-nothing professors breathing their inanities on hapless students. These too were symptoms of the intellectual struggle and of our defeat.

On the military front, our political leaders disavowed any intent to win the war in Vietnam. They just wanted the North Vietnamese to stop the aggression and go home. They feared that a military counteroffensive against enemy forces in Laos, Cambodia and North Vietnam would bring Red China into the war. So they fought on in South Vietnam in a war which ravaged the country and sacrificed the population of our ally, a war without end. The spectacle of the United States of America, commanding as it did vastly superior power, paralyzed by fear of North Vietnam and Red China, recalls the serum which makes a tomcat fearful of a mouse. The same psychosis can be induced in men through diplomacy.

Though our fighting men have won every battle, our political leaders are defeated. They have renounced victory and so must embrace defeat. To explain their policies, politicians advance the most outlandish claims. Some assert that the United States cannot win this war. They say that guerrilla warfare cannot be defeated by conventional war-making, a piece of ignorant nonsense. Now they have us retreating toward victory!

What has happened to our generals? How can they rationalize a war which wastes the youth, the wealth and the prestige of the country in futile combat? What has brought them to acquiesce in defeat?

Aware of the intellectual nature of the issue, Soviet leaders have mobilized the propaganda resources of the socialist world to engage in the struggle. Their minions are active not only behind the Iron Curtain, where the struggle of North Vietnam is exalted as the focus of class warfare, but in every country of the Free World. Soviet agents and sympathizers use the freedom of the West to attack and discredit the defense of the West. Because the socialist ideology reaches into powerful political elements of the Free World, it is not difficult for Soviet polemicists to depict the war as a violation of democratic principle.

The movement against the war culminated in the Moratorium Days of October and November, 1969. Under the veneer of a march for peace, the hard-core Marxists mounted public displays to mislead the people and intimidate the government. Some people were misled by the lie that such marches could advance the cause of peace. Others anxious to avoid a confrontation between the revolutionary left and the police sought to endow the occasions with an aura of respectability.

In the black wards of our big cities, Black Panthers prepared for the class warfare. They assembled caches of arms and ammunition, trained leaders for the planned violence, indoctrinated black youth with a hatred of the United States as the bastion of capitalist imperialism. This too was a facet of the war for Vietnam. Soviet strategists knew that the military power of the United States was invincible but that the national will was vulnerable.

To spread domestic disaffection and accelerate recruiting among the proleteriat, the war resisters blamed the war for prevalent poverty. They alleged that the war was diverting to Vietnam resources which should have been applied to domestic social problems. Many of the black leaders took up the cry against the war on this score. White political leaders, too, used this complaint against the war.

Against these pressures of an aggressive enemy, the American political system performed pathetically. It moved instinctively for compromise, for accommodation, for capitulation.

Paternalism is the eternal enemy of human freedom, and it is the everyday currency of politics. The father image is the symbol of the successful politician. He could do more for the people if only he had the power, the authority, the money. In time he acquires all power, all authority, all money. Then the citizen is a slave, as he is in the Soviet Union.

In our American political system, the public official is the servant. But it is difficult—perhaps impossible—to keep him from assuming the father role. We have not adequately impressed on the minds of our people the vital importance of relating the father image to the citizen, the servant image to public officials. Consequently we have seen in the decade of the Sixties a sharp change in the character of American government. In this period, the Democratic Party, guided by its socialist theoreticians and instrumented through its control of the legislature, the executive and the judiciary, moved boldly to extend the federal power. In its 1964 platform, the Democratic Party dared to assert that the federal government should assume state powers which the states failed (in the judgment of the Party) to exercise. *That* for the Constitution!

The Supreme Court moved in full harmony with the central government to diminish state authority and extend the federal realm. Through its decisions, the federal powers were extended to reach the personal and local behavior of citizens, a realm from which the Constitution had carefully excluded the federal authority. In consequence, the central government became a reservoir of paternalism and demogogy. No ache or pain of any citizen anywhere in the country was excluded from the concern of a profligate Congress.

An early casualty was the dollar. We saw it rejected in corners of the earth where it had once been prized. The currency was demonetized. Silver was withdrawn from circulation. Gold backing of the currency was voided. Now the dollar bore only the good faith and credit of the federal government; and the deficit financing practiced by the Congress put that value in question.

The Republican Party regarded this scene from the sidelines during the Sixties. It lacked the vision and the courage to challenge Democratic error. It was in reality committed to the same political premises which controlled Democratic policy. It could only wait like a jackal for the Democratic Party to strangle on its own corrupt administration and hope then to win the presidential office.

The country lived through the Sixties without an opposition party. There was no organized political force capable of opposing the prevailing error. Organized labor and civil rights activities had their own axes to grind. The great financial interests of the country were content with the reigning political philosophy.

Television emerged as a new political force in the decade; but it existed in hidebound adherence to ritual liberalism and to sensationalism. The news media became a mouthpiece for the federal government, conveying to the people the self-serving propaganda of federal bureaucrats. Even as they condemned conformity, the liberal intelligentsia practiced it religiously.

The confusion of intellectuals who could not comprehend the nature of the war they were in was aptly described by Douglas Pike, who had served as a junior officer in the United States Information Agency in Saigon:

> Vietnam was a Kafka-like nightmare to anyone seeking facts. Even simple data, the population of a province, for example, were unobtainable. Beyond simply the dearth of statistics lay the domain of obfuscated information, or what Marshal Foch called "the fog war." One came to believe that the struggle in Vietnam had many faces, all of them false. The falsehoods consisted on the one hand of nontruths born of the events themselves: the partial account, the uncertain rumor, the contradictory report. When an event took place, an assassination, for example, immediately there was spun around it like a cocoon around a silk worm larva, an involved thread of interpretation. Those remote from the events, say, in the United States, were never able to separate fact from speculation and after a period even the eyewitness in Vietnam began to doubt his memory. On the other hand there was that honest misperception or misinterpretation, the result of conflicting patterns of thought held by persons, each conditioned by his own peculiar national psychological frame

of reference and moving from his own peculiar national psychological base. One despaired of ever learning the truth, much less the Truth.[1]

What do all these considerations have to do with the war for Vietnam? Everything! They are the heart of the matter. Just as the skill and conditioning of a prize fighter will determine his performance in the ring, so the health—especially the mental health—of a nation will determine its performance in war.

War is not measured alone by the clash of the men and weapons on the battlefield. War is a conflict of nations and its outcome is determined by the wisdom and skill which the two sides bring to the struggle. A nation which has the power to win a quick victory and restore peace may renounce victory and choose instead to fight a prolonged war. If its vision is clouded with illusion, if its resolution is weakened by fear, it may make the choice unwittingly in the misguided belief that it has acted wisely.

We are therefore concerned in our assessment of war not alone with the battlefield but with the philosophy and wisdom of the participants, with the intellectual and moral contest which conditions the battlefield.

The war for Vietnam has provided a magnificent display of ranging human error and wisdom. Only when a great power is falling into decadence does history furnish such an exhibition. Because of its power, the great nation can indulge error and suffer losses which for a lesser power would be fatal.

It staggers on, bereft of vision and courage, adhering to its misconceptions, wasting its strength and its prestige, until the barbarians are at last emboldened to attack.

That was the course of Imperial Rome. There were interludes when emperors of great vision and courage seemed on the verge of reviving the ancient virtues of Rome. But these interludes were short-lived and they occurred with decreasing frequency. As the whole nation drifted from its ancient virtues into a growing corruption, no human force could stem the decay. Rome was dying.

The condition of a sick civilization is revealed in the quality of its leadership. Demagogues empty of concern for the public welfare and seeking only to humor the public fancy are lifted to high office. Lacking vision and wisdom and courage, they are influenced by the strictures of expediency. They face the barbarians in fear and trembling. They fumble and retreat, forever rationalizing cowardice as prudence.

When, in the spring of 1970, President Nixon at long last launched an attack against the Cambodian sanctuaries, American liberals raised a new clamor of criticism. It had so long been an article of their faith that an attack on the sanctuaries would expand the war that they could not view the event rationally. Disregarding the significant political and military achievements of the action, they deplored the consequences they feared, the events which never happened.

Vietnam is a curious war, a baffling war, only to those who take the protestations of political leaders at face value. If this classification embraces most of the people of the Free World, that is because our demagogues have so skilfully concealed from the people the true nature of the conflict. The mystification of the people measures the success of politicians and the decline of civilization.

II THE VIETNAMESE PEOPLE

★   ★   ★

THE VIETNAMESE ARE A FIGHTING PEOPLE. THEIR HIS-
tory covers centuries of struggle against Chinese overlordship.
Sometimes the Vietnamese were successful and enjoyed periods of independence. At other times they were for long periods
under Chinese suzerainty.

Their kings were fighting kings, men who established dynas-
ties by their skill in war and in government. Their heroes are
men who led the people in the continual wars for independence. It is this history and character which explains the
tenacity of their fight for independence, the patience with
which they endure sacrifice even when hopes are faint.

In the dim light of tradition, it is believed that the Viet people
lived originally in the lower valley of the Yangtse River in
South China. About the third Century B. C. they were forced
from their homeland by more powerful Chinese tribes. They
trekked across the Himalaya Mountains into the fertile valley
of the Red River where they seized lands from the Kingdom of
Champa. In succeeding centuries they expanded to the South
against the Kingdom of Champa and the Kingdom of Cambodia
until by 1714 their empire extended from China to the Gulf of
Thailand.

In 1792, Nguyen Anh, ruler in the far south of the country, used the assistance of Monsignor Pigneau de Behaine, Bishop of Adran, to modernize his army and extend his rule throughout the country. He became the Emperor Gia Long.

The last Chinese occupation of the country had ended in 1428 in consequence of rebellion led by Le Loi, founder of the Le Dynasty. Four hundred and thirty years later, the approach of a new overlordship was sounded when a French naval flotilla moved into the port of Tourane (Danang) and seized the city. This was the French response to the Court at Hue, which had refused a French request for establishment of a consulate in Tourane.

In 1861, the French seized Saigon. In 1868 they annexed Cochin China in the south as a colony. In 1883, they extended their dominion to Annam in Central Vietnam and to Tonkin in the north.

The French exercised a direct control of government in Cochin China and Tonkin but allowed the Emperor a nominal rule over Annam. Cochin China and Tonkin sent representatives to the French Chamber of Deputies. Dual citizenship in France and Vietnam was offered Vietnamese who by talent or wealth or position qualified for the distinction.

The dominant religious influence on the Vietnamese people came from China. Confucian precepts guided the people. The concept of an ordered human structure in harmony with nature gave every man his rights and duties in society. The family hierarchy was the tree of life. Ancestors were honored in formal rites.

For many Vietnamese, the worship of Buddha was in full harmony with their Confucian precepts. The Buddhist temple became a supplement to the home altar. Buddhist religious practice became an important element of national culture, though it operated without formal national organization until 1963.

Taoism too was absorbed into the national religious culture and harmonized with the basic precepts of the Confucian ethic. In general, the people of Vietnam have shown a toleration of any religious practice which did not threaten the existing imperial authority.

Two important sects native to the country have substantial followings. The Cao Dai is a reform Buddhist sect which has incorporated into its doctrine and practice elements of Taoism, Confucianism and Christianity. It originated in the Delta and now has about one million adherents.

The Hoa Hao is another reform Buddhist sect which had its origins in the Mekong Delta. It was founded in 1939 by Huynh Phu So. He stressed the importance of spiritual development and prayer. He limited prayer to Buddha, ancestors and national heroes.

Both the Cao Dai and the Hoa Hao entered into politics and became important factors in the national scene. Huynh Phu So is believed to have been ambushed and killed by the Viet Minh. Both sects have divided into rival factions.

With the establishment of French hegemony, and the advent of French education, the Christian religion gained new prestige in the country. With the best schools French-based, the elite of the country tended to be French-educated.

As the French governments of the period were generally anti-clerical, the Christian churches were accorded no special privileges. But their schools provided the training so essential for service in a French administration and therefore had the privilege of educating the most promising youth of the country. In consequence of this association and the selfless example of the Christian missionaries, some 7 percent of the population was converted to the Christian faith before independence.

Until the advent of French hegemony, education in Vietnam followed the Confucian model. The Chinese script was used. Education was designed for the public servants and scholars required to serve the state. Elementary education centered in the Confucian classics was given in the villages of the country. Examination of candidates for higher education was held in the provinces and finally at the capital city of Hue. Candidates received awards and positions in the governmental hierarchy according to their performance in the examinations.

With the introduction of romanized script and the printing press in the latter part of the Nineteenth Century, the spread of education to the masses became possible. The French introduced schools on the French model for education from elementary to university levels and sought to standardize instruction. Many Vietnamese went to France for advanced degrees.

Since the advent of independence, education has been a chief concern of government. Compulsory free education for all children from ages 6 to 11 is prescribed by law. About one-third of elementary schools and two-thirds of secondary schools are private institutions. They operate under the supervision of the Ministry of Education and often with governmental assistance.

About 75 percent of the people are engaged in agricultural work. Rice growing is the chief activity but rubber and tea also are export crops. In addition, a wide variety of tropical products is produced on a smaller scale. Dalat is a center of vegetable production. Light industry is engaged in processing agricultural and forest products and in some manufacturing. Coal and salt are mined. Exploration for oil and for mineral ores is being made.

We see then a people tough and resilient, living close to nature. They are disciplined by a Confucian tradition, moderated by the intrusion of Western culture, while the cities display the cosmopolitan diversity and confusion of voices so typical of modern urban societies.

Because they have so recently been subject to great-power domination, the people are fiercely devoted to their own independence. They have suffered the agony of protracted war with patience and perseverance.

III THE COLONIAL LEGACY

★   ★   ★

THE FEVER OF EXPLORATION AND COLONIZATION EX-
cited by the Renaissance in Europe was directed chiefly to the
new American continents and to the west coast of Africa. In the
Sixteenth Century some adventurers and missionaries reached
out to the closed societies of the Far East. In 1615, the first
Christian missionaries arrived in Danang.

The foreign presence was tolerated or not according to the
whims or judgments of succeeding emperors. Some of the people were converted to the Christian faith and suffered periods
of oppression. But the foreign presence was never large or powerful until the new colonialism of the Nineteenth Century
breached the closed societies of the East.

The competition for markets and resources sent European
rulers of the late Nineteenth and early Twentieth Centuries
searching the world for new conquests. In their era of industri-
alization, they had unlocked many of the secrets of nature and
had developed powerful armaments. The ancient arms of the
East were no match for Western weapons. Submission was the
only prudent response.

The new colonialism was not based on colonization. It was an
export of management for the organization of the more primi-

tive societies, for the introduction of new products, for the development of agriculture and industry. These projects and investments required for their success the security which could be assured by the intervening Western state.

This new colonialism shattered the ancient culture of the closed societies. Although the Western powers were interested primarily in economic development and did not interfere in social and religious customs compatible with the new order, the very presence of the foreign power was a shock to the ancient order. Moreover, the wonders of power and machinery developed in the West could not fail to excite the interest of the Eastern scholars and diplomats.

This colonialism brought great benefit to the Eastern peoples in opening to them vistas of modern science and technology. (It also brought to the subject lands a culture of personal worth and freedom which would destroy colonialism.) Against these benefits, the consciousness of superior power and knowledge could not fail to implant in colonial administrators a sense of superiority. This was to be a subtle poison which would end, in due time, in the administrators' doubting the capacity of the subject people to rule their own country.

At the same time the political example of Western freedom, of rule by the people, would inevitably create in the people governed a conviction of their own right to self-government. Colonialism was consuming itself.

Between 1858 and 1884, France moved in successive steps to occupy Tourane, to occupy Saigon, to occupy Hanoi and to establish hegemony over Cambodia. In 1893, France extended its rule to Laos to complete its protectorate of French Indochina. Also in 1893, the Emperor Ham Nghi revolted against French rule and was subdued. The French presence was firmly established.

As the French brought new economic development to the country, they created new elites of the Vietnamese population serving the French administration, sharing in the economic development, building new fortunes. Some entered the officer corps of the French military services, receiving their higher education in France. Some became millionnaires.

Adjusting to the mutual advantages of scientific and economic progress, the colonial relationship passed through an era of development in which the underground of rebellious dissent was subordinated to cooperation. The new Marxism of the wobblies was reaching out in all lands, but with only minor influence in the colonial areas.

The ascendancy of Lenin in Russia and the creation of the Union of Soviet Socialist Republics gave new impetus to the revolutionary fervor. In the Twenties the young revolutionary Nguyen Ai Quoc, son of a disaffected minor official of the Imperial Government, later to become the venerable Ho Chi Minh, established his leadership of the Communist cause in French Indochina.

Nguyen Ai Quoc had shipped out for France in 1911. After two years at sea he worked as a kitchen helper in the Carlton Hotel in London until 1917. He then went to France where he became active in the Socialist Party and finally in the Communist Party. He was sent to Moscow in 1924 and 1925 for advanced training. He returned to Vietnam to organize the Association of Vietnamese Youth in 1925 and the Indochinese Communist Party in 1932. In 1927 he stated his purpose: "I intend to form an Indochinese national revolutionary movement, whose leaders will bring its members step by step to orthodox communism."

The quick French collapse in the West in World War II destroyed the image of France as the invincible overlord. During the war, while the Vichy Government continued to administer French Indochina, the Japanese were the new overlords directing the French Administration. This ascendancy of an Asian power gave new impetus to the revolutionary cause and to the expectation of independence.

In this twilight period of World War II, the allies fought the Japanese in China, in India and Burma, in the Pacific Islands. Indochina was a backwater area remote from the march of war.

Early in the war, Nguyen Ai Quoc was sent to South China to

work for the organization of a Communist underground. He had previously lived in China and spoke the language fluently. In 1941, he assembled a few of his fellow Vietnamese exiles to organize the Viet Minh Front of National Liberation. Posing as a patriot whose only purpose was to liberate his country from the Japanese conquest, he adopted the pseudonym of Ho Chi Minh. He received the support of the Chinese Government, the American Office of Strategic Services and British Intelligence. He established a network of informers in French Indochina to gather information on the Japanese forces which he could furnish to the Allies.

When the war ended, Ho was first with the most in Vietnam. His organizational work during the war had built his own Communist underground which could now support his seizure of power. On September 2, 1945, as General Douglas MacArthur was receiving the Japanese surrender on the battleship *Missouri* in Tokyo Bay, Ho Chi Minh proclaimed in Hanoi the establishment of the Democratic Republic of Vietnam with himself as president.

The effort of Ho's lieutenants to seize power in the South was short-lived. British forces designated to receive the Japanese surrender moved in quickly and dispersed the Viet Minh provisional government in Saigon. French forces followed to restore French rule.

In the North, where the Chinese were designated to receive the Japanese surrender, Ho Chi Minh was more successful. Without conflict with the Chinese forces, he proceeded to build his own government.

In November he dissolved the Indochinese Communist Party and operated with the same men through the Viet Minh United Nationalist Front. In January 1946, Ho held elections for a National Assembly of 444 seats, which was of course dominated by his Viet Minh delegates. The Assembly met in March.

On March 6, 1946, as it prepared to succeed the departing Chinese occupation forces in the North, France negotiated with Ho Chi Minh on recognition of Vietnam as a free state within the French Union. The status of South and Central Vietnam would be determined by separate referenda. The Viet Minh would not oppose the return of French troops to the north. France would station 15,000 troops there, the numbers to be gradually reduced.

Ho's negotiations with the French continued through the summer and fall of 1946. This was a period of turmoil in France, too, as the people strove to establish a new postwar government. In October, France adopted a constitution which made no provision for independent states within the French Union. In November, the Democratic Republic of Vietnam adopted a new constitution which made no reference to French hegemony. As negotiations broke down, Ho Chi Minh, who had been assiduously building his military strength, struck at the French. On December 19, 1946, he ordered a general offensive against the French in North and Central Vietnam. The war was on.

In the hindsight of later years, some critics have belabored the French for not supporting Ho Chi Minh in Vietnam and allowing him to build a Titoist, if Communist, regime in the country. According to this view, Ho was a nationalist who would have maintained his independence against any encroachment from Red China or the Soviet Union. Sometimes the hindsight is more obscure than the foresight.

Americans familiar with the fatherly image affected by Ho Chi Minh and ignorant of his life story were readily deceived about his designs. Ho used nationalism as a tool in establishing communism. But in 1945 he relentlessly exterminated other nationalists who might have challenged his leadership of the Viet Minh movement. His long and faithful service as an agent of the Cominterm should have warned anyone familiar with his record against the dangers of wishful thinking.

Ho Chi Minh was without question a remarkably shrewd and ruthless leader. He long maintained the posture of an earnest nationalist in his dealings with French governments and effectively exploited their socialist predilections. He served the French colonial administration by betraying to it other leaders of the independence movement, thereby earning income and trust from the French administrators while he disposed of non-Communist competitors.

In the North, Ho exploited his opportunities to build his power until the French returned. Then, when he could no longer maintain his public position against the superior French military forces, he moved into guerrilla warfare.

IV

THE DEFEAT OF FRANCE

★ ★ ★

THE FRENCH FAILURE IN VIETNAM MUST BE CHARGED not to its neglect of Ho Chi Minh but to its rejection of the aspirations of the Vietnamese people. That rejection had varied roots and disastrous consequences.

After the experience of its own occupation by a victorious German Army, France was not disposed in the hour of ultimate victory to shed any of its dominions. All pressure upon the provisional government of General de Gaulle was for the reconstitution of empire. In the new government under a new constitution, this influence continued powerful.

Moreover, the Communist domination of the Viet Minh movement, and the threat which the movement posed to the whole structure of French investment and influence in the country, sparked a clamorous opposition from the entire French and French-influenced elites of the country. For the prosperous Vietnamese no less than the French merchant, the threat was to his life. The French Governor General, living close to these elites, shared their concern. It was natural to respond to the Communist attacks with resistance.

There was also the factor, though its importance is difficult to assess, of doubt about the capacity of the Vietnamese to rule themselves. After sixty years of French rule, a French ruling class had been established. However competent and friendly individual Vietnamese might be, the prospect of turning over to a Vietnamese government complete political control over all French investments and citizens in the country must have caused nightmares to French officials.

For these and other reasons, France failed to take the one course which could have enhanced its investments in the country by winning the cooperation of a people destined inevitably to be free. By offering Vietnam complete independence, by setting up responsible government through due process of law, by supervising and protecting a free government in its initial stages of operation, France could have established a free, friendly and non-Communist government in Vietnam.

Some will demur that there was no non-Communist organization to fulfill such a role in the country. It will be said that Ho Chi Minh was so popular, no other leader could command the support of the people. But that opinion does not bear analysis.

It is true that Ho Chi Minh, virtually unknown to the people of Vietnam before the war, built up his prestige after the war. He did this by fighting the French overlords and offering himself as a rallying point for all Vietnamese who prized freedom. In a very real sense, Ho Chi Minh was made into a significant public figure by the attempt of France to re-establish colonial rule in Vietnam.

By mid-1946, when France had re-established its military presence in both Hanoi and Saigon, Ho Chi Minh had been unmasked. His earlier pose as a nationalist leader had been destroyed by his liquidation of the non-Communist leadership of the Viet Minh movement. An alert French intelligence no doubt knew of the tensions within the movement. A wise French policy would have moved, not to draw the non-Communist elements to the support of France, but to commit France to the non-Communist independence movement. Perhaps the French governments of the period were too riddled with Communist influence ever to draw such a distinction.

France tried instead to restore the Emperor Bao Dai as a puppet ruler. It declared war against communism. It divided the Vietnamese people. Some joined Ho Chi Minh in the belief that only Ho offered an avenue to freedom. Others supported the government in the belief that communism was worse than French rule and that independence could be obtained only from France. So the tragic war continued, fueled by the inertia and obtuseness of French policy.

At first, the forces of Ho Chi Minh were outgunned by the French military formations. There was nothing Ho could do but retire to the countryside and build his organization. From 1945 to 1947, the Viet Minh movement was in a quiescent stage, preparing for future operations when its strength should be adequate. It negotiated with the French, it recruited and trained forces, it employed the Emperor Bao Dai for a period as advisor to the new government, it intimidated or executed opposition.

In 1947, the period of open battle with the French forces began. Still the strength of the Viet Minh limited it to guerrilla operations, harassing the French military units, terrorizing and subverting the countryside. In this period, South China was held by Nationalist Chinese forces, so Ho was dependent on his own resources and the help Stalin could supply.

In 1949, Mao took control of mainland China. His forces occupied the South China provinces of Yunnan, Kwantung and Kwangsi which border on Vietnam. Mao sent supplies, troops and military leadership to support Ho's war against the French. Now the Viet Minh had aid from both the Soviet Union and Red China. The assistance of Mao, providing geographical as well as material support, had special importance.

In 1950, Ho Chi Minh stepped up his incursions against the French. He could now operate from a secure base in Red China. He had built a formidable Red Army in the North to challenge French control of territory.

The French understood the new threat to their position in Vietnam. They brought the Emperor Bao Dai from his exile on the French Riviera to resume his position as nominal ruler of

Vietnam. They brought their distinguished Marshal Jean de Lattre de Tassigny to command the French military forces in the country.

Marshal de Lattre de Tassigny infused the French fighting forces with new life and vigor. At Hoa Binh, west of Hanoi, he delivered a crushing blow to the Viet Minh forces in November 1951. Thereafter General Vo Nguyen Giap used his Viet Minh forces more prudently while de Tassigny was in command for France.

The restoration of Bao Dai was a futile French effort to build popular support. Although the Emperor was a personable individual, well liked by his associates, his lack of leadership qualities was too widely known to make his rule credible. He had served as puppet ruler for France, for Japan and for Ho Chi Minh. He again asked the French to give more power to the Vietnamese Government, but he lacked the capacity or the interest to press the cause of independence effectively with the Government of France.

Ho Chi Minh used the restoration of Bao Dai as a sign of French determination to keep Vietnam in subjection. He attacked the puppet regime as a catspaw of France and recruited citizens to his cause by depicting the impossibility of winning independence in any other way. He continued to build his military forces against the day when they could successfully engage the French in open warfare. Meanwhile, he ensured an incessant attrition of the French forces through guerrilla warfare.

From 1950 to 1953, Ho Chi Minh received major support and assistance from both the Soviet Union and Red China. The prosecution of the Korean War did not cause Mao to neglect the war front in Vietnam. But with the conclusion of an armistice agreement on the Korean Front in July 1953, new resources of men and materials in China became available for transfer to Vietnam.

President Truman had opened the door for U. S. military assistance to France in Indochina through the Mutual Security Agreements of 1949 and 1950. Moderate amounts of war materials were furnished until the termination of hostilities in Korea posed the new threat of Chinese assistance to the Viet Minh. Special measures were then initiated to increase materiel support of the French war effort, but the aid could not save the French position.

The relentless drive of the Communist powers is illustrated in the strategic coordination of their worldwide operations. In Europe, Stalin followed his coup in Czechoslovakia in 1948 with the move against Berlin which provoked the Berlin Airlift. In Asia, the armistice on the Korean front was not long in operation before massive new Chinese support of the war in Vietnam pressed against the French defenses.

We might easily conclude that the attack against the French military forces in Vietnam was the less important part of the war. Because war is essentially a question of morale, the Communist aim is to destroy the morale of its bourgeois victim. Guerrilla warfare or open battle may contribute to that goal, but so also does the propaganda war. And in free nations laboring under the burden of illusions that they are at peace, propaganda strikes at the heart of morale, the will to fight.

A free nation at peace opens the minds of its citizens to the deception of the enemy. The enemy can clandestinely own and direct the news media of the country. It can pay handsomely the political factions, the talented individuals and the accomplished polemicists of the country without having these citizens even be aware of the source of their income. It can attack the government, discredit the war effort with every lie or sophistry and confuse the public. It can enlist against the government political factions which seek a domestic advantage from the embarrassment which a long, inconclusive war causes to the party in power.

The art of this coordination of military and political action was illustrated in the defeat of France. There was no important defeat on the battlefields of Vietnam. Dienbienphu was a minor setback when dissociaed from the psychosis which had been induced in the French public.

The military role in the Communist strategy was to keep up

a war of attrition against the French forces in Vietnam. It was not important to hold ground. It was important to wage a war of terror which would strike fear into the hearts of potential opponents, show that the French could not protect their adherents from reprisals, and steadily cut down the French troops committed to the war. It was important to build up in the minds of the French public and of French politicians the idea that this war could not be won, that it would go on and on and on, killing and maiming the flower of French youth.

In France as in other countries, there is scant defense against such an attack on the morale of the nation. Western intellectuals are profoundly ignorant about the most elementary aspects of war. It is a matter of class honor with them to attribute the conflicts and dissensions of modern society to sociological conditions. Thus the artful prosecution of the war by Communist cadres operating freely if surreptitiously in the bourgeois society is beyond the comprehension of bourgeois intellectuals.

In consequence, the communications media are readily aligned against the government. Especially in countries where strong socialist prejudices promote illusion about both war and communism, the enemy attack pierces the vital defenses with ease.

In early 1954, the United States, the Soviet Union, Great Britain and France met in Geneva with other countries involved in the Korean War to seek a resolution of that conflict. Fighting had been terminated by the armistice of July 1953 and nineteen nations assembled. The Korean question was discussed without conclusion from April 26, 1954 to June 15, 1954; the Communists would not allow international supervision of free elections in North Korea.

The Geneva Conference opened at a time of high tension in Vietnam. The timing of the conference had been arranged by the Communist participants to coincide with a major military effort against the French forces in Vietnam.

In order to protect the Kingdom of Laos—a state of the French Union—from the attacks of the Viet Minh, the French Commander, General Henri-Eugene Navarre, had occupied the small French fortress of Dienbienphu near the Laotian border west of Hanoi with some 15,000 troops. General Giap moved his Viet Minh forces to the attack. By isolating the garrison and bringing up heavy artillery to pound the fortress into submission, General Giap forced a French surrender on May 8, 1954.

The siege of Dienbienphu had evoked desperate French cries for American succor and some soul-searching in the Eisenhower Administration, now in office for a year. After surveying the problems of launching modern armed forces into the primitive jungle terrain of Vietnam, General Matthew B. Ridgeway, the Army Chief of Staff, counseled against intervention. But this was not the counsel which prevailed. As President Eisenhower has recounted in his memoirs, he offered to intervene if Great Britain would join the United States in the venture. Thus the possible use of United States military forces in Vietnam was left to the discretion of the British leaders. The event showed that President Eisenhower had learned nothing at all from the record of Korea in which British restraint of United States power had controlled war policy. He did not seem to grasp the fact that Britain dared not act against the interest of Red China for fear of jeopardizing its rich colony in Hong Kong.

The incapacity of the United States to act in the face of British opposition has been the consistent pattern of our foreign policy since the death of Franklin Roosevelt. One of the most tragic examples occurred in the Hungarian Revolution of 1956.

Western intelligence had never calculated that the Hungarian Army, so carefully schooled to Soviet Communist discipline, would ever be on our side. But when Hungarian soldiers had to shoot their own people or turn against the Russians, they turned against the Russians. If, at that time, President Eisenhower had obtained a request from the Hungarian Government for U.S. support, if he had flown U.S. troops and supporting aircraft to the Budapest airport, as he was later to do in Lebanon, the Soviet Union would have had no choice but to withdraw. We had the legitimate government on our side.

Tragically, the British Government saw in this event not a free Hungary needing assistance but a chance to strike at Suez

while the Soviet Union was too involved in Hungary to offer
opposition. It struck hastily and failed. But it also murdered
free Hungary.

The United States should have acted alone. It had such nuclear superiority that it really had nothing to fear from the
Soviet Union. But the United States was simply incapable of
acting in such an emergency without British support. Soviet
leaders saw the paralysis of U.S. policy and struck to smash the
Hungarian resistance.

Britain vetoed United States combat aid to the beleaguered
French at Dienbienphu and the fortress fell. That expected but
shocking event immediately turned the powers at Geneva to
discussion of a Vietnam settlement. And there, by ill fate, the
Vietnamese question was taken up by a conference chaired by
the Soviet Union—and Great Britain! By some strange de-
mentia the Western powers continued to believe Great Britain
could represent their interests in Asia.

The Geneva Conference addressed itself to the Vietnam
question in seven plenary sessions between May 8 and June 10.
The gap between Communist demands and solutions was great.
The government of Premier Laniel did not want a political
settlement at that time. Before another session could be held,
a change in French Government brought Premier Pierre
Mendes-France to the Conference on June 17 as replacement
for Georges Bidault, the Foreign Minister of the Laniel government.

Pierre Mendes-France, leader of the small Radical-Socialist
Party in the French Chamber of Deputies, sensing the deep
discouragement of the French people with the wasting character of the war in Vietnam, had offered to lead a government
which would negotiate peace on whatever terms could be arranged. So complete was the defeat of France that Mendes-
France was indeed designated to lead a new government.

After a series of secret conversations and consultations, the
delegates met in an eighth plenary session on July 21, 1954 to
ratify the cease-fire agreement signed by French and Viet Minh
representatives and to announce a general agreement to which

all conferees except Vietnam and the United States subscribed.

Pierre Mendes-France had met the demands of the Communist victors. Once again, as so often in recent history, the Western powers had delivered a people to Communist rule in the vain illusion that they were making peace.

No doubt Premier Mendes-France felt that he had saved half of Vietnam for France and freedom. He had preserved the integrity of Laos and Cambodia. But the common judgment of experienced observers held even these to be shortlived victories. The French defeat was so complete, the visible strengths of the retained states were so frail, that the early triumph of the Viet Minh in all of French Indochina seemed inevitable. It was considered improbable that the fragmented South Vietnam could survive more than six months. No one expected Ho Chi Minh to respect the agreements made at Geneva.

The phenomenon of the defeat of France has been little understood in the West. Other Western powers observe the event and see nothing. They fail to recognize the conditions of a free society which open it to conquest without war. For France was not in a declared war: it was merely attempting to subdue an insurrection. Others have failed to assess the enemy method of defeating a bourgeois nation without war and to see how the tactic can be applied to their own positions.

We can state the case briefly. A free society in time of peace is organized to allow a maximum of freedom to its citizens consistent with the maintenance of public order. In this condition, the society has a high tolerance for dissent, even to the point of violence. As an open society, it offers every opportunity for the advancement of ideas incompatible with the preservation of personal freedom and national independence. It is the general judgment of the free societies that this toleration of dissent is essential to the preservation of freedom.

Whether it is possible for a free nation to survive under these conditions of internal division in time of peace is debatable. The outcome will depend upon the course pursued by the ship of state.

It is beyond debate, however, that a free society cannot defend itself against assault by a hostile power while maintaining at home the freedom of dissent to which the society subscribes in time of peace. Under these conditions, a national consensus cannot be achieved or maintained, the defense of the country cannot be managed. In this state, the society is an easy target for enemy conquest.

It is therefore imperative that the free nation under assault by a hostile power suspend the right of dissent, unify the people in a common dedication to survival and defeat the enemy. A free society so aroused and unified is a formidable power, far surpassing in its potential any similar mobilization of a closed society.

Their own survival requires free men to understand that in the face of grave threat from an outside power they must put aside their internal differences until the enemy is defeated. Only then can they safely restore the freedoms suspended by war. The traditional call both to warn and to unify the people is a declaration of war.

All this is well known to the Communist strategists. Their design of conquest therefore provides for undeclared war, waged at a level which will bleed and weaken the victim without ever provoking him into a declaration of war. In the ensuing conflict, a Communist power geared for war engages a non-Communist power geared for peace. The aim is not for a military victory which might provoke declared war but for a steady attrition of blood and treasure which in time demoralizes and defeats the victim without engaging in decisive battle.

This is the tactic used by the Communists against the United States in Korea. For two years after President Truman asked for a truce, they held him in a continuing war of attrition which accounted for more than half the U. S. casualties of the conflict.

This is the tactic which defeated France in Vietnam. The will of the French people was shattered when they realized that their political leaders were incapable of bringing the war of attrition to an honorable conclusion.

This is the tactic which defeated France in Algeria. The long war of terror and sabotage could not be resolved by governments incapable of offensive action.

We see the same tactic taking its toll of the United States in Vietnam. It is not necessary to invade the United States. It is required only to destroy public confidence in the national leadership. When leadership fails, the most valiant people can behave as quitters.

France had a final chance to save its honor at Geneva. After the disaster of Dienbienphu, in view of the dire straits of his country, Ngo Dinh Diem had consented to accept the post of Premier of Vietnam. Diem was convinced that even at this late hour he could rally the people and defeat Ho Chi Minh if France would grant full independence to Vietnam. With the continuing support of France for a short transition period while national forces were being created, he believed a free government would attract the support of the great majority of Viet Minh fighters who were patriotic nationalists and not Communists.

Diem was not to have his chance. The French people were too demoralized to brook any delay in negotiating a cease-fire. Reflecting their psychological prostration, Premier Mendes-France ended the fighting at whatever cost to Vietnam and to the cause of freedom.

V

THE GENEVA SETTLEMENT

★ ★ ★

THE DISCUSSION OF POLICY HAS BEEN SO CONTAM-
inated with lies and purposeful propaganda about the Geneva
settlement of 1954 that some clarification is required to establish an accurate perspective.

The essential reality of the conference was the defeat of
France. Premier Mendes-France tried to salvage some interests and prestige from the negotiations but he was largely at
the mercy of the Communist powers.

The Communist powers were not, however, in a position to
dictate unconditional surrender. They had won a battle but
they were still inferior militarily to the French forces in Vietnam. They had used the battle to fasten on France a sense of
hopelessness about the war. However, the French malaise was
subject to change. Outrageous demands might arouse the national conscience and spark a renewal of the war effort.

As a further factor the United States was strongly opposed to
making any territorial concessions to the Communist side. It
might be induced by arrogant demands to support France in a
continuation of the war.

Premier Mendes-France brought all these factors into play in
the agreement reached. He gave Ho Chi Minh North Vietnam,

the prime Communist objective. He camouflaged the cession with verbiage about a "provisional" division of the country and subsequent voting so as to make it appear in France and the United States that the people would have the final decision on separation. Of course he knew that Communist regimes do not submit their tenure of power to vote of the people. The provision for future elections was a fraud.

The basic document of the Agreement, and the only document to be signed, was the "Agreement on the Cessation of Hostilities in Vietnam." That paper provided for the regroupment of forces north and south of a demilitarized zone at the Seventeenth Parallel; for free movement of peoples who wished to move from one area to the other; and for the stabilization of military strengths at present levels, permitting replacement but not increases. It was further agreed that, pending elections to reunify the country, each force would have full jurisdiction in its own area. Finally, the cease-fire established an International Supervisory Commission of Canadian, Indian and Polish membership to oversee the provisions of the agreement. This cease-fire was signed by Brigadier Henri Delteil for the French High Command in Indochina and by Brigadier General Ta Quang Buu for the Viet Minh.

The conferees also issued a Final Declaration of the Conference, unsigned, which received the approval of all except the delegates representing the United States and Vietnam. This declaration confirmed the cease-fire arrangements. It added the familiar verbiage by which cynical Western governments continue to deceive their peoples about the validity of agreements reached with Communist countries. Geneva was another Yalta.

The Final Declaration stated in part: "The Conference recognizes that . . . military demarcation line is provisional and should not in any way be interpreted as constituting a political or territorial boundary. . . . General elections shall be held in July 1956, under the supervision of an international commission composed of the Member States of the International Supervisory Commission." To deepen the affront to truth and honesty, the Declaration stated: "The Conference declares that, so far as Vietnam is concerned, the settlement of political problems, effected on the basis of respect for the principles of independence, unity and territorial integrity, shall permit the Vietnamese people to enjoy the fundamental freedoms, guaranteed by democratic institutions established as a result of free general elections by secret ballot." How, we ask, could Anthony Eden, the British Chairman, subscribe to such a statement even as he was delivering the people of North Vietnam to the ruthless tyranny of Ho Chi Minh? Foreign Minister Tran Van Do of Vietnam, representing his country in the conference, cabled Premier Diem in Saigon: "Absolutely impossible to surmount the hostility of our enemies and the perfidy of false friends." The cynical quality of the call for future free elections in North Vietnam was illustrated by the experience of earlier sessions of the same conference given to the question of Korea. Attempts to arrange a free election throughout that country foundered on the Communist refusal to allow United Nations supervisors in North Korea. The delegates could hardly have been as innocent about future elections in North Vietnam as they pretended to be.

The provision of the Geneva Settlement for elections in July 1956 has been cited by propagandists for Hanoi who accuse President Diem of refusing to hold elections in the South. Before that date, the South had indeed held free elections by secret ballot to constitute its own government. In the North, no elections were held because the ruling Communist apparatus was firmly in control and the question of alternative government was not entertained.

Before the time specified for the election, Ho Chi Minh had stopped the exodus of his people to the South and had excluded the representatives of the International Control Commission from supervision of the cease-fire agreement. There was no possible way to force Ho Chi Minh to hold free elections by secret ballot on the question of his own eviction from power. When President Diem announced that the election *would not* be held in the South, he was simply acknowledging that the election *could not* be held in the North.

This outcome was of course fore-ordained by the conditions of the cease-fire. The provision for an election was purely a face-saving gesture for French and British politicians.

Some of our scholars have gone to extreme lengths to avoid this simple truth. Bernard B. Fall and others have promulgated the myth that President Diem avoided the election because he knew the people would choose Ho Chi Minh. In this cause, Fall wrote, "As President Eisenhower was to remark in his memoirs later, every responsible observer estimated that the North Vietnam leader Ho Chi Minh could win even an uncoerced pan-Vietnamese election by 80 percent of the popular vote. With elections only two years away, there was no reason for the Communists to risk precious cadre personnel on short-term adventures." What President Eisenhower actually wrote was this: "I have never talked or corresponded with a person knowledgeable in Indochinese affairs who did not agree that had elections been held as of the time of the fighting, possibly 80 percent of the population would have voted for the Communist Ho Chi Minh as their leader rather than the Chief of State Bao Dai." When he approved these lines, Dwight Eisenhower of course knew that the people of the South had voted 98-plus percent to replace Bao Dai with Ngo Dinh Diem. It is entirely credible that Ho Chi Minh too could have carried an overwhelming majority *against Bao Dai* before the country was divided. But that fact, if it is a fact, is irrelevant to the situation in 1956. By 1956, the "love" of the people of the North for Ho Chi Minh had been demonstrated by those who voted with their feet, leaving home and possessions in the North to move to the South. By 1956, the South was unified and was healing the wounds of war. It was entering upon the economic prosperity which was to endure for the rest of the decade.

In the North, some 800,000 citizens had fled south. Of those who remained, some 100,000 persons not deemed useful to the Communist regime had been executed. The Communist Party had fastened its cruel tyranny on the people. It seems incontestable that if the people of the North had been given access to the

secret ballot in 1956, they would have voted overwhelmingly for
the dismissal of Ho Chi Minh. To present this ruthless despot
as a popular leader after he took power in North Vietnam is
journalism as irresponsible as so depicting Gomulka in Poland
or Castro in Cuba.

Another facet of the Geneva mythology alleges that Ho Chi
Minh was betrayed at the conference by Soviet and Red Chinese delegates seeking accommodation with the West. A likely
story! As Douglas Pike puts it:

> Britain maintained its reputation as a wise world-power
> middleman valued for its good offices. . . . Only the Viet
> Minh, the winners, lost. Or were sold out. Ho Chi Minh
> somehow was persuaded—apparently by a joint Sino-
> Soviet effort—to settle for half the country on the grounds
> that the other half would be his as soon as elections were
> held, which would be within a year's time. His willingness
> to accept partition after Dienbienphu proves as nothing
> else can, his deep loyalty and fidelity to international com-
> munism. The shock of understanding that they had been
> betrayed, when it came a year later to North Vietnamese,
> must have been great indeed—nine years of sacrifice in
> the name of independence and unity washed down the
> river of abstraction. (In 1965 and 1966, Southern Viet Minh
> cadres in the ranks of the NLF expressed undiminished
> bitterness over the settlement and were prejudiced
> against any political settlement of the later struggle for
> fear it might lead to a second sellout.)[1]

Despite his deep study of the Viet Cong, Douglas Pike has not
grasped the capacity of Communist apologists to rationalize
present policy. Consistency is to them a negligible virtue.

It is a misjudgment to regard Dienbienphu as a decisive military battle. It was a serious setback to French arms but not
decisive to the balance of military forces in Vietnam. It was not
the military consequence of the battle which defeated France;
it was the psychological impact on an already weakened
French public opinion which did the job. Ho Chi Minh was not
in a position to demand unconditional surrender.

That the South Vietnam of Bao Dai and the French would soon succumb to Communist subversion or assault was the general consensus of Western observers after the Geneva settlement. It is reasonable to suppose that the Viet Minh made the same judgment. However, that prospect was changed by the energetic leadership of Premier Ngo Dinh Diem, who guided the country in dismissing both Bao Dai and his French mentors. Premier Diem united the South, pacified the countryside and restored a prosperous economy. But we should not expect Viet Cong propagandists to credit Premier Diem with defeat of the Communist hopes.

There has been loose talk also about "going back to the Geneva Agreement." Those who have entertained the false view that the North was cheated out of an election victory by President Diem's refusal to hold elections imply that elections would now mend the damage. But as we have seen it is the North which will not submit to internationally supervised elections by secret ballot. Surely the South would have everything to gain by such elections if they could be held. It is the North which will never comply with the election provisions of the Geneva settlement.

Moreover, the Geneva agreement provided that all military forces of the North should be withdrawn to positions above the Seventeenth Parallel. Thus, to propose in the mid-Sixties a return to the Geneva settlement was tantamount to demanding of the North the unconditional abandonment of the war against the South. It was symptomatic of the peace prostration of the Johnson Administration in 1965 that the President and the Secretary of State actually advanced the proposal.

VI PEACEFUL INTERLUDE

★ ★ ★

THE GENEVA SETTLEMENT LEFT SOUTH VIETNAM IN A frightful state of chaos. Although the chief strength of the Viet Minh was in the North, its military operations had ranged over the whole country. Government forces assembled in the South were dispirited and discredited. Government prestige was at a low ebb.

The economy of the South had been ruined by the long war. The hidden structure of the Communist underground remained to intensify its subversion. Citizens were badly divided. The private armies of the Binh Xuyen gangsters and of the Cao Dai and Hoa Hao sects were protecting their own interests. There was no semblance of national unity except in the weak government of Bao Dai.

Ngo Dinh Diem arrived in Saigon on June 26, 1954 to receive from Bao Dai his portfolio as Premier. Bao Dai then departed for France, to rule from more comfortable environs. Premier Diem was left with the prostrate country and with divided authority. He did not control the Army, then commanded by General Nguyen Van Hing, Chief of Staff to the Emperor; and although the country was now legally independent of France, French influence had hardly diminished. On July 7, 1954,

Premier Diem introduced his first cabinet.

Douglas Pike aptly described conditions in South Vietnam when Premier Diem took office:

> From an organizational viewpoint, the government of South Vietnam in 1954 was an incredible mess. French bureaucrats who had managed the South and held all key positions in the colonial government panicked after Dienbienphu, sold what they could of their personal belongings, and fled. . . . The new government under Diem began in just about as total an organizational vacuum as is possible. . . . What Diem did possess was a record as a man untarred by the colonialist brush, a patriot of integrity who opposed the Communists, sects and other narrow interest groups not for the sake of his own self-interest but because of deep moral and religious beliefs.[1]

Premier Diem moved energetically to unify the country. He moved against the domain of General Le Van Vien, leader of the Binh Xuyen and vice king of Saigon. Using the Army, he smashed the private army of the Binh Xuyen. He moved against the private armies of the Cao Dai and the Hoa Hao, taking some of their elements into the nation's armed forces. Diem's personal integrity, courage and determination and his obvious independence of French control won the confidence of the people.

In October of 1954, Senator Mike Mansfield made his "Report on a Study Mission to Viet Nam, Cambodia and Laos." He recognized the honesty and competence of Premier Diem and recommended sending U. S. economic assistance to South Vietnam. In November, General J. Lawton Collins was sent to Vietnam as U. S. Special Ambassador. General Collins arranged for U. S. aid to refugees moving into the South to be given directly to the Diem Government and not through the French as formerly. He also arranged for an American Military Mission to take over from the French the training of the Vietnamese Army.

After these arrangements were completed, the prospects for the South brightened steadily. Premier Diem still faced the monumental task of receiving and resettling 800,000 refugees from the North, of restoring order and industry in the country. He worked without the French civil servants who had been repatriated, depending upon a slender corps of trained Vietnamese personnel. But he welded all his resources into a hardworking, dedicated government which could face and overcome great obstacles.

At the end of a year in office, Premier Diem announced that the government would hold a national referendum in October, 1955 to determine whether the country should continue with the monarchy or should establish a republic. The people voted overwhelmingly for the republic. A constituent assembly was formed, a constitution was written, and Ngo Dinh Diem was elected President of the Republic of Vietnam. In a year as Premier, Ngo Dinh Diem had become an authentic national hero, the man who would lead the people to independence in freedom. From 1955 to 1960, the Republic of Vietnam knew a period of relative peace and prosperity. The country was united and not under assault. Although Communist subversion increased its terror in the later years of the period, these attacks were not in serious dimension. Under the prevailing security, commerce and industry were revived and expanded. South Vietnam once again became a rice-exporting country.

These gains for the country were not made without some hazard to the Diem Government. In dispossessing the vice interests in Saigon, Diem had made powerful enemies. In taking one million acres of land for the resettlement of refugees and for agrarian reform, Diem antagonized wealthy landholders. But no doubt he made his most unforgiving enemies in evicting the French overlords and their satraps from positions of power in the country.

Although Premier Diem, a lifelong advocate of national independence, had opposed the French rule from his youth, he had never taken up arms against the French. He wanted France to restore the independence of Vietnam by mutual agreement. He was even more adamantly opposed to Communist rule by Ho Chi Minh than to the French rule. Diem saw the removal of all vestiges of French political control of the country as an absolute requirement of independence. The people could never believe in the independence of any government while the French political consuls remained. That is why Diem dismissed French civil servants from government when he could ill afford to lose their services. That is why he asked the United States to take over the training of the military forces.

From these events, some French partisans have built a new mythology. They accuse the United States of using President Diem as an agent to expel French interests from South Vietnam. Some perspective on this accusation is gained from the knowledge that in 1959 American new investment in the country was $1.0 million; French new investment, $22.0 million! The charge smacks of Communist condemnation of U. S. imperialism, but it has a curious twist of claiming that the anti-Communist Diem was used to oppose French anti-communism. Aside from these claims, there is no doubt that Ngo Dinh Diem was reckoned an enemy of France. He had bitter enemies among the Vietnamese exiles living in France in the shadow of the court of Bao Dai.

Fortunately for Premier Diem, United States foreign policy was in 1954 in the hands of a competent Secretary of State who understood the imperatives of the new government in South Vietnam. John Foster Dulles respected the need of the country for genuine independence. As long as the Diem Government could administer effectively the aid provided, Dulles was content to leave the entire management of internal affairs in Vietnamese hands. His policy with South Vietnam as with other allies was to foster its independence and prestige, not to undercut the nation with arrogant United States dictation of internal policy. Substantial credit for these years of peace and prosperity must be given to the sound policies of the United States shaped by Secretary Dulles.

Secretary Dulles did more than sustain the pride and independence of South Vietnam. He saw the disunity of the free nations participating in the Geneva Conference and realized that new institutions to assure common action in self-defense were needed. The Truman Doctrince had proclaimed United

States policy of assisting free nations threatened by Communist aggression, but the United States had been unable to organize a consensus for the defense of Vietnam. Consequently, North Vietnam had been delivered to the Communist aggressor. The experience demonstrated the need for local regional organization of mutual security.

Secretary Dulles moved with his usual energy to consult the interested powers and to assemble in Manila a conference on Southeast Asia. Although Mr. Dulles had considered a general pact of the free powers on the Pacific littoral, he was moved by British and French objections to exclude the Republic of China and the Republic of Korea from the scope of this conference. When the Manila Pact was concluded on September 8, 1954, the signatories were Thailand, Pakistan and the Philippines, the United States, Great Britain, France, Australia and New Zealand. Cambodia, Laos and South Vietnam were protected by the treaty.

The Southeast Asia Collective Defense Treaty negotiated in Manila has, with its Pacific Charter and protocol, come in recent years to bear the name of the Southeast Asia Treaty Organization which it created, SEATO. The treaty united the signatory powers in a pact of opposition to conquest within the covered area either by overt aggression or by subversion. Due to the sensitivities of British and French participants, the pact did not mention communism.

The treaty created a secretariat with headquarters in Bangkok. It called for cooperation of the signatory powers in military planning and in economic activity but did not create a standing military organization. The proposal of Thailand for a standing military organization ready for action was supported by the United States but was opposed by Britain and France.

This treaty does not include the NATO provision that "an attack on one is an attack on all." Instead it describes the common purpose of resisting aggression and subversion and leaves to the signatory powers determination of the measures which they will take in each instance.

In the light of later history, one American reservation in the treaty has special importance. The United States reserved the right to act against aggression in the area individually or jointly with other powers as circumstances might require.

On February 1, 1955, the treaty was approved by the United States Senate by a vote of 82 to 1.

The prompt negotiation and ratification of the Collective Defense Treaty reflected the urgency with which the Eisenhower Government then regarded the loss of North Vietnam to communism. This rallying of neighboring and sustaining powers to the cause of South Vietnam gave inspiration and confidence to the work of Premier Diem. It is easier to rally the people to your cause when the success of that cause seems assured.

Not until the next decade was President Diem to learn how insubstantial a piece of paper can be.

Ngo Dinh Diem did not come to the Premiership as a novice in Vietnamese politics. Although he had held no official position since he resigned in 1933, at the age of thirty-two, as Minister of Interior to the Emperor Bao Dai, Diem had kept in touch with Vietnamese political leaders. Through the years he had refused repeated calls of Bao Dai to return to government service. In 1945, he had refused an invitation of Ho Chi Minh to serve the Democratic Republic of Vietnam. As a lifelong patriot and political leader, he was well prepared to assume the national leadership.

Diem had no party, no following. He could only appeal to all factions which respected his independence of both the French and the Viet Minh. He had, however, a political philosophy to offer his people. He saw the future of Vietnam in the confluence of two streams of culture embodied in his own life and inherited traditions.

Diem's ancestors had been converted to Catholicism in the Seventeenth Century and had adhered to the faith through intermittent persecution. Through the centuries, his forebears had served the Emperors as Court officials. Thus the Christian faith was one foundation of Diem's philosophy.

But Diem was also very proud of his Confucian heritage. In Vietnam, the Catholic faith and the Confucian culture had been welded into a harmonious blending of related and sustaining ethical principles. Diem cherished the Confucian disciplines of his people and sought their enhancement in the life of his country.

As a man of the East and of the West, Diem sought for his people the best of what he had found in both. He was a modern man, aware of the vitality and the productivity of Western science and technology. He was an ancient man, steeped in the philosophies of both East and West. He was a man of action, trained in law and administration.

In his youthful service, Diem had been both District Chief and Provincial Governor before moving to the Emperor's cabinet. He knew the needs and the aspirations of the people from direct daily contact with them.

As a political leader, Diem had to pull together a sustaining political structure. Around his policies he organized the National Revolutionary Party of Vietnam. His younger brother Nhu organized a national labor movement in support of the government. Madame Nhu organized a women's auxiliary.

President Diem in Vietnam, like President de Gaulle in France, maintained his popular support by direct appeal to the people. He disregarded the parties and factions but courted the public with frequent visits to the provinces and with energetic prosecution of public programs.

Diem moved in 1955 to inaugurate a program of agrarian reform. Action was made imperative by the flood of refugees from North Vietnam. Annual rentals for tenant farmers were limited to 25 percent of the major crop. Government lands were distributed to landless peasants and private land holdings were purchased for distribution. By 1960, about one million acres had been distributed to some 300,000 tenant farmers. In addition, tenant purchase direct from land-owners had been financed by government loans. By 1962, 98 percent of the peasant farmers tilled their own land.

Through government loans and technical assistance, agriculture and industry were revived and extended. Rice production doubled. New light industry was organized by private capital.

Foreign investment was invited and encouraged.

Within three years, South Vietnam had become a model to the Free World of successful resistance to Communist subversion. In 1957, President Diem visited Washington as the guest of President Eisenhower. He received similar acclaim from other countries of the Free World.

In the aftermath of the Geneva Agreement, Ho Chi Minh too was busy, establishing his power in the North. As with all new Communist regimes, his first task was the extermination of any potential leadership around which a counter-revolution might be organized. In every community of the country, persons of substance who could not wholeheartedly embrace the new Communist tyranny were charged with treason and executed. Then, with undisputed tyranny established, the regime disciplined the people to automatic response to Communist direction.

He had first to stop the exodus of citizens fleeing to the South. In 1955, he terminated supervision by the International Control Commission and stopped the refugee outflow.

In 1955 and again in 1956 when President Diem inquired about plans to hold free elections in the North in compliance with the Geneva Settlement, Ho Chi Minh ignored the inquiry. His purpose and his method were clear.

He realized meanwhile that the leadership of President Diem in unifying the South had defeated his plan to take the South by internal subversion. He knew also that the South could not be taken by direct assault: the 45-mile front at the Demilitarized Zone was too narrow and too easily defended. In order to attack the South, he would have to move through Laos and attack South Vietnam across its western border.

Such an operation offered no insuperable obstacle to Ho Chi Minh. As leader of the Indochinese Communist Party, he already controlled the Communist forces in Laos and Cambodia. He had only to reinforce the Pathet Lao, his Communist Party in Laos, and establish a line of communication through Laos to the western border of South Vietnam.

The first step had to be the seizure of the Plaines des Jarres airfield. Because of the mountains and the lack of roads between Hanoi and Laos, air resupply would be required to support the larger forces planned for the attack. The Plaines des Jarres airfield provided the essential air terminal in Laos.

When in 1957 North Vietnamese soldiers disguised as Pathet Lao moved against the Plaines des Jarres, the government of Laos cried out in alarm. The United Nations considered sending observers to the scene. Then, without such intervention, the attack against the Plaines des Jarres subsided.

It was subsequently reported that Secretary Dulles had called the Soviet Ambassador to the State Department and said in effect: "Mr. Ambassador, I want you to tell Premier Khrushchev that if he doesn't stop that aggression in Laos, I'll cause more trouble for him in Eastern Europe than he can possibly handle. Thank you. Good day." The story was credible, coming in the aftermath of the Hungarian Revolution. It reflected also the realism with which Secretary Dulles regarded the Soviet initiatives.

But then Secretary Dulles sickened and died. In the last years of his administration, President Eisenhower was served by Christian Herter, a sick and inadequate Secretary of State who fell subject to the fears, the illusions and the timidities of the departmental bureaucracy. In these years, Premier Khrushchev launched the "Spirit of Camp David" to entrap Eisenhower with the exhilarating notion that he could negotiate peace for the world.

Meanwhile, Khrushchev's proconsul in Cuba took over that island and Ho Chi Minh resumed the attack in Laos. Through the defection of the neutralist paratrooper Kong Le, North Vietnam obtained the use of the Plaines des Jarres airfield for the Pathet Lao buildup which ultimately dispossessed Kong Le. In the end, Khrushchev closed his peace charade with a slap in the face to President Eisenhower at Paris. The Americans were hurt and uncomprehending as usual.

As President Eisenhower transferred the reins of government to his successor, he called Senator Kennedy's attention not only to the Bay of Pigs plans but also to the very serious situation in Laos. There, Soviet planes were flying 30 tons of supplies daily from Hanoi to the Plaines des Jarres in violation of the sovereignty of Laos, a nation we were pledged to protect against Communist aggression. President Eisenhower had done nothing about the violation because one does not mention such trivia when one is engaged in negotiating the peace of the world!

As he mounted his new plan for the conquest of South Vietnam, Ho Chi Minh also revitalized his cadres within that country. He opened the first phase of his guerrilla campaign, the building of organization and the opening of minor terror operations in the South.

Bernard Fall, who tried hard to attribute the increasing guerrilla activity in the South to the intensified police operations of the Diem government rather than vice versa, nevertheless demonstrates by his cited figures that the sharp escalation of guerrilla activity occurred after President Kennedy took office. He reports that the rate of Viet Cong killing and kidnaping of village officials jumped from about 450 per year in January, 1958 to 750 per year in January 1960 and to 4000 per year in May 1961. He cites Viet Cong guerrilla strength at 3000 in 1959, 15,000 in mid-1961 and 80,000 in early 1965. The correlation of these figures with Ho Chi Minh's over-all plan of conquest is apparent. They show that while the Viet Cong were present and active in South Vietnam in the late 1950's, the scale of their operations was relatively small. The real war was launched against John F. Kennedy.

We see in summary that this peaceful interlude for South Vietnam opened in a time of internal chaos following the Geneva Settlement. It was shaped by the leadership of President Ngo Dinh Diem and nurtured by the prudent diplomacy of the United States. In the end, it was threatened by a growing insurgency as Ho Chi Minh launched his war against the South and President Eisenhower abandoned the prudent defense of his allies to nibble at the bait of peace.

Through the default of President Eisenhower, President Kennedy faced a mounting aggression which he had either to oppose or accommodate. His decision would be fateful for America.

VII

THE THEATRE
OF WAR

★　　★　　★

AS WE APPROACH THE GROWING INVOLVEMENT OF THE
United States in the war in Southeast Asia, let us examine in
some detail the lands in contest. The growing struggle will be
shaped in large measure by considerations of geography.

The theatre of war comprises the countries of Vietnam, Cambodia, Laos and Thailand. Its area is about 486,000 square miles
and its population is approximately 81 million.

The chief geographical features of this area are: the Himalaya Mountains, the continental chain bounding the area on the
north; the Annamese Mountains, a spur of the continental
chain dividing Vietnam from Laos; and the Mekong River, one
of the great rivers of the world, which rises in the highlands of
Tibet and flows through or bounds Southwest China, Burma,
Laos, Thailand, Cambodia and Vietnam, emptying into the
South China Sea near the southern tip of Vietnam. These features have influenced the historical development of the subcontinent.

Thus the Vietnamese migrated from China, bearing Chinese
culture into Southeast Asia, but they were limited by the Annamese Mountains in the west until, farther south, they could
move into the Mekong River Valley. Thus the Annamese Moun-

tains in the north and the Mekong River in the south came to define the limits of Chinese culture.

In the west, the Thais too were a Chinese people who had migrated south to settle in warmer climes. But the Thais did not spread a Chinese culture. They embraced the Indian culture which they received in the subcontinent. By their prowess at arms, they dominated the middle area extending east to Vietnam and west to Burma.

In early history, populations settled chiefly in the coastal lowlands and in the fertile river valleys. The highlands were left to more primitive tribes. The coastal areas of Vietnam could support a large population. The remote areas of Cambodia and Laos were relatively isolated and sparsely populated. This distribution is reflected in the areas and populations of the countries, as follows: North Vietnam, 61,000 sq. mi.—20,700,000; South Vietnam, 66,000 sq. mi.—17,400,000; Laos, 91,000 sq. mi.—2,800,000; Cambodia, 70,000 sq. mi.—6,600,000; Thailand, 200,000 sq. mi.—33,700,000. Overland communications in the subcontinent were, prior to the war, severely limited. Since the onset of the war, both sides have made major additions to the road network.

In Vietnam, there is a coastal railroad from Saigon to Hanoi. There are two rail lines from Hanoi to China, to Kunming in the west and to Nanning in the east. In Thailand there are rail lines from Bangkok to Phnom Penh, Cambodia; to Vientiane in Laos; and to Chiang Mai in western Thailand.

The climate of the subcontinent varies from tropical to subtropical. Temperature ranges vary with latitude, altitude and prevailing weather patterns. Weather is influenced by air movement between the continental land mass and the ocean areas but varies by region according to the local patterns. Rainfall is seasonal, with marked rainy and dry seasons. Heavy rainfall, to include typhoons, strikes the coastal areas during the storm season from May to October.

Temperature and rainfall sustain a heavy land cover. In primeval forest areas, great trees dominate the land, overshadowing and killing off smaller growth. Where land has been cleared for cultivation and then abandoned, dense jungle growths appear. In the savanna lands a thick growth of kunai and other grasses covers the land.

In past millennia, the Himalaya Mountains have provided a barrier limiting southward migration from mainland China. They have enabled the people of Southeast Asia to control their own affairs with only occasional interference from the more populated and powerful Chinese empire.

So too the protection of the Annamese Mountains has enabled the Lao people, ethnically related to the Thais, to live in their remote kingdom with limited intrusion from the more warlike Vietnamese.

In this age of air transportation, these barriers have lost their effectiveness. Now the more powerful nation can see what happens beyond the mountains and can, by air, sustain large forces in conquest of the once-remote area. It is not necessary to pierce the mountain barrier with roads and railroads. In this age, those facilities follow after the air communications have been established.

The bearing of these geographical considerations on the war in Vietnam is apparent. The remote and formerly secure land of Laos is now neither remote nor secure. In this new age of air transportation, Laos is a power vacuum sucking into its vortex both Red China and North Vietnam. Western powers which formerly regarded this as an inaccessible and unimportant piece of territory unfortunately cling to past shibboleths while the energetic Communist powers exploit the tools of modern technology.

The simple reality today is that the Free World has in the angle of the Himalayan and Annamese Mountains a boundary with the Communist world on the boundary of Laos. This is a frontier which the SEATO powers are pledged to protect. The natural barrier of the mountains gives them a defensible position. Will they, through ignorance or weakness, allow the Red Chinese and the North Vietnamese to take Laos and advance the ideological frontier to the Mekong River at Vientiane? How can they then protect Thailand and Cambodia from further conquest? These are crucial questions which geography poses to the SEATO powers and which those powers have refused to face.

The Geneva Treaty of 1962 which neutralized Laos was an act of self-deception. SEATO powers pretended that the North Vietnamese would withdraw from Laos as the treaty required. North Vietnamese forces remained in Laos. They are using it in the war on Vietnam. Toleration of this treaty violation by the SEATO powers is an invitation to North Vietnam to take the rest of Laos. The violation measures the weakness of SEATO.

What could Cambodia do? The country was too weak to oppose the intrusion of North Vietnamese forces. If the SEATO powers would not secure Laos, they could not protect Cambodia. Cambodia submitted to superior force. The Communist aggressors had an open road to the Gulf of Thailand.

These considerations define some of the crucial questions posed by the war in Vietnam and conditioned by geographical factors. The country which will not fight from a strong position may find that retreat has sacrificed its capacity to survive. Perhaps it has also sacrificed its right to survive.

VIII

CAST OF CHARACTERS

★ ★ ★

OUR CHARACTERS ARE NATIONS, THE CHIEF ACTORS IN the war. In this still bi-polar world, we could claim that all the nations of the world have become involved in the Vietnam war, if only through the emotional partisanship of their citizens. Such counting would reveal the Free World divided, the Communist world united.

We are not interested in that counting except in a general sense. Our concern now is that nations, like people, have characters and interests and that these can have a crucial bearing on their address to war. We shall examine only the chief characters, those having had a significant bearing on the course of the war.

We have examined the Vietnamese character and the division of the country, North and South. Other countries in the theatre of war are Laos, Cambodia, Thailand and Red China. Pakistan, the Philippines, Australia and New Zealand are supporting powers in the general area. France and Great Britain, the Soviet Union and the United States are the more remote supporting powers.

Laos is a pawn. It is weak. It is at the mercy of the powers in conflict and must depend upon a balance in the general conflict for its own survival. The serious question for Laos must be whether to continue to play the neutralist game or to throw in its lot with one side or the other. We can expect Laos to accommodate the inevitable. Its fate will be determined by the resolution or the irresolution of the SEATO powers.

Cambodia is a relic of French rule. It has Thai people in the west and Vietnamese people in the east. It had a ruler who bowed prudently to the varying winds sweeping his country. When the United States came to Southeast Asia with power and purpose, Prince Sihanouk welcomed U.S. military aid and accepted a Military Mission. When President Kennedy made clear his intention of withdrawing U. S. forces from Vietnam, Prince Sihanouk quickly adjusted to the new order. He dismissed the U. S. Military Mission, refused all aid and went to Peking to make his peace with the other side. When he was told that he must allow North Vietnamese troops to operate from Cambodian soil in the war against Vietnam, he agreed. What else can a little fellow do?

Thailand, with a population half again as big as that of North Vietnam, is the other chief nation of Southeast Asia. It has been on the fringes of the Vietnam war, a committed and supporting power with a division of troops serving in South Vietnam and with the U. S. Air Force operating from Thai bases.

Thailand maintained its independence throughout the colonial period through prudent treaties with both Britain and France. In this age of conflict it has cast its lot with the Free World and against Communist aggression. It has spoken and acted boldly for strong action by the SEATO powers. Its distinguished Foreign Minister, Thanat Khoman, is a leader of moves to build cooperation and collective security among the free countries of Asia.

The Thais, who have had an historic hegemony over Laos and over parts of Cambodia, have viewed with grave concern the intrusion of communism into the subcontinent. They know that Laos is the back door to Thailand, the country's most vulnerable portal. They have faced Communist guerrilla activity on their own soil. Red China has publicly designated Thailand as the target of the next "war of liberation" in Southeast Asia.

The Thais are courageous and loyal allies. In the past, they have been willing partners in any undertaking which the United States would wholeheartedly support. Their grave concern and danger is of course that a weak United States administration will abandon its interests in Southeast Asia and leave Thailand to stand alone against the aggression of Red China.

People's Republic of China. After their conquest of the mainland, China's Communist leaders moved quickly to strengthen the Viet Minh war in Vietnam. For all their differences with Soviet leaders, the Red Chinese leaders are dogmatic Communists, wedded to the doctrines of Lenin and Stalin as expounded by Mao. If in their domestic programs they have appeared to show a touch of lunacy, that is only the logical reaction of Communist fanaticism to the insoluble problem of the Chinese family. Desperation provokes strange deeds.

In their international relationships, the Chinese leaders have been prudent with the wisdom of Lenin. They intervened in Korea only when they were assured that their base in Manchuria would be secure. Against India, they took only the border provinces to which China had an historic claim.

The Western caricature of the Red Chinese leaders as an assembly of megalomaniacs is sheer fiction. These men and women have been coldly practical about the problem of destroying capitalism. Their continuing support of the conquest of South Vietnam is assured, but only within limits which do not risk the Communist base on the mainland. Red Chinese support with both munitions and manpower is an important factor in Hanoi's war effort. The Soviet Union supplies sophisticated equipment but Red China supplies small arms and ammunition for the North Vietnam forces.

Pakistan was an earnest participant in framing the Southeast Asia Collective Defense Treaty in 1954. In later years it discovered that the United States was more partial to neutralist India than to its ally, Pakistan. It saw the United States under President Kennedy planning to abandon South Vietnam and withdraw from the war. Pakistan, like Cambodia, made its own peace with Red China. It is not active in SEATO.

The Philippines is an ally with troubles at home. It has had a checkered career. Its great President Ramon Magsaysay is reputed to have been the father of SEATO. He first suggested the alliance to John Foster Dulles.

With a population roughly equal to that of Thailand, the Philippines is one of the important regional powers. However, its effectiveness varies with leadership because of a strong inclination to internal disruption. It has in the past been effective as a member of SEATO and it can be strong again. At this time it is again plagued with internal dissension.

It remains to note in all fairness that the leftward tendencies and consequent weakness of the Philippines, as well as of other United States allies, are but a pale reflection of similar tendencies in the United States. It is not to be expected that our allies will stand alone while weakness in the United States undermines their confidence in the alliance.

Australia is big in territory but small in population. It has fewer people than South Vietnam. Nevertheless, Australia has been a staunch supporter of SEATO both in its formation and in its subsequent action. Australia moved promptly to supply forces to the Vietnam war after the United States made its commitment to ground combat in 1965. Australia can be counted upon to do its share in collective defense of the region.

New Zealand, with a population approximating that of Laos, is one of the smaller SEATO powers. It has been, like its neighbor Australia, a staunch advocate of collective security in Southeast Asia and Australia. In 1965, New Zealand sent a contingent to South Vietnam with the Australian expeditionary force. Within SEATO, New Zealand has been a constructive advocate of common defense.

France has a greater economic stake in South Vietnam than any of the other SEATO powers. Yet France has been a reluctant member of SEATO from the beginning and an inactive member in recent years. Since it recognized Red China, France has declined to participate in SEATO maneuvers. The French move to make peace with Red China, like similar moves by Pakistan and Cambodia, was made at a time when it appeared that President Kennedy would withdraw from South Vietnam and deliver the country to communism through a coalition government. At that juncture, it must have seemed to French policy makers that recognition of Red China offered their best chance of salvaging French interests in Vietnam. That was a serious misjudgment, not alone because the Kennedy plan failed, but because recognition of Red China opened France to intensified Communist subversion at home.

It is not to be expected today that France would contribute anything to the defense of Southeast Asia. It has given no support to South Vietnam.

Great Britain is a power of the second class, ranking below the Soviet Union and the United States. It had long played the balancing role in Europe, before World War II. Since that war, it has played a balancing role on the world scene, between the Soviet Union and the United States. The concept is that Socialist Britain represents a middle ground between the communism of the Soviet Union and the capitalism of the United States. Britain must be the intermediary, the peacemaker, between the hostile powers.

Because the United States and Britain have ties of a common heritage and present alliance, it is relatively easy for Britain to influence United States policy. The financial and professional ties between the two countries, especially the ties nurtured by decades of Rhodes Scholarships, provide easy access to policy making.

On the other hand, the Communist countries have no such sentimental regard for Britain. They will accept British services only as long as those services bring adequate benefits to the Communist cause.

The consequence of these relationships is that Britain brokers to the Soviet Union and Red China her capacity to restrain the United States. In Korea and in Vietnam, the decisive influence on American policy has been the irrational fear of expanded war, pressed by British diplomacy. In both wars, Britain has prevailed on the United States to allow sanctuary to the Communist side, in contravention of international law.

We should note that Britain can play the balancing power only because the United States obediently accepts the role of antagonist which Britain has assigned to it. While it is true that the United States is the ultimate target of Communist conquest, it is not the immediate target. Free countries bordering the Iron Curtain are the first objective. It would of course be a serious setback to U.S. interests to have the Soviet Union seize West Germany, but it would be a disaster for Britain to have Soviet power lodged across the North Sea. Today the United States protects Britain no less than West Germany.

The realities of power and position establish that the United States can accomodate any weakness of western Europe which is tolerable to Britain. It is a reproach to American policy that our leaders allow Britain to play the intermediary for communism. The spectacle of our European allies criticizing our Vietnam policy and urging U.S. withdrawal reflects the vacuous quality of American leadership.

The free world alliance will be strengthened when the United States requires Britain to stop acting as a broker for communism.

We have noted how Britain refused to aid France in Vietnam after Dienbienhphu and effectively blocked United States intervention. We have seen Britain chair the conference which delivered North Vietnam to the Communist side. Within SEATO, the British role is to oppose any military action against Communist aggression.

During and following World War II, when the Communist forces were isolated in northwest China, British policy and propaganda were hostile to the Government of China, favorable to the Communist rebels. Britain knew that Chiang Kai Chek had proclaimed the Kuomintang's purpose of ending all foreign enclaves on Chinese soil; and that the citizens of Hong Kong, raised in the tradition of freedom, would demand reunion with a Free China. But these citizens have no desire to exchange their freedom for the tyranny of Communist China. Their loyalty to Britain is now assured.

Even so, Britain holds Hong Kong on sufferance of Red China.

Mao can reclaim the concession at any time, and it is some embarrassment to him not to do so. But as long as Britain can induce the United States to fight losing wars in Korea and Vietnam, that advantage to the Communist cause more than compensates for the foreign occupation of Chinese soil.

The ideological climate of Britain, reflected in its Socialist governments, harmonizes with the role of service to communism which Britain has played. Nevertheless, British policy is essentially pragmatic and self-serving. We find Britain unequivocably opposed to Communist aggression when its own interests are at stake.

In the Vietnam war, Britain is an ally of Red China. Her shipping supplies the Communist war effort. Her diplomacy keeps the port of Haiphong open, restrains the bombing of Communist military installations and confines the allied ground effort to South Vietnam. Britain does nothing to help the fight against Communist aggression; and yet Britain in SEATO and in Washington is at the center of decision-making for our side. We must discover what quality of the American intellect tolerates such an arrangement.

The U.S.S.R. is the chief enemy. It is the originator and instigator of the war in Vietnam. In its true perspective, the war in Vietnam is a satellite war waged by the Soviet Union for the purpose of undercutting the power and prestige of the United States, wasting its substance and demoralizing its people. The war is only coincidentally a war between North and South Vietnam. That dividing line between the Soviet satellite and our ally just happened to be the most propitious place to wage war against the United States.

This perspective on the war is illustrated by the fact that the United States has been spending $30 billion per year on the war while the Soviet Union has been spending $1 billion per year for the same purpose. Since the United States has roughly twice the industrial capacity of the Soviet Union, the advantage to the Soviet Union in continuing the war is apparent. Surely one of the most fatuous aspects of the war has been the assumption of United States diplomats and presidents that we and the Soviet Union have a mutual interest in ending the war. How the

Soviet leaders must have guffawed when President Johnson sought their assistance in ending the war!

The Soviet Union has avowed its purpose to destroy the capitalist societies, of which America is the chief one. It has grown steadily in power and has never wavered in purpose. It is more dangerous today than the empire of Stalin ever was.

Nevertheless, the Soviet Union, like Red China, acts within the strictures of Lenin. Its leaders are indoctrinated with an abhorrence of adventurism. They push vigorously wherever advantage can be gained but they will not risk their base in reaching for new conquests. It is grossly irrational to suppose the Soviet leaders would risk war with the United States as a cost of persistence in the war against South Vietnam.

The United States is the bulwark of all Free World defense. Only the power of America has protected the free countries of Europe and Asia from Communist conquest. No other country has the power to deter the Soviet Union and Red China.

As the bulwark of the Free World, the United States is also the principal target of Communist aggression and subversion. Soviet strategists move where they can, but always with the ultimate target in view. The United States can be weakened by direct attack or by undermining its prestige and the confidence of its associates.

In recent years, the United States has shown self-deception about Soviet purposes and an inclination to appeasement which raise serious doubt in the minds of allied leaders. Is the United States a dependable ally? The attitudes assumed by some United States political leaders who command world attention argue that it is not. Aside from the question of loyalty to commitments assumed, there is the question of competence. Does the United States have a realistic comprehension of the proper use of its power? If it does not, the weight of its power will be correspondingly diminished or even nullified. This becomes a serious question when a nation charged with crucial world leadership treads uncertainly from defeat to defeat by countries of vastly inferior resources. Human intelligence remains the most critical factor in war.

If a country endowed with power and responsibility bedazzles itself with impractical notions about peace and war, it renders itself unable to avoid war or to win peace. There is so much of this in the past three decades of United States history as to raise a serious question about the capacity of the country to survive.

These are our chief characters. As we shall see in the unfolding drama of war, it is the interplay of their strengths and weaknesses, their fears and illusions, their hopes and ambitions which charts the course of history.

IX THE POLICY MAKERS

★　　★　　★

WE HAVE TOUCHED IN EARLIER CHAPTERS ON SOME AS-
pects of the Viet Minh strategy against the French regime in
Vietnam and on Ho Chi Minh's new plan for a war against the
South after conquest by subversion failed. We must, however,
engage a more comprehensive view of Communist strategy if
we are to understand the course of war.

It is essential first to understand that Communist strategy is
global in scope. The objective of world conquest requires such
a perspective and Communist philosophy provides it. Whatever
the differences between the Soviet Union and Red China have
been, the two countries have been as one in all confrontations
with the Free World. They are as one in support of North Vietnam.

When a power such as the Soviet Union, commanding about
one-half as much industrial power as the United States, sets out
to conquer the world, it faces real obstacles. It is too weak to
strike directly at the United States. It must by indirect attack
undermine the prestige and power of the United States, while
building its own military power and prestige, until victory in
confrontation is assured.

The Communist philosopy builds in its adherents a contempt

for the intellectual integrity and the moral resolution of the bourgeois powers. It depicts the capitalist society as a decadent order which will collapse before the forces of Communist reality. But it also tempers the confidence so created with thunderous strictures against adventurism. No Communist must ever throw away his conquests by overreaching, as Napoleon and Hitler did. Lenin forged in the party leadership a combination of aggressiveness and prudence which has marked the policies of all Communist countries.

Thus the conquest of the capitalist world is regarded as both easy and inevitable. It is necessary only to persist in a continuing offensive in order to topple the corrupt capitalist society.

These beliefs give to Communist strategy a character distinctly different from that engendered by the Free World philosophy. The Communist strategy is aggressive, persistent and timeless. It conceives a continuing duty to attack, but not to achieve at any specified rate because the final triumph is in any event inevitable. Advantage must be taken of every opportunity to weaken the capitalist powers, with assurance that every advance contributes to the ultimate victory.

Therefore, in such wars as those in Korea and Vietnam, the Communist side persists as long as the terms of warfare are advantageous to it. How long the war continues is not important. But if the terms of warfare are so changed as to become disadvantageous to the Communist side, as President Eisenhower threatened to change them in Korea, that condition must be terminated by prudent measures, such as an armistice.

The Communist powers are continuously at war with the capitalist powers. Whether at any given time there is open warfare, as in Korea and Vietnam, is purely a question of relative advantage. When such measures can hasten the fall of the United States, they will be used. But they are only one of the avenues of destruction, in the long run less important than political warfare.

The submission of an enemy to your will is only in part a question of relative military strength. The real object is to bend his will to your own, and this aim is furthered by a variety of means and methods. You can mislead him about your intentions so that he will think it is unnecessary to defend himself. You can frighten him with threats of (nuclear) destruction so that he will prefer submission. You can soften him with propaganda about convergence so that he will regard submission as tolerable. You can separate him from his friends and supporters so that he will stand alone, and afraid. You can debauch him with immorality so that his will to fight is destroyed. You can so confuse him with false hopes of peace that his capacity to repel aggression is paralyzed. And you can do all this without committing one soldier to battle.

Lest the reader think that striking at the will of the enemy is new to warfare, let him know that the tactic is as old as war itself. Genghis Khan and Napoleon had agents who preceded their armies to excite fears and spread false information about the impending invasions. Lenin added the idea of continuous warfare for the destruction of the bourgeois world. He raised the formerly preparatory stage of subversion through political warfare to be the chief gauge of battle. He visualized formal military organizations as a sustaining force, but he thought the class warfare would be decisive as it had been in Russia. What Lenin did was to develop the application to political warfare of the principles enunciated by Karl von Clausewitz for conventional warfare.

The task of Soviet strategy in Vietnam was therefore to create conditions which would bleed the United States, would undermine its self-confidence and would eventually destroy its internal coherence. These objectives were to be achieved while avoiding any measures which would jeopardize the Communist base in North Vietnam or risk war with the United States. The achievement of all of these aims, demonstrated in recent years, represents one of the most consummate achievements of grand strategy in modern history.

The perfection of this strategy depended upon obtaining from the United States certain decisive advantages. It was essential that the United States and its allies not strike back against North Vietnam in such a way as to threaten the Communist regime or involve Red China in the war. Such action would negate the whole plan and risk the loss of Communist rule in North Vietnam, in China, or in both countries.

To achieve this purpose, it was necessary to persuade American political leaders that limiting the war to South Vietnam would serve the cause of peace. It would be necessary to have sanctuary for North Vietnamese forces in Laos and Cambodia as well as North Vietnam, or the war could not be prosecuted at all.

It might seem to less ambitious strategists a hopeless task to persuade any country not to strike back when it is attacked by a neighbor. The difficulty is multiplied by the fact that international law clearly defines the right of the victim to strike back against the aggressor. But Soviet strategists were not so inhibited. They knew that the United States had submitted to such a restriction in Korea.

In that instance, Britain had prevailed upon President Truman to limit the war to the Korean Peninsula in order to avoid confrontation with the Soviet Union. But a decision on one side to limit war is an invitation to the other side to extend the war. With assurance that its base in Manchuria was secure, Red China attacked the United Nations forces and drove them out of North Korea. The result was inevitable, given Manchurian sanctuary. United Nations forces could not hold the line of the Yalu River without using artillery and airpower against an enemy attacking from Manchuria. When President Truman allowed a Manchurian sanctuary, he surrendered North Korea to the Communists. Truman's advisers apparently did not comprehend that reality, but Soviet strategists saw it very clearly.

The crucial question in Vietnam was whether Britain could once again paralyze the United States response to aggression. Once again Britain rendered this service to communism. As in Korea, British diplomacy urged that the war be limited to South Vietnam. It raised the spectre of Red Chinese intervention, Soviet involvement and a nuclear holocaust if the United States allowed Vietnam to strike back at North Vietnamese forces attacking from Laos. It opposed naval blockade or mining Haiphong Harbor for fear of damaging a Soviet vessel and starting war. It urged restraint in bombing North Vietnam. It brought a steady pressure first for the bombing pauses, then for cessation of bombing.

These British warnings are of course trivial and insubstantial. They picture Red China and the Soviet Union as ready to go to war with the United States when in fact it was the abiding necessity of both powers to avoid such war. They imply that the Communist powers would risk the destruction of their homelands rather than desist from the aggression against South Vietnam—a ridiculous premise. They build on misinterpretation of the Korean experience the notion that the Communist powers cannot abide an American presence on their borders, when we know very well that it was the grant of sanctuary which caused Red China to strike in Korea.

If the United States were to grant Red China a sanctuary from American bombing for fear that such bombing would lead us into World War III—as the British aver—China would of course be free to intervene in Vietnam. She could suffer no damage except to her forces committed to the battle.

On the other hand, if Red China intervenes in Vietnam Red China becomes a belligerent, and international law subjects it to United States attack. If Chinese leaders know that in these circumstances the United States will bomb mainland installations, not even the prospective loss of North Vietnam could induce Red China to intervene in the war. The Communist leaders in Peking are too prudent to risk their hold on China for any advantage to be gained in Vietnam.

Yes, the British protestations are trivial and insubstantial. How then have they come to dominate United States policy? There can be no doubt of the effect—we have too many stories about the responses of Presidents Kennedy and Johnson to have any doubt about their mental paralysis. One example will illustrate the effect of British influence on United States action:

When North Korea seized the U.S.S. *Pueblo* on January 23, 1968, the admiral commanding the U. S. Pacific Fleet is reported to have started a couple of carriers moving toward

Korea. When word of the movement reached the White House, the admiral's orders were countermanded by President Johnson. The President is reported to have said as he defended the White House action, "I am not about to start a war."

Who in the world led the President to think that the admiral's action might start a war? The admiral had no such intention. He knew that if he appeared at the port of Wonsan and said, "Give back the *Pueblo* and crew or I'll blast your entire air force out of the air," the North Koreans would return the ship and crew. The North Koreans didn't want to start a war and they didn't want to lose their planes. They just wanted to take the *Pueblo* and crew if President Johnson would let them have it.

It is obvious that no Soviet Ambassador in Washington has such access to the President of the United States as to influence these decisions. We know that in the case of President Kennedy the British Ambassador did have such access to the President. In fact, Theodore Sorensen has assured us that President Kennedy did not act on major issues of foreign policy without consulting the British Ambassador.

It is not established that British Ambassadors have had such rapport with President Johnson. But that rapport, while desirable for Britain, is not necessary. Britain has structure.

The people who saw President Kennedy daily, or frequently, on foreign policy were Dean Rusk, McGeorge Bundy and Senator J. William Fulbright. As a former member of the Senate Foreign Relations Committee, the President had great respect for the Senator from Arkansas. John Kennedy also had an open door for Walter Lippmann and other opinion makers. His brother Robert, the Attorney General, was consulted on all policy. But Rusk, Bundy and Fulbright were his chief advisers, with Walt Whitman Rostow also playing a key role at the State Department.

SENATOR J. WILLIAM FULBRIGHT is a former Rhodes Scholar and an ardent anglophile. He may occasionally criticize minor faults of British policy to create an impression of independence but his position in foreign affairs is a faithful reflection of policy at 10 Downing Street. When Britain serves Communist policy, Senator Fulbright serves Communist policy. When Britain breaks with Lyndon Johnson, Senator Fulbright breaks with Lyndon Johnson.

DEAN RUSK, too, was a Rhodes Scholar. While his fellow alumnus, Guy Burgess, was betraying the British Ambassador in Washington, Dean Rusk, as Assistant Secretary of State for the Far East, was busy working British policy into American action. His speeches of the period reveal a solicitude for the Communist "agrarian reformers" in China and a hostility for the Government of China which were quite in keeping with the British interest. He bore the brunt of shaping United States policy in Korea, with the help of the later-discredited China hands and with the ready concurrence of Dean Acheson, another notorious anglophile. But Dean Acheson had a first preoccupation with Europe.

It is one of the remarkable diplomatic feats of the Sixties that Dean Rusk, while faithfully serving British policy, has managed to project an image of staunch resistance to Communist aggression. The word is quicker than the mind.

As we have seen, the critical factor in the Communist strategy is the retention of sanctuary for its forces in Laos, Cambodia and North Vietnam. As long as Britain secures these military positions against attack by allied ground forces, she fulfills the Communist requirement.

Throughout his service as Secretary of State, Dean Rusk was adamantly opposed to any invasion of the sanctuaries. When, during Senate hearings, Senator Long of Louisana suggested that our forces should invade the sanctuaries, Rusk replied, "Senator, you can start a world war any time you want to." This was of course the pat British response to any criticism of our sanctuary policy.

As long as you preserve the sanctuaries, you can be the biggest hawk in the world *within South Vietnam.* Nothing the United States can do there will threaten North Vietnam or Red China or force the Soviet Union to end the war. When he was adamant against breaching the sanctuaries but insistent that the United States must fight an endless war of attrition, Dean Rusk was fulfilling exactly the service which Britain had undertaken to render to the Communist cause.

MCGEORGE BUNDY, President Kennedy's Assistant for National Security Affairs, came to the White House from Harvard. He had served as a political analyst for the Council on Foreign Relations and as an assistant professor of government at Harvard before taking his post as Dean of the faculty of Arts and Sciences at Harvard.

WALT WHITMAN ROSTOW moved from the Center for International Studies at the Massachusetts Institute of Technology only briefly to the post of Deputy Special Assistant to the President for National Security Affairs at the White House until his security clearance for service in the State Department could be arranged. He then took the post of Chairman of the State Department Policy Planning Council until 1966 and thereafter became Special Assistant to the President for National Security Affairs. He had been a Rhodes Scholar, an instructor in economics at Columbia University, a State Department employee, Professor of American History at Oxford University in 1946-47 and at Cambridge in 1949–50. During the war he had served as an officer in the OSS.

MAXWELL DAVENPORT TAYLOR retired from the United States Army in 1959 after a distinguished career culminating in service as Chief of Staff. In retirement, he served successively as Chairman of the Board of the Mexican Light and Power Company, Limited and as President of the Lincoln Center for the Performing Arts in New York City before returning to government service with the Kennedy Administration. After the Bay of Pigs disaster, General Taylor was called to the White House staff as Military Adviser to the President. He then served successively as Chairman of the Joint Chiefs of Staff, as Ambassador to the Republic of Vietnam, as Special Counsultant to the President and as President of the Institute for Defense Analysis. He was the chief military architect of our disastrous war policy.

These were the chief sources of advice for President

Kennedy. He, of course, consulted with other congressional leaders but these meetings were generally planned to inform the legislators, not to get advice from them.

In the Johnson Administration, the phalanx of advisers was little changed. President Johnson was at pains to keep continuity with the Kennedy policymakers. Besides, he didn't know anyone but Bill Fulbright who knew anything about foreign policy, he thought. When McGeorge Bundy retired to the presidency of the Ford Foundation, Walt Rostow was drafted from the State Department Policy Planning Office to fill the National Security Post. There he remained for the balance of the Johnson tenure.

It is clear that our management of foreign policy is frightfully unbalanced with British interest. The point is not that Rhodes Scholars are disloyal to the United States or conscious agents of Britain. It is merely that their Oxford education gives them a strong partiality to British attitudes and a natural amenity to British persuasion. It is incontestable that if our policy making offices were equally weighted with men who had studied at the Sorbonne (John Foster Dulles had), we would have a very different foreign policy.

The problem we face is that the Rhodes Scholarship program draws many of our most gifted young men to Oxford for advanced education. When they finish the course, they are accepted as specialists in international affairs. Whether they go directly to government service or first to banking and law offices in New York City, they are marked for high policy positions. Inevitably, they attain rank in the State Department. Cecil Rhodes has been repaid.

It is clearly imprudent for the United States to allow this condition to continue. We have an ample supply of talented American lawyers, bankers, educators and government officials who have never been indoctrinated with the interests of any other power. It is of course desirable to have a representation of American scholars who have done foreign studies, but these should be deliberately balanced to include men schooled in Germany, France, Italy, Spain,

Japan and the Republic of China as well as Britain.

Some American scholars who have noted with dismay the continuing sacrifice of our national interests to accommodate Communist aggression have sought explanation of our course in Soviet infiltration of our policymaking offices. That is the wrong scent. Because the Soviet Union has in the past been highly successful in penetrating policy-level positions of other countries, we must suppose that the practice continues and has not been fully exposed by counter-intelligence agencies. Nevertheless we have reason to believe that such penetration is limited and cannot explain our national policies.

Herman H. Dinsmore, a former editor of the *New York Times* International Edition, in his analysis of the *Times* opposition to U.S. policy in Vietnam, attributed policy to a mysterious "balance of power." He wrote[1]: "In brief, the New York Times has rebuffed the war in Vietnam—sought to make it unpopular and advocated on many occasions that the United States follow a course that in the past has led to the erection of Communist governments and the loss of countries to the free world.

"The arc of reasoning that is responsible for the balance of power stems chiefly from the Left side of the political spectrum. Of course, it draws full support from the Communist party, which in turn acquires strength from the power and resources of the Soviet Government, financial and otherwise. Unless we can say these things and discuss them without hysteria or blinders we shall be multiplying our dangers. Every form of appeasement is akin to dishonor and can only lead to defeat."

Mr. Dinsmore's evidence showed the parallel course of British and *New York Times* policy. Nevertheless, he seemed unaware that it is Britain which frames a policy to restrain the United States and the *Times* which dutifully complies. The *New York Times* is the chief mouthpiece of British policy in America, though it is hardly more zealous than the wire services and the television networks.

A closer examination of recent history will reveal that the United States was partial to Soviet interests only when Britain was partial to the same interests. The continuing British influence on United States policy is evident. We shall see this British role documented as the war develops.

It may appear from these observations that the Soviet successes are due not so much to good Soviet strategy as to basic American weakness. However, it is the province of strategy to deal with forces as they are. In their manipulation of Great Britain to win American accommodation of Communist aggression, the Soviet leaders are using the world as it is.

These critical decisions at the highest levels of government were decisive for the course of the war. The resulting slaughter, even as our leaders professed their hopes of peace, was inevitable. Nevertheless, Soviet strategy was not content to rest on these achievements. It sought by every means available to increase the punishment of the United States and to conserve its own resources.

A first requirement of strategy is to make a correct assessment of the enemy leadership. Soviet policy respected the realism of John Foster Dulles, backed up as it was by the support of the President. But when Dulles died, the Soviet leaders knew that United States policy would change radically. The pro-British sentimentality which Dulles had restrained would now have free rein and would doubtless affect the President. Premier Khrushchev moved swiftly in Cuba and in Laos to take advantage of the new opportunities.

And yet, with a general in office, there was always some question with Soviet leaders as to how far they could press an issue. Eisenhower had moved into Lebanon in the face of Soviet threats (because of the British interest in Jordan) and he might be aroused to take similar action in the last months of his administration.

With the election of John F. Kennedy, the lid was off. Soviet strategists knew him well, especially his naivete. They knew the men who would form his cabinet and shape his policies. They knew it was now safe to proceed with an openly-declared "war of liberation" against South Vietnam. In this way the real war, the class war, the political war would be launched in earnest.

In the month following the election of John F. Kennedy as

President of the United States, the National Liberation Front of South Vietnam proclaimed its program for the liberation of South Vietnam:

Program of the National Liberation Front of South Vietnam, published in a manifesto issued on the day of its founding, Dec. 20, 1960.[2]

I. Overthrow the camouflaged colonial regime of the American imperialists and the dictatorial power of Ngo Dinh Diem, servant of the Americans, and institute a government of national democratic union.

II. Institute a largely liberal and democratic regime.

III. Establish an independent and sovereign economy, and improve the living and conditions of the people.

IV. Reduce land rent; implement agrarian reform with the aim of providing land to the tillers.

V. Develop a national and democratic culture and education.

VI. Create a national army devoted to the defense of the Fatherland and the people.

VII. Guarantee equality between the various minorities and between the two sexes; protect the legitimate interests of foreign citizens established in Vietnam and of Vietnamese citizens residing abroad.

VIII. Promote a foreign policy of peace and neutrality.

IX. Re-establish normal relations between the two zones, and prepare for the peaceful reunification of the country.

X. Struggle against all aggressive war; actively defend universal peace.

In the language of communism, this was a declaration of war. But in the Kennedy councils in Washington, no one understood. Filled with impractical notions about peacemaking, these men did not understand the war they were in.

X THE KENNEDY POLICY

★   ★   ★

WE MUST SYMPATHIZE WITH THE YOUNG PRESIDENT who received such a mess of problems from his predecessor. President Eisenhower had lost Cuba through sheer ineptitude and as a lame duck was preparing an expedition to overthrow the Castro regime. He had watched with the apparent approval of silence while Soviet planes flew supplies from Hanoi to the Plaines des Jarres in Laos for the North Vietnamese invasion of that country. He had embraced the peace initiatives of Premier Khrushchev only to have the balloon burst in his face and a new freeze descend on Soviet-American relationships.

President Kennedy was not unfamiliar with the problem of Indochina. In 1951, on his return from a visit to Saigon, he had said:

> In Indochina we have allied ourselves to the desperate effort of a French regime to hang on to the remnants of empire. . . . To check the southern drive of communism makes sense but not only through reliance on the force of arms. The task is rather to build a strong native non-Communist sentiment within these areas and rely on that as a spearhead of defense rather than upon the legions of General de Lattre. To do this apart from and in defiance

of innately nationalistic aims spells foredoomed failure."[1]

In 1953, Senator Kennedy met Mr. Ngo Dinh Diem, then an exile in the United States, at a luncheon tendered by Supreme Court Justice William O. Douglas.

In his quest for the presidency, John Kennedy had assiduously built up his image as the man of action. Contrasting his youthful vigor with the elderly, golf-playing, staff-oriented Administration of Dwight Eisenhower, he had promised new leadership to the country. According to the press notices, Secretary Rusk would not make decisions on foreign policy in the new Adminstration; he would recommend policy and President Kennedy would make the decision. So it ran in every Department until John Kennedy was portrayed as a superpresident.

The reality was quite different. John Kennedy had been an indifferent student of foreign policy. He accepted the support of the socialist-oriented elements of the Democratic Party because he knew that support was necessary to gain party leadership. In victory, he was committed to the inclusion of these elements in his cabinet. They dominated the field of foreign policy.

The new Administration took power with a show of confidence. There would be no more of the stumbling of the Eisenhower years. The Kennedy elite intended to assure world peace. As Arthur Schlesinger was to write, "The Kennedy Presidency began with incomparable dash."

President Kennedy set aside the carefully-designed structure of the National Security Council to depend upon more congenial personal relationships with his advisers. As Townsend Hoopes put it: "President Kennedy, acting upon the advice of McGeorge Bundy and Walt Rostow, scrapped the entire structure of the NSC and chose to rely on small groups of flexible composition that were given responsibility for both policy formulation and execution with respect to particular countries, regions or functional problems."[2]

The essential rationale of the new Kennedy policy was rever-

sal of the Truman Doctrine. The old policy had mobilized the
Free World to oppose Communist expansionism but it had, according to the Kennedy theory, projected United States power
up to the borders of the Soviet Union. This, it was said, explained Soviet hostility and belligerence. If detente between
the two worlds was to be advanced, the United States must
withdraw from these threatening positions and allow the
Soviet Union a reasonable sphere of influence. Walter Lippmann said so.

But this change of policy was not proclaimed in these terms.
There was no great debate. Rather, it was simply announced
that the Kennedy Administration would open new initiatives
for peace. In due time the initiatives were revealed: return of
the RB-4 crew members, refusal to defend Laos, tragic fum-
bling at the Bay of Pigs.

Nikita Khrushchev had some initiatives too, and they were
not of withdrawal. At Vienna, he evicted the United States
from Laos. He seized East Berlin and closed off the flow of
refugees to the West. He launched a series of nuclear tests on
an unprecedented scale, tearing up the voluntary test ban
which the United States had been observing.

These contrasts of style and purpose were to persist throughout the Kennedy presidency. As the United States turned to a
soft approach, a policy of conciliation, the Soviet Union became
more aggressive. If the Kennedy policy had been practical and
pragmatic; it might have been adjusted to this experience. But
the policy was not pragmatic; it was syllogistic, and messianic.

The basic premise of the Kennedy policy was that the world
must prevent nuclear war because nuclear war could destroy
civilization. Of course, only the Soviet Union and the United
States really held enough weapons to destroy civilization.
Therefore, it was the most basic obligation of foreign policy to
prevent differences between the United States and the Soviet
Union from increasing to the point of war.

From this conclusion, it is obvious that all other elements of
policy must be subordinated to detente. If Soviet diatribes are
insufferably arrogant, they must be suffered passively because

to respond in kind would jeopardize detente. If the Soviet Union wages satellite war against you, you must suffer patiently because your losses in Vietnam are, after all, small compared with the consequences of nuclear war. After the Soviet invasion of Czechoslovakia in 1968, the French Foreign Minister said that the most important obligation of the Atlantic powers was not to lose faith in detente!

The total paralysis of the Free World initiative in its confrontation with Soviet aggression is the dominant characteristic of Western foreign policy today. The free nations show only good will, never hostility. They never threaten or intimidate, even when they have the power to do so with assurance.

The pressures on President Kennedy were mounted even before he took office. Arthur Schlesinger reported on the shaping of the inaugural address: "Walter Lippmann contributed ... by suggesting, when he was shown a draft of the speech, that references to the Soviet Union as the 'enemy' should be replaced by 'adversary'—a word which expressed Kennedy's intention more precisely and which he employed for the rest of his life."[3]

But the game is carried far beyond the idea of passive defense. The passion to save the world from nuclear warfare can become so compelling that the affected nation entertains delusions, such as the belief that unilateral disarmament will be emulated by the conquering enemy. It drives statesmen to unequal treaties in the belief that any semblance of progress is worth while.

Perhaps the most abject evidence of the psychosis is in the United States obsession with disarmament. It is quite normal for a capitalist power to want to save money for welfare projects by reducing armament. But it is clearly not rational to suppose that a power committed to the conquest of the world wants to save money by disarmament. To such a power, the only useful potential of disarmament is to disarm its victim.

Even the capitalist mind tries to maintain an appearance of rationality. The United States has therefore postulated that the Soviet Union is not conquest-oriented but is like the United

States a peace-loving power interested only in its own security. All pacts, all international meetings, all disarmament conferences are framed in these terms. The Soviet Union is assumed to be a peace-loving power interested in world peace and order.

This assumption is of course belied by mountainous evidence of conquest-oriented philosophy, doctrine and behavior. But the Western detente mind does not admit these realities because it could not then conceive a means of avoiding nuclear war. False or not, it is *necessary* to make the peaceable assumption about the evolution of Soviet purposes.

As Ambassador George F. Kennan, a reputed authority on Soviet policy, put the matter to the House Subcommittee on the Far East and the Pacific:

> I have never felt that the Soviet government had intentions of embarking on an aggressive path by the same methods that Hitler used. For this reason, I felt our responses, too, had to be different ones. I think this has been proven correct over the years. And so far as the Soviet government is concerned, if we can get through with this present crisis over Vietnam in some way that does not entirely destroy our relations with the Soviet Union, we need not despair of an evolution of the nature of Soviet power, of its attitude toward its world relationships, which would permit an improving relationship with ourselves. That is my feeling.
>
> Since that possibility exists and since it is the only hopeful one I can see in a world where you have loose such things as nuclear weapons, I think we should be very, very careful not to damage it.[4]

This frame of mind is not unlike that in which President Roosevelt recognized the Soviet Union.

The prior policy of non-recognition had been eloquently explained by Secretary of State Bainbridge Colby in 1920:

> It is not possible for the government of the United States to recognize the present rulers of Russia as a government

with which the relation common to friendly governments can be maintained. . . . The existing regime in Russia is based upon the negation of every principle of honor and good faith, and every usage and convention underlying the whole structure of international law. . . . The responsibile leaders of the regime have freely and openly boasted that they are willing to sign agreements and undertakings with foreign powers while having not the slightest intention of observing such undertakings or carrying out such agreements. . . . Responsible spokesmen of this power . . . have declared that . . . the very existence of Bolshevism in Russia . . . depends . . . upon the occurrence of revolutions in all other great civilized nations, including the United States, which will destroy and overthrow their governments and set up Bolshevist rule in their stead.

In the view of this government there cannot be any common ground upon which it can stand with a power whose conceptions of international relations are as entirely alien to its own, so utterly repugant to its moral sense.[5]

In 1933, President Franklin D. Roosevelt put these objections aside. The Soviet regime had not changed for the better. If there was some extenuation of the revolutionary fervor of 1920, there could be none for the coarse Stalinism of 1933.

But the new Roosevelt policy was not based on realism. It simply assumed that through extending diplomatic relations to the Soviet Union, the United States would be able to influence Soviet behavior. Stalin made one of those promises he had sworn not to fulfill—that he would stop subversive activity in the United States.

In 37 years there has not been a scintilla of evidence that the United States has in any way moderated Soviet behavior. But there is a continuous history of Soviet subversion, intrigue and influence on United States policy. The continuing record of Soviet duplicity and enmity did not influence Roosevelt or his successors because, regardless of past failures, it was argued that diplomatic relations afforded the only chance of influencing Soviet behavior.

The Kennedy policy reverted to the principles of the Roosevelt pro-Soviet policy, temporarily sidetracked by the Truman policy, but now reinforced and rigidified with the fear of nuclear damnation. Under the new policy, disasters mounted in frequency and dimension, from the Bay of Pigs and the Berlin Wall to the war in Vietnam.

Let us be clear about the enormous error of this policy. It is true that we must avoid nuclear war. But it is not true that you can advance that aim by pretending that the Soviet leaders represent a peace-loving regime. It is not true that the ambitions of a conquest-oriented state can be defeated by the good will of the victim.

It is also true that the Soviet Union must avoid nuclear war. It is realistic to recognize that the Soviet leaders are as concerned to protect their institutions as we are to protect ours. Policy must be based on this reality.

It is a serious misjudgment of reality to suppose that every military initiative could escalate into nuclear war. The nuclear possibility requires both sides to be prudent. But if one side is so fearful of nuclear conflict that it retreats in fear from every requirement for military action, the other side is invited to wage sub-nuclear military aggression.

In a national foreign policy for the nuclear age, the United States must use its conventional power forthrightly to defend its legitimate interests, in confidence that the Soviet Union would not risk nuclear war to attack those interests. Such a posture would deter Communist aggression and promote peace in the world.

If this analysis makes clear the pervasive error of the Kennedy policy, it may help to explain why the United States, launched on a quest for peace, marched ever deeper into the morass of war.

XI NEUTRALIZING LAOS

★　　　★　　　★

LAOS WAS ONLY ONE OF THE CRITICAL PROBLEMS which President Kennedy found on his White House doorstep. He had to attend to it while Premier Khrushchev was pushing hard in other quarters of the globe.

In his final briefing of the President-elect on January 19, 1961 Dwight Eisenhower had stated his concern about Laos. "Eisenhower said that he had hoped that the Southeast Asia Treaty Organization would take charge of the 'controversy' but that the British and the French did not want SEATO to act. . . . If a political settlement could not be arranged in Laos, then this country must intervene. Eisenhower added that Laos was the key to all Southeast Asia."[1]

In Laos, the Communist Pathet Lao, reinforced by North Vietnamese forces, continued their offensive. In an effort to deter the foreign invasion, King Savang Vathana on February 19, 1961 proclaimed the neutrality of Laos and called upon all foreign powers to respect it. The United States and Great Britain pledged support of the declaration. Prince Souphanouvong, leader of the Pathet Lao, condemned it. The attack continued.

On February 24, 1961 Prime Minister Robert G. Menzies of Australia, visiting President Kennedy in Washington, expressed grave concern about the Communist aggression in Laos. On March third, New Zealand Prime Minister Keith J. Holyoake, on a state visit, expressed similar concern.

At a meeting on March 20, 1961 the National Security Council "discussed the possibility of moving a small number of American troops into the Mekong Valley not to fight the Pathet Lao but to deter them by their presence and provide a bargaining counter for an international conference. Walt Rostow argued persuasively for this limited commitment; but the Joint Chiefs opposed the sending of ground forces to the mainland of Asia, drawing a lurid picture of an all-out Communist response, with thousands of Viet Minh pouring into Laos and the ultimate possibility of war with China. Their recommendation was for all or nothing: either go in on a large scale, with 60,000 soldiers, air cover, and even nuclear weapons, or else stay out."[2]

On March 23, 1961, while SEATO military advisers were meeting in Bangkok, President Kennedy held a nationally televised and broadcast news conference to inform the American people about the critical situation in Laos. The President issued a stern warning to the Soviet Union, speaking in part as follows:

Firstly, we strongly and unreservedly support the goal of a neutral and independent Laos tied to no outside power or group of powers, threatening no one and free from any domination. Our support of the present duly-constituted government is aimed entirely and exclusively at that result.

Secondly, if there is to be a peaceful solution there must be a cessation of the present armed attacks by externally supported Communists. If these attacks do not stop, those who support a truly neutral Laos will have to consider their response. . . . No one should doubt our resolution on this point.

Thirdly, we are earnestly in favor of constructive negotiation among the nations concerned and among the leaders of Laos which can help Laos back to the pathway of independence and genuine neutrality. We strongly support the present British proposal of a prompt end of hostilities and prompt negotiation.[3]

On March 24, 1961 the SEATO Military Advisers issued a final communique on their three-day meeting in Bangkok. They reported unanimously that Communist support to the insurgent Pathet Lao guerrillas "had created a dangerous situation. This had emphasized the need for continued solidarity among the eight nations to safeguard the freedom of the peoples of the non-Communist states. . . . The ability of SEATO's defenses, supported by powerful added air and naval forces, has up to now been an effective deterrent to overt aggression."

On March 25, the *New York Times* reported, "Sources close to the top-secret military conference indicated that the top-ranking allied commanders in the Asian area had determined that Laos must be defended in the . . . Mekong basin, which includes the Laotian administrative capital at Vientiane and the royal seat of Luang Prabang." On the same day, the *London Observer* reported: "The British . . . fear that any threat of military action by SEATO will fatally prejudice the chances of diplomatic settlement." It was clear that the British Foreign Office would not sustain its military representatives.

On March 27-29, 1961 the SEATO Council of Foreign Ministers met in Bangkok. Dean Rusk represented the United States, Lord Home represented Great Britain and Couve de Murville represented France. According to Arthur Schlesinger, Jr., "Dean Rusk went to a SEATO conference at Bangkok on March 27 and secured troop pledges from Thailand, Pakistan and the Philippines, though French opposition prevented the organization as a whole from promising anything more specific than 'appropriate' measures."[4]

The final communique spoke in part as follows:

The Council notes with approval the present efforts for a cessation of hostilities and for peaceful negotiations to achieve an unaligned and independent Laos. If those efforts fail, however, and there continues to be an active military attempt to obtain control of Laos, members of SEATO are prepared, within the terms of the treaty, to take whatever action may be appropriate in the circumstances.[5]

SEATO seemed reduced to making idle threats. The resolution expressed by President Kennedy on March 23rd had dissolved in the face of British opposition. The *London Observer* of March 25 illustrated the British method of undermining resistance to Communist aggression when it voiced British fears that any threat of military force "would fatally prejudice the chances of diplomatic settlement." This British view was palpable nonsense, but it prevailed.

To assume in the face of aggression that stopping the aggression would jeopardize the possibility of diplomatic settlement is of course erroneous. Stopping the aggression establishes a basis for diplomatic settlement. If the aggression remains unopposed, the advance of the aggressor steadily undermines any diplomatic settlement except surrender. Britain simply refused to oppose Communist aggression in Asia which was not directed at her own possessions.

It seems unlikely that the cogency of the British argument persuaded President Kennedy to abandon his defense of Laos. Rather, there was just an American incapability of going it alone. As with Eisenhower at Dienbienphu in 1954, President Kennedy could not bring himself to maintain an independent posture. He accepted, perhaps unconsciously, a British veto on American policy.

At his June 3-4, 1961, meeting with Premier Khrushchev in Vienna, President Kennedy entered the summit meeting at which he intended to order the peace of the world. He came away badly shaken by the threatening bombast of the Soviet leader. He didn't seem to understand that Khrushchev had put on a dramatic act designed to scare him.

The President and the Premier agreed to neutralize Laos. The communique of June 4, 1961 stated in part as follows: "The

President and the Chairman reaffirmed their support of a neutral and independent Laos under a government chosen by the Laotians themselves, and of international agreements for insuring that neutrality and independence, and in this connection they have recognized the importance of an effective cease-fire."[6]

Britain had been working to reconvene the fourteen-nation conference which negotiated the Geneva Settlement of 1954. The new conference on Laos had opened at Geneva in May with Under-Secretary of State W. Averell Harriman representing the United States.

As the conference on Laos was meeting in Geneva, Walt W. Rostow, now Assistant to the Special Assistant to the President for National Security Affairs, spoke at Fort Bragg, N. C. in June, 1961:

> The truth is that guerrilla warfare, mounted from external bases—with rights of sanctuary—is a terrible burden to carry for any government in a society making its way toward modernization. . . . There will be no peace in the world if the international community accepts the outcome of a guerrilla war, mounted from outside a nation, as tantamount to a free election.

> The sending of men and arms across international boundaries and the direction of guerrilla war from outside a sovereign nation is aggression: and this is a fact which the whole international community must confront and whose consequent responsibilities it must accept. Without such international action, those against whom aggression is mounted will be driven inevitably to seek out and engage the ultimate source of aggression they confront. I suspect that in the end the real meaning of the conference on Laos will hinge on this question: It will depend on whether or not the international community is prepared to mount an International Control Commission which has the will and the capacity to control the borders it was designed to control. . . .[7]

Mr. Rostow should have known the answer to that question from previous performance of the Soviet Union in the "international community." Its purpose was to conquer these small free nations, not to preserve them. Mr. Rostow should have learned from experience with the Geneva Agreement of 1954 that the Communists will not abide the restraint of any international commission even when they have agreed to do so.

The first six months of the Kennedy Administration had shown talk but no fight. Under date of July 9, 1961, *New York Times* reporter Robert Trumbull reported from Hong Kong:

> Growing uncertainty over Washington's policies in Asia has seriously shaken the confidence of its Eastern allies in its determination to defend the area against Communism. Especially since the inconclusive Southeast Asia Treaty Organization Conference on Laos in Bangkok recently, the question has been raised in a number of Asian capitals whether the United States can be depended upon for early decisive steps to curb the advance of Communism regardless of cost.

> What these Asians want to know is whether the United States, in the final analysis, is willing to fight or will just keep talking as the Reds advance. . . .

> The Chinese Nationalist Foreign Minister, Shen Chang-huan, spoke even more bluntly this week: "The United States lacks courage to fight for international justice," he asserted. Despite official utterances to the contrary, neutralist sentiment is known to be proliferating in Thailand and Japan. . . . Australians in Singapore were heard to ask "If the United States will not defend Southeast Asia, will she defend Australia?"[8]

The Geneva negotiations dragged on without significant progress. Communist representatives required a surrender of all of Eastern Laos to their control so that they might wage from that territory the war against South Vietnam. They had not won such a position militarily but they were determined to get it in the conference. The free Asian powers, including the government of Laos, demurred. The conference became a process of American bludgeoning of Laos to accept the Communist terms.

It was not that President Kennedy didn't have better advice. There was awareness of the real issue in our governmental field personnel if not in Washington. Senator Thomas J. Dodd of Connecticut reported on his trip to Southeast Asia:

> I traveled through Southeast Asia just before the conclusion of the Laotian armistice.
>
> I talked to many people at that time. It is true that the armistice was favored by our Ambassador in Laos and it obviously must have had the support of important members of the State Department hierarchy. But the personnel of our embassies in Saigon and in Bangkok did not conceal from me their apprehensions over the consequences of such an armistice for Vietnam and Southeast Asia.
>
> All of this I reported on confidentially upon my return.[9]

The Communist side sought to accelerate the negotiations by starting an offensive against the Laotian government forces which cut the Vientiane-Luang Prabang road. In May 1962 President Kennedy moved about 5,000 U. S. troops into Thailand for possible use in the defense of Laos. He called on the Soviet Union to restrain the violation of the 1961 cease-fire. Premier Khrushchev warned that the United States action could lead to another Korean War.

This Soviet tension was too much for President Kennedy. The Laotian representatives at Geneva were given an ultimatum by Averell Harriman to comply with the Communist terms or else. It is an interesting sidelight on American policymaking that Harriman had said in Saigon in 1961, "We have to give some places on the Government of Laos to the Communists."[10]

On June 11, 1962 the reorganization of the Laotian government was announced from Khong Khay, Laos. The anti-Communist Premier Boun Oum would retire. The country would be divided into three areas with the Pathet Lao taking the eastern sector, the neutralist forces holding a middle region on the Plaines des Jarres and the Government forces holding the western sector. The neutralist Prince Souvanna Phouma would become Premier of the new tripartite government. He had earned that distinction by courting Red China and the Soviet Union. He saw, as did all Asians, that the United States would not support the pro-Western government of Prince Boun Oum.

Premier Khrushchev hailed the "agreement" in a message to President Kennedy. "The results achieved in the settlement of the Laotian problem strengthen the convictions that success in solving other international problems which now divide states and create tension in the world can be achieved on the same road as well," he glowed.[11]

President Kennedy at his press conference on June 14, 1961 was more sombre: "We have to wait now and see whether we can make this agreement . . . work. If we can, then it will be an encouraging step forward to more amicable relations between the Soviet Union and the United States and we can discuss other problems."[12] Behind him lay the Bay of Pigs and the Berlin Wall. Ahead lay the Cuban missile confrontation. The war in Vietnam was increasing in scale and intensity. Still he spoke hopefully. He could not face reality.

The Conference agreement, endorsing the changes in the Laotian government and providing for the withdrawal of all foreign forces, was signed on July 23, 1962. Prime Minister Harold Macmillan of Britain sent congratulations to the conferees. The agreement would, he said "afford the people of Laos the chance to pursue their own peace and prosperity to which all parties in Laos are devoted."[13]

The game was played out. Pious implications that the Communists had changed their stripes were spoon-fed to the American people. The United States had reneged on a solemn treaty obligation not because our allies in the area were unwilling to fight but because we would not support them. Republicans and Democrats had concurred in the President's decision. The stock of gumption was falling very low.

Maybe the shortage was one of comprehension. In retreating

from his March statement, President Kennedy had run scared. He told congressional leaders that the defense of Laos might require hundreds of thousands of American soldiers if Red China intervened. Who scared him with such idle fears?

The defense of Laos required *no* American soldiers. This was an area of Thai hegemony. The Thais had twice the population of North Vietnam. Would they stop the North Vietnam invasion? Yes, with American support. All the United States had to do was to keep China out, and that was comparable to keeping the Soviet Union out of West Berlin. The Thais would do the rest.

In April, 1970 in response to a question why the 1962 agreements on Laos had not been effective, Ambassador Averell Harriman, who had been our chief negotiator, said:

> I have no idea. . . . We thought that the co-chairmen were going to have responsibilities. It's written into the agreement that the British and the Soviet Union have responsibilities for the observance of the agreement, and they haven't done it. Of course, the Soviets are the ones that should have kept North Vietnam in line. They didn't keep the agreement for a single day, you know. We took out all of our military persons, some 660-odd, and the other side had some thousands and they left at least five or six thousand in the country.[14]

Of course Ambassador Harriman and President Kennedy knew in 1962 that the Communists were flouting the treaty. Why didn't they require compliance by North Vietnam? They were so addled by their fears and hopes that they could only pretend peace. As the Soviet Union and Great Britain knew, the surest way to stop a man is to confront him with an insoluble problem, imaginary though it be.

XII

THE DEFENSE OF
SOUTH VIETNAM

★ ★ ★

THE NEW KENNEDY GOVERNMENT IN WASHINGTON
was crippled not alone by its fateful approach to detente with
the Soviet Union but by a host of related attitudes, misconceptions and misjudgments. It seemed to have absorbed some of
the socialist rationalization of social phenomena in developing
societies. It showed a motherly solicitude for the modernization
of South Vietnam, a confidence in its own infallibility and an
intolerance of any contrary prescriptions. Policy seemed to be
in the hands of a theorizing and tragically impractical crew
only recently liberated from the halls of academia.

As the war mounted in scale, the regnant theoreticians
sought to explain the disaster not in terms of their own mistakes but in the imagined mistakes of their predecessors. Arthur Schlesinger, Jr. wrote:

> The commitment to South Vietnam, like the parallel attempt to make the languid country of Laos a bastion of
> Western power, followed directly from the Dulles conception of the world as irrevocably split into two unified and

hostile blocs. In such a world, the threat of Communism was indivisible and the obligation to oppose that threat unlimited. . . .

A more discriminating view might have regarded Ho Chi Minh, the boss of North Vietnam, less as the obedient servan of a homogeneous Sino-Soviet bloc than as the leader of a nationalist communism, historically mistrustful of the Chinese and eager to preserve his own freedom of action. It might have taken a more relaxed attitude toward the evolution of Vietnam; and it might have decided to draw the American line on the Siamese side of the Mekong River, where both the political and military foundations for an American position were a good deal stronger.[1]

As though to escape from using the power which it had, the Administration advanced new theories about guerrilla warfare. The idea was that we must develop our guerrilla warfare techniques to keep the level of conflict low and thereby avoid conventional war. Walt W. Rostow explained the need to men receiving guerrilla training at Fort Bragg, North Carolina:

What is happening throughout Latin America, Africa, the Middle East, and Asia, is this: Old societies are changing their ways in order to create and maintain a national personality on the world scene and to bring to their peoples the benefits modern technology can offer. This process is truly revolutionary. It touches every aspect of the traditional life—economic, social and political. The introduction of modern technology brings about not merely new methods of production but a new style of family life, new links between the villages and the cities, the beginnings of national policies and a new relationship to the world outside.

Thus our central task in the underdeveloped areas as we see it, is to protect the independence of the revolutionary process now going forward. . . .[2]

Douglas Pike made a similar comment about change in the villages of Vietnam:

The fundamental assumption here is that when people, especially those in developing societies, are exposed to new ideas, new methods, new social structures, certain things happen, and neither they nor their society are ever again quite the same. This assumption seems to me to be beyond debate. The Communists have brought to the villages of South Vietnam significant social change and have done so largely by means of the communication process. This process is what this book is all about.[3]

Certainly the authoritarian Communist regime is a decided change from the Confucian family system. But it is not a progressive change. It is an oppressive change growing not from communications but out of the barrel of a gun; a change which people flee when they can. No Communist system in any land could survive a free vote of its people.

A third view of the same process was given by Richard Barnet, a more radical Administration consultant:

It should be our major task to help create a framework for tempering the violence which accompanies the modernization of ancient societies, while at the same time supporting that process. The goals of "stability" and "order" cannot be achieved by alliances with the groups in those societies whom the people wish to overthrow. If we need a slogan, it should be, "Let us make the world safe for revolution." . . . What is needed is time to find ways to ease the world into the next century, in which familiar ideologies and the familiar patterns of nationhood will almost surely be profoundly altered.[4]

None of these views, I submit, grapples realistically with the real problem of change: the determined, ruthless, systematic destruction of the free society, wherever it may be, by cadres trained to subvert, terrorize and destroy all who resist the Communist tyranny. Our progress is smothered not by feudalism but by the illusions of socialism.

Mr. Rostow was confident of our capacity to handle the Vietnam problem. He said:

I am confident that we can deal with the kind of operation now under way in Vietnam. It is an extremely dangerous operation, and it could overwhelm Vietnam if the Vietnamese—aided by the Free World—do not deal with it. But it is an unsubtle operation by the book, based more on murder than on political or psychological appeal.

When Communists speak of wars of national liberation and of their support for "progressive forces," I think of the systematic program of assassination now going forward in which the principal victims are health, agriculture, and education officers in the Vietnam villages. . . . With resolution and confidence on all sides and with the assumption of international responsibility for the frontier problem, I believe we are going to bring this threat to the independence of Vietnam under control. . . .[5]

Where indeed did Mr. Rostow get the idea that the Soviet Union would approve of closing frontiers which its satellite must cross in the conquest of South Vietnam?

That aberration seems strange, for Ho Chi Minh was already intensifying his assault on South Vietnam. The guerrilla war moved into its second stage of stepped-up assassination of officials, more attacks on government installations and small-scale clashes with home guardsmen. Between January and May 1961 estimates of Communist guerrilla strength increased from 9,000 to twelve thousand. A more realistic perception of events was held in the United States Embassy in Saigon. Senator Dodd reported:

Our Embassy personnel in Saigon expressed the fear that the conclusion of the Laotian armistice would enable the Communists to infiltrate men and material on a much larger scale and would result at an early date in a marked intensification of the Viet Cong insurgency. . . .[6]

On April 9, 1961, President Diem and Vice President Ngugyen Ngoc Tho were elected to a second five-year term. Despite the intensified guerrilla activity, the people voted in large numbers. Diem and Tho received 85 percent of the vote, running against two opposing slates.

On May 4, 1961 Senator Fulbright, Chairman of the Senate Foreign Relations Committee, met with President Kennedy and later announced that he would support sending U. S. combat troops to South Vietnam and Thailand. He had opposed sending U. S. troops to Laos but he considered that the present question was different because the Thais and the South Vietnamese had shown determination to defend themselves against communism. The next day, President Kennedy announced that he was sending Vice President Johnson to Asia to examine the need for additional aid to South Vietnam.

In Saigon, Vice President Johnson pledged U. S. support of the war against communism. On May 13, he announced a joint program negotiated with President Diem for an additional $40 million of aid to increase and strengthen the civil guard and the army and to support public works and social welfare programs. On his return to Washington and after consulting with President Kennedy, the Vice President announced an additional $100 million of U. S. aid to go chiefly to South Vietnam, Thailand and Pakistan.

Meanwhile, the scale of warfare continued to increase. On September 19, 1500 guerrillas overran the city of Phouc Minh, 60 miles north of Saigon and a provincial capital. On October 2, President Diem announcd that a real war was in progress with the enemy attacking in regular formation, fully armed and equipped.

In October, General Maxwell D. Taylor, Special Assistant to the President, flew to Vietnam for a survey of needs. He urged national mobilization and expressed his confidence in the South Vietnam defenses. Arthur Schlesinger was to write of this report: "With Rostow, Taylor felt the situation in Vietnam required a shift in the character of the American effort from advice to limited partnership, and he expressed the conviction that Vietnamese performance across the whole political-military-economic-social spectrum could be substantially improved if more Americans were prepared to work side by side with them on key problems."

On December 11, the first contingent of United States Army helicopters and 400 crewmen to operate and serve them arrived

for support of the South Vietnam Army. Fighter planes and
B-26 bombers with U. S. crews were also being moved into South
Vietnam.

As the year closed, President Kennedy assured President
Diem, "We shall promptly increase our assistance to your defense effort."

No doubt President Kennedy was taken aback by the intensity of the Communist attack. Within the year, the enemy had
moved first to intensified guerrilla attacks and then to open
warfare.

According to the Kennedy theory of international relations,
his agreement at Vienna to neutralize Laos should have
removed one point of conflict with the Communist powers and
opened up new avenues of cooperation. He found instead that
the other side only intensified its pressures in South Vietnam.
With new assurance of a secure line of communications
through Laos, Ho Chi Minh moved swiftly to attack.

The first response of the President was to defend South Vietnam. It had been relatively secure when he took office. To lose
it after withdrawing from Laos might be more than an administration could stand. Thus, he moved to support South Vietnam. But even at this early date, President Kennedy bore the
fatal flaw which was to make his defensive measures futile. He
would not countenance what had to be done to stop the aggression.

Whatever the confusion in Washington and London, there
was no uncertainty in Saigon. President Diem knew what had
to be done to win. In an address to the United States Senate on
February 23, 1965, Senator Thomas J. Dodd of Connecticut explained the issue:

> The hub of the Ho Chi Minh Trail is the town of Tchepone,
> inside the Laotian frontier, just south of the Seventeenth
> Parallel, the dividing line between North Vietnam and
> South Vietnam.

> I recall that when I met with President Diem in April of

1961, he urged that Americans assist him and the Laotian government in pre-emptive action to secure three centers in the Laotian panhandle—Tchepone, Saravane and Attopeu—in order to prevent the large-scale infiltration which is today taking place.

I still have a copy of the marked map which he gave me in outlining his project. Had Diem's advice been followed there would have been no Ho Chi Minh Trail. But this was at the time of the Laotian armistice and we were not disposed to take any actions which might provoke the Laotian Communists. So nothing was done.[7]

President Diem was quite right. South Vietnam could not be defended by waiting within its boundaries for the enemy to attack. It could be defended only by moving out to strike the forces and installations of the attacking enemy. That truth is as old as warfare.

Why didn't President Kennedy understand this? Who could have persuaded him to cripple South Vietnam by giving sanctuary to the aggressor?

The argument for appeasement is always insidious: "If you limit your operations, you will limit the war. If you attack the enemy you will expand the war. Restraint in the use of force serves peace. If you cross the border, Red China will intervene. If you bomb a Soviet ship, we shall have war with the Soviet Union." A pack of lies—but there is no doubt that they were marshaled against President Kennedy by his own staff.

President Kennedy was reaping the tragic harvest of his error. The United States had maintained a Military Advisory Group in South Vietnam since 1954 to train the military forces. In the six years before 1961, the size of the group had increased from about 300 to about 700 men. In that time, not one American soldier had been killed in hostile action. Then American casualties began to reflect the mounting action. In July, 1961 the first American soldier was killed in action. By the end of the year, U. S. forces had been increased to more than 4,000 and combat support was being given to the Army of South Vietnam.

At first, the political work of the Communists in South Vietnam was done by the Lao Dang Party of North Vietnam, the Communist Workers' Party. As the revolutionary activity increased in 1961, Hanoi became concerned to preserve the appearance of an internal revolt. It organized the Peoples Revolutionary Party in South Vietnam on January 1, 1962, to do the cadre work of the National Liberation Front. An internal document informed the party cadre:

> The new Party must maintain the outward appearance of a separation from the Lao Dong so that the enemy cannot use it in his propaganda. . . . Within the party it is necessary to explain that the founding of the PRP has the purpose of isolating the Americans and the Ngo Dinh Diem regime and countering their accusations of an invasion of the South by the North.[8]

The Soviet Union joined in the attack on South Vietnam, setting a pattern for the Communist parties in all countries. In a note to Britain, co-chairman of the Geneva conference, on January 10, 1962, it condemned the United States for gross interference in the internal affairs of South Vietnam and for open violation of the agreements on Indochina. The Soviet note also accused President Diem of abolishing all democratic liberties and creating a military dictatorship based on ruthless terror.

These Soviet charges set a line of attack not only for Communist parties but for elements of the President's own party which had a constitutional aversion to resisting Communist aggression. Of course the Government of South Vietnam had tightened its internal security arrangements and suspended normal peacetime processes, just as the United States had done during World War II. The country was at war, though an undeclared war.

The President's critics berated the suspension of peacetime due process in South Vietnam and opposed the increased U. S. military support of the Diem Government. Some argued that this was a civil war, that the Viet Cong were merely rebelling against the feudal rule of the Diem regime and that the United States should stay out of the conflict. These critics seemed to regard the Communist revolutionary war as an exercise in argumentation which would be refuted by the example of people having a decent government.

This criticism of the Diem government by Washington bureaucrats, and especially by unnamed spokesmen in the State Department, emerged in the early days of the Kennedy Administration. It intensified as frustration grew because President Diem would not meet the Communist onslaught with the increased civil liberties which the Communists demanded.

Increasingly these critics asserted that President Diem had lost the support of the people. On July 25, 1962 Homer Bigart of the *New York Times* reported after a half-year stay in South Vietnam: "The United States by massive and unqualified support of the regime of President Ngo Dinh Diem, has helped arrest the spread of Communist insurgency in South Vietnam. But victory is remote. The issue remains in doubt because the Vietnamese President seems incapable of winning the loyalty of his people."

There was indeed confusion in the country as the Communist terror attacks mounted and the United States would not permit the South Vietnam government to make the declaration of war which could unify the country. The people were confused and fearful and many sought security in neutralism. Diem faced the reality of war while his critics, with American support, assailed him for not maintaining the freedoms of peacetime— the right to criticize the government, to oppose the war effort, to advocate neutralism, et cetera. United States policy was playing into the hands of Soviet strategy.

During 1962, the scale of conflict grew. The South Vietnamese Army was increased to about 200,000 men. Organized Viet Cong military forces were estimated to number 25,000 men. The United States forces, now under a new Military Assistance Command headed by General Paul D. Harkins, had increased to 11,000 men. Americans remained in support and advisory roles but were often in battle. They had orders to fire only if fired upon. Fifty-one were killed in action during the year.

In December of 1962, President Diem reported to the National Assembly that the war had turned for the better. Everywhere the Army had taken the offensive and had overcome the advantages won by the Viet Cong the previous year. The optimism seemed warranted, despite the increased Communist strength, notably by the progress being made in the strategic hamlet program.

During 1961, Great Britain had sent Sir Robert Thompson, a guerrilla war authority with experience in Malaya, to South Vietnam to assist with the counter-guerrilla operations. On his recommendation the government began early in 1962 a program of building strategic hamlets which would assemble the people of rural areas into defended villages. By providing security to the people, this program isolated them from the Viet Cong. It denied the Viet Cong the protection and resources of a cowed people. It built up local defense forces to exclude small Communist units from the protected areas.

The government of South Vietnam, under supervision from the President's brother and special assistant, Ngo Dinh Nhu, prosecuted the program with vigor. Some said that Mr. Nhu was pushing the program too fast and alienating the rural people. But after one year, Sir Robert Thompson was to report that the Diem government had "turned the corner and was winning the people back from the Communists."

The year 1963 opened in that spirit. There was optimism not only in the South Vietnamese government but in the American command. Ambassador Frederick Nolting, Jr. and General Harkins were optimistic about the military progress in the countryside, though they were concerned about political conflict of the factions in Saigon.

The favorable military prospect did not inspire unalloyed joy. Some Americans were deeply concerned about the scale of U. S. involvement in South Vietnam and about increasing U. S. participation in the war. American soldiers trained to attack and destroy the enemy could not comprehend that President Diem did not want to wipe out the enemy—they were his people, though they were now under control of Communist cadres.

In February, 1963 the Mansfield panel of four United States Senators submitted to the Senate Foreign Relations Committee a report of investigation of the U. S. aid programs in South Vietnam, Laos, Cambodia, Thailand, Burma and the Philippines. The Senators expressed concern about the U. S. aid program for South Vietnam which was running at $400 million per year and requiring 12,000 Americans for military support. They expressed hope that a general reassessment of security requirements in Southeast Asia would make savings possible but they also cautioned against the danger of cuts which would help the Viet Cong. They were worried about the United States taking over from South Vietnam the principal responsibility for the defense.

In a personal note, Senator Mansfield compared the situation in South Vietnam with that which he had found there during his 1955 visit. "What is most disturbing," he wrote, "is that Vietnam now appears to be as it was then, only at the beginning of coping with its grave inner problems. All of the current difficulties existed in 1955, along with the hope and energy to meet them. But it is seven years later and $2 billion of U. S. aid later. Yet, substantially the same difficulties remain, if, indeed, they have not been compounded." Senator Mansfield just did not understand what had happened, and in this he was as one with other members of the Senate Foreign Relations Committee.

After the battle of Ap Bac on January 2, 1963, in which a Viet Cong battalion escaped from an Army of Vietnam trap, U. S. advisers imprudently aired their criticism to the press. The resulting publicity raised Vietnamese resentment which Ambassador Nolting sought to soothe. But this kind of idle criticism by gung-ho American officers who did not understand the different Vietnamese attitude toward the war was to be a source of continuing friction. Because the press widely published such criticism and scoffed at official reports on the war, the American people, too, were badly misled.

On March 9, 1963, in statements which seemed to bely the Sino-Soviet divorce, Moscow and Peking accused the United States of using poison gas in Vietnam. The United States first denied the charges, but then, concerned about world-wide criticism, curtailed its use of non-toxic gases.

As the war continued, the familiar criticism of the Diem government as a dictatorship (though it had been re-elected in 1961 by overwhelming vote of the people in free elections); the condemnation of the legislature's declaration of an emergency, suspending judicial process in security cases; and resentment of the restriction on public assembly were exploited by a hostile press. Strangely enough in a country where the President's brother was Attorney General in charge of the F.B.I., the similar relationship in Saigon—where Mr. Nhu served the President as a personal, unpaid assistant—was roundly criticized by the American press. It was nepotism in Saigon but true brotherhood in Washington.

All this criticism, derived largely from a base of propaganda planted by the world-wide Communist parties and exacerbated by the truly blundering quality of United States policy, did not seem to dismay President Kennedy until the charges of religious persecution were launched. In the war to date, President Kennedy had maintained a solid, bi-partisan support. But in a brief six months the Buddhist campaign, ably seconded by American news media, was to split the alliance, overthrow the Diem government and plunge the defense of South Vietnam into a state of chaos.

XIII

THE BETRAYAL

★ ★ ★

IN AN ADDRESS ON MARCH 26, 1964, SECRETARY OF DE-
fense Robert S. McNamara said:

> In early 1963, President Kennedy was able to report that
> "the spearpoint of aggression has been blunted in South
> Vietnam." It was evident that the government had seized
> the initiative in most areas from the insurgents. But this
> progress was interrupted in 1963 by the political crisis
> arising from the troubles between the government and the
> Buddhists, students and other non-communist opposition-
> ists. President Diem lost the confidence and loyalty of his
> people; there were accusations of maladministration and
> injustice.[1]

In these few sentences, Secretary McNamara told the not
credible Administration story of what had happened in 1963.
President Diem was winning the war—and that meant his popular support was increasing. Suddenly the people turned
against him and he was overthrown.

That story is for children. President Diem did not lose the
confidence of the Vietnamese people. The November coup
against him was conducted by a handful of generals who acted

under specific direction from the United States government and for reasons which they have explained. American officials involved in the plot have given no honest account of their involvement so we can only surmise their motives from the course of events.

While American military forces, working constructively with the government of South Vietnam, had indeed contributed to the favorable security situation cited by President Kennedy in 1963, American political forces were working against that strategy. The querulous, naive academicians and the associated left-wing zealots whom President Kennedy had brought to Washington were busy wielding their new and unaccustomed power. They seemed to feel a mission to change the world.

We have noted the December 1960 proclamation of the National Liberation Front condemning the Diem government as a corrupt fascist regime and calling for its overthrow. This war cry circled the globe with the speed of the Communist communications media. It was reflected back from the Kennedy Administration in a United Press International dispatch from Washington on May 7, 1961 that "American planners also hope Diem will rid himself of the taint of corruption. This stems not from his own actions but from riches acquired by his relations through their inside positions with the regime."[2] How did Communist lies so quickly reach into the policy-making echelons of the State Department?

Could the anonymous spokesman have been Averell Harriman, the Assistant Secretary of State for Far East Affairs? This was the same Averell Harriman who later in the year was to forecast American policy favoring a coalition government in Laos. Was he so sensitive to Soviet policy through his prior service as Ambassador to Stalin's Russia or so responsive to British suggestion that his course was already set? Why had a former Secretary of Commerce, Governor of New York and Presidential aspirant accepted the lowly post of Assistant Secretary normally reserved for bright young men?

Whatever the source, that voice was never silenced, in the

State Department or in the *New York Times.* It was a curious thing to have the Secretary of State making the usual speeches about alliance solidarity and resistance to communism while his subordinates were undermining the one ally engaged in a shooting war.

Communist propaganda claimed that the government of South Vietnam was repressive and dictatorial. Diem's critics, in Saigon and in Washington, shared the view. Douglas Pike, who from his post in the U. S. Information Agency office in Saigon had a close view of the affair, gave us the American rationalization of this posture. He wrote that in 1959, the government alienated

> persons and families of persons victimized by improper administration of law 10/59 which provided for "repression of acts of sabotage, of infringements of national security, and of attacks upon the life or property of citizens." Special tribunals from whose verdict there was no appeal heard these cases and could mete out only death or life imprisonment sentences; often the tribunal became a weapon of local vendettas, quite without the knowledge of Saigon.[3]

What "improper administration"? All tribunals are fallible, but charges of malfeasance should not be stated in broad terms without supporting evidence. Neither Pike nor any other critic has to my knowledge sustained the charge so broadly made.

We know that war was being waged against South Vietnam when the National Assembly authorized summary procedures. The action was prudent. Of course it was resented by those South Vietnamese who were of or closely associated with the Viet Cong. It did not alienate the people whom the law protected.

Douglas Pike was the victim of a propaganda line which he did not comprehend. He spoke in terms of the prevailing political passions. But when in July 1965, after 20 months of unmitigated disaster following the overthrow of the Diem Government, the GVN decreed the death penalty for Viet Cong terrorists, corrupt officials, speculators and black marketeers, the United States confessed at last the necessity and the justice of such measures.

These general charges of loss of public support were advanced by Professor Bernard Fall, who argued that the growth of the Viet Cong rebellion measured public disaffection with the government. The contention may be acceptable to academicians who regard communism as a sociological response to oppression, but it has no correlation with reality. The April 1961 elections showed that Diem was more popular, if that were possible, than he had been in 1955; for in 1961 he faced two opposing candidates and not merely an absentee Emperor.

Facts to the contrary notwithstanding, the sniping at Diem persisted. Arthur Schlesinger, Jr. voiced the perspective of the Kennedy approach when he wrote:

> Diem, a profound traditionalist, ran a family despotism in the Oriental manner. He held power in his own hands, regarded opposition as treason, showed disdain for the shallow institutions of Western democracy, and aimed to restore the ancient Annamese morality. . . . Living standards, indeed, had risen faster in South than in North Vietnam where Ho Chi Minh concentrated on investment rather than consumption.[4]

The worst smears were directed at Diem's brother, who held no power except in service to the President. Diem's integrity was too widely known for attacks on it to be credible. Mr. Nhu was charged with mistakes and chicanery. Americans affected not to understand his philosophy of personal responsibility as opposed to state responsibility, so far had Americans forsaken their own heritage:

> Ngo Dinh Nhu particularly sought to work almost exclusively in the spiritual domain. For instance, in a significant speech on April 17, 1963, he defined the events of the moment in Vietnam as a struggle "for the salvation of the Fatherland . . . against feudalism, colonialism, and com-

munism, against underdevelopment and disunity. . . . To build a new society, a new life with new values, to live by his own means, to work for his own security and with his own strength, starting from the infrastructure of the hamlets and quarters to pervade the superstructure of the State—is not this the profound and real operation of our people?" . . .

The language was not in terms of the state serving the people, nor of a government acting for its people; it was a declaration that the people must do for themselves what they wanted done. . . . None of this related to the idea that by providing social services and by performing other civic action tasks the government of Vietnam could prove to the rural people that it was worthy of their support, that their interest lay in supporting that government. . . .

Under United States pressure Ngo Dinh Nhu agreed to go along with efforts to provide social services to villages, paid for by the United States, although he continued his spiritual exhortation work, chiefly using "personalism" as his doctrinal instrument.[5]

But the sociologists and political theorists are so enamored of their hypotheses that they have tried to rewrite history accordingly. They found, for example, that the Diem government did not have a proper balance:

For the Diem government the Northern refugee group became a major manpower recruitment pool; many of these people were trained, efficient, dedicated and, in addition, uninterested in Southern political infighting. The GVN's civil service soon became asymmetrical, too sectarian, too exclusively Northern; Diem was accused of "loading the government with Catholics," which most of the Northerners were, yet the refugees were the only significant source of trained personnel available.[6]

In this charge too, the critics have disregarded facts to repeat common canards. Although Catholic leadership in the government and in the Army was in higher percentage than in the total population, the Catholics were a distinct minority in both institutions. But worse than their misrepresentation is the inference that religion and "Northernness" either were or should be criteria for filling government posts. They were not, because these considerations were not significant in Vietnamese society. Men were selected or promoted for ability and for their loyalty to the country.

Of course, these and myriad other aspersions against the Diem government and the Ngo family were rife among the factions of Saigon. A society which could register more than 60 separate political parties after the death of Diem, obviously had that propaganda talent. But these factions had no roots in the countryside. They were vociferous but impotent. Diem understood the difference, though Americans did not.

Perhaps the American misjudgment was best stated in one sentence by Pike: "The third weakness, stemming from the first two, was the highly conservative nature of the government in a political situation calling for liberal or even radical government policies." That is precisely what the American would-be reformers thought, but they were tragically wrong. Their "liberal and even radical" measures which Diem resisted were grossly inept and impractical; it was Diem who regarded the situation realistically.

Schlesinger described the conflict more colorfully:

> The Americans did tend to regard Vietnam, in the Vice President's words, as a "young and unsophisticated" nation, populated by affable little men, unaccustomed to the modern world, who if sufficiently backed up by instruction and encouragement might amount to something. The Vietnamese, regarding their nation as infinitely older and more sophisticated than the United States, looked on the Americans as impatient, naive and childlike, lacking all sense of form or history.[7]

It was of course the responsibility of Communist intelligence to know about the conflicts and to exacerbate them in every way possible. This was the real battlefield.

Some critics have regarded the May 8, 1963 riot at Hue as a spontaneous spark which started the violence of the following months. The theory of spontaneity is not credible. There is too much evidence both that the conflict with police was deliberately incited and that careful preparation for the event had been made.

The incident arose over flying the newly-designed flag of the General Buddhist Association in violation of law during a celebration of Buddha's birthday. In an effort to promote nationalism and de-emphasize factionalism, the government had prescribed that other flags must be subordinated to the national flag in all public ceremonies. The General Buddhist Association raised its flag above the national flag in its procession. When police sought to correct the offense to the national emblem, strife ensued, explosions occurred, people were killed and injured.

Tensions ran high and were skilfully directed against the government by the Buddhist leader, Thich Tri Quang. The government alleged that persons had been killed and injured not by police fire but by a plastic explosive detonated among the people. But the Buddhists had been first in the world press with their account of police brutality.

The ensuing events had all the spontaneity of a planned campaign. Charges were made against the government. Catholic oppression of Buddhism was alleged. Punishment of the police "murderers" was demanded. A public funeral for the "victims" was organized to incite anti-government feelings.

When President Diem appointed a special commission headed by Vice President Nguyen Ngoc Tho, a Buddhist, to negotiate with the Buddhist protest leaders, Diem's brother Nhu objected. He urged that the demonstrations were a serious threat to the security of the State and that they must be stopped by force. Diem, however, was seeking an amicable resolution of differences. He overruled Nhu's objections.

Vice President Nguyen Ngoc Tho represented the government in negotiations with Buddhist leaders. He agreed that the government would compensate the injured but he would not

admit guilt. Negotiations deadlocked. On June 11, 1963 an elderly monk, Thich Quang Duc, committed public suicide by
burning, with the help of two brother monks. Brother monks
poured on the gasoline, Duc lit the match.

Buddhist demonstrations followed throughout the country
and other immolations occurred. American newsmen worked
in collusion with representatives of the General Buddhist Association to film and report the planned suicides and to maintain
in the daily press through the wire services a veritable storm
of innuendo about the oppression of the Diem regime and the
innocence of the persecuted Buddhists. That these reports were
palpably untrue and grossly misleading was of scant concern to
the reporters at the scene or to the editors back home. The press
was making world headlines.

The attack on President Diem was led by the *New York Times*
and the Associated Press. From their cue, the whole American
newspaper establishment fell into line for one of the most
tragic hoaxes ever foisted on the American people. Paul Jones,
a columnist for the *Philadelphia Bulletin,* has described the
schizophrenia of the time:

> Since I was the only man on my paper who had ever been
> to South Vietnam (at that time), I thought my views might
> carry some weight. In vain. If I disagreed with the *Times*
> version of the meaning of events in South Vietnam, or
> even of the nature and organizational structure of Bud-
> dhism in that country, I must be wrong. The paper chose
> to follow the *New York Times* lead right down the line, as
> did the rest of the American press.[8]

There were individual exceptions. Joseph Alsop visited Saigon and likened the zeal of the young reporters for Diem's head
to a similar zeal which he had seen among the young American
reporters in Chungking who had reviled Chiang Kai-shek during World War II. Marguerite Higgins did a superb job of reporting events as they were, both in the war in the field and in the
politics of Saigon. She went to the Buddhist command post at
the Xa Loi Pagoda in Saigon where she interviewed Thich Tri
Quang, the militant Buddhist leader. She remarked his lack of

concern about the war against the Communists. "It is possible the current disorders could lead to Communist gains. But if this happens, it will be Diem's fault, not ours," he said.[9] His solution to the war was neutralism. "We cannot get an arrangement with the North until we get rid of Diem and Nhu," he said.

Among the Saigon reporters, only Miss Higgins and Rev. Patrick O'Connor of the National Catholic News Service seemed to grasp the reality that Thich Tri Quang and his handful of seditionists were victimizing the Buddhists of Vietnam no less than the American news media. Thich Tri Quang was giving aid and comfort to the enemy.

The Buddhist Association of Tri Quang had organized an efficient propaganda operation and "suicide promotion" squads to recruit candidates for immolation. Innocent monks from the countryside were told outrageous tales about government persecution of the Buddhist religion. They were told that by volunteering to sacrifice their lives they would gain great merit and high rank in their next reincarnation. The entire routine of sacrifice was worked out in detail, with the assistance of other monks where needed.

A few monks, who through inadvertence learned of the lies which had been told them, evaded their grisly ordeal. But many completed their directed suicides.

Thich Tri Quang did not act alone. From the first incident in May right through the summer, the American government stood in support of Quang and opposed to the South Vietnam government. At first there was only the unidentified Washington spokesman who wanted to end corruption in the Diem government. Then there was the anonymous statement to the *New York Times:* "What do you want us to do? We're in a box. We don't like that Government but it's the only one around. We can't fight a war and a revolution at the same time, so lay off."[10]

Finally there was public censure by the President of the United States on September 2, 1963: "I don't think that the war can be won unless the people support the effort and, in my opinion, in the last two months the Government has gotten out of touch with the people."[11]

These were not expressions of concern for an ally. They were attacks on an ally. Suggestions regarding the internal affairs of an ally are transmitted confidentially, not in public print. The effect, and we must assume it was the planned effect, of these statements was to undermine the President of South Vietnam. They were so interpreted in Saigon and throughout the world.

The coordination of Quang's campaign with U. S. policy was emphasized when a Buddhist spokesman said to Marguerite Higgins in August 1963: "When Lodge gets here there will really be some excitement."[12]

Henry Cabot Lodge was indeed a key piece on the 1963 checkerboard. He had been living in Paris, working for a NATO affiliate, the Atlantic Institute. Paris was of course a refuge for wealthy Vietnamese emigres who hated President Diem. French elites, too, resented Diem's expulsion of the French and his turn to the United States for assistance. Who inspired Lodge to ask for the Ambassadorship in South Vietnam? Or did John Kennedy know enough about Lodge's views to feel that Lodge would do the hatchet job? How felicitous to have a Republican hangman!

The announcement of Lodge's appointment was made by the President on June 27, 1963, seven weeks after the Hue riot and two weeks after the Duc suicide. Lodge went first to Washington for briefing by the President and the State Department, then to Saigon. He arrived in Saigon on August 22, one day after the government raid on pagodas harboring seditious monks and protecting their activities. He pointedly called on the monk Tri Quang before presenting his credentials to President Diem.

Once again the U. S. news media grossly misrepresented an event to the American people. The police raids of August 21 were falsely reported as striking at the Buddhist religion. In fact, only twelve of the 4,000 pagodas in the country were raided. About 1,000 were arrested and after questioning, all but a few dozen of the apparent ringleaders were released. The false propaganda of the Buddhist militants was relayed by American news media to sustain the allegations of massive oppression by the Government.

The raids of August 21 had been prompted by information

that certain pagodas were being used to store explosives and ammunition unlawfully. President Diem proclaimed martial law and publicly stated the Government position:

In the face of recent Communist-instigated international events, especially in Southeast Asia and Laos, which have had a direct influence on the frontier, while in our country the entire people and army are putting forth the utmost effort to struggle against Communist aggression, our compatriots have seen clearly for three and one-half months the government's extremely conciliatory good-will towards settling problems raised by the General Buddhist Association.

However, the efforts have not been answered by a number of political speculators who have taken advantage of religion, and the extremely conciliatory attitude of the Government, to carry out repeated illegal actions in order to create a confused situation to sabotage this policy and to hamper the doctrine of democratic jurisdiction. This is very prejudicial to the good name of Buddhism and is beneficial only to communism.

Therefore, by virtue of Article 44 of the Constitution of the Republic of Vietnam, I proclaim the promulgation of martial law throughout the national territory on 21 August 1963, and I entrust the Army of the Republic of Vietnam with using fully all means and taking all necessary measures specified in the decree promulgating martial law in order to restore public security and order, to defend the nation, to vanquish communism and to build democratic freedom.[13]

General Ton That Dinh, Military Governor of the Saigon area, reported that arms, ammunition and plans for assassinating both Vietnamese and American officers had been taken in the pagodas. But Ambassador Lodge reported to the State Department his criticism of the Government and support of the Buddhists. He deplored the declaration of martial law as a repudiation of Diem's promise to be conciliatory.

On August 25, the Voice of America radio broadcast openly

criticized the martial law, the armed forces of the Republic and the Ngo Dinh Diem family. The die had been cast. Roger Hilsman later said: "After the closing of the pagodas on August 21, the facts became irrelevant."[14]

On August 24, the State Department instructed Ambassador Lodge that unless Diem accepted U. S. direction, the Embassy should support a military revolt against the President. The message was leaked to the press and soon became public knowledge in Saigon.

Thich Tri Quang, the chief Buddhist agitator, escaped the August 21 dragnet and sought asylum in the American Embassy. Against firmly-established U. S. diplomatic practice, Lodge granted asylum. His action was a deliberate affront to the government of South Vietnam. It signaled U. S. interference in the Buddhist crisis.

The State Department message of August 24 had been crafted by Roger Hilsman and Averell Harriman. It went out on a Saturday without the knowledge of Secretary McNamara or of C.I.A. Director McCone. Some critics have accused Harriman and Hilsman of sending this critical message without proper authority or coordination.

The lack of coordination seems established. The Defense Department and the C.I.A. would have opposed such action. But why didn't they protest on Monday and have the policy changed? The apparent answer is that State had cleared the message with the President. No one in government overthrows a friendly ruler without presidential sanction.

It was approved policy. State may not have persuaded Defense and C.I.A. of the wisdom of its policy, but it had persuaded John F. Kennedy.

In noting this seeming manipulation of policy by subordinates in government, it is relevant to note the President's physical handicap. As a sufferer from Addison's disease, he was required to take regular medication. His condition deteriorated gradually and was periodically restored by medicine. The opportunity for informed insiders to approach the President with difficult policy decisions and to get his approval of desired action could be enhanced in periods of fatigue and depression prior to medication. That individuals did get such decisions, without National Security Council coordination, in the Bay of Pigs and other crises, is well established.

In this instance approval was obtained from the President while he was vacationing at Hyannisport. The event had all the aspect of a pre-planned operation in which only the triggering was required.

On September 2, the *Times of Vietnam* revealed that the August events had been precipitated by an American plan to overthrow the Diem Government. According to this account, elements of the Central Intelligence Agency working from the American Embassy had plotted with the subversive Buddhist agitators in the Xa Lai Pagoda, offering subsidies of $24 million. The plan called for the creation of unrest and discontent among the people, the mobilization of youthful dissent, the subversion of labor and civil service groups, the presentation of an ultimatum to the President to resign or to send his family into exile, and the establishment of a military junta if the President resigned. The report said the government was well informed of these activities but "could not believe such action was possible from allies, at a time with victory so near."[15]

This was obviously a government-inspired report printed in a semi-official newspaper controlled by Mr. Nhu. When an American visitor calling on President Diem questioned the authenticity of the story, the President showed him documents supporting the charges. Moreover, Marguerite Higgins testified that in Washington, D. C. on August 23 an old friend at the State Department told her: "Diem will be overthrown in a matter of days."[16]

The American Embassy denied the *Times* charges. When all copies of the newspaper disappeared from newstands, the *Times* reprinted the story on September ninth. These, too, quickly disappeared. That night the *Times* presses were smashed by persons unknown.

After the August 21 raid and the attendant worldwide publicity, sixteen Afro-Asians expressed their concern to Secretary General U Thant at the United Nations. On September 20 the United Nations accepted "The Violation of Human Rights in South Vietnam" as an agenda item. Before it could be discussed, President Diem invited the United Nations to send a fact-finding commission to Vietnam.

A commission chaired by Afghanistan and including delegates from Brazil, Ceylon, Costa Rica, Dahomey, Morocco and Nepal visited South Vietnam between October 24 and November 3, 1963. Their report was never adopted by the United Nations because the overthrow of the Diem Government had made the issue moot; but the report found no evidence of violation of human rights in South Vietnam. President Diem had cooperated fully with the commission.

That the coup did not occur as planned in August was due apparently to the resistance of General Ton That Dinh, the military governor of Saigon. Dinh was a vain man; it would take some weeks of flattery by the other conspirators to induce him to betray President Diem. After the November coup, General Dinh told Father Raymond de Jaegher that they simply had to overthrow the Government because of United States pressure, and he produced documents to substantiate that pressure.

There was no easing of Ambassador Lodge's hostility to the Diem Government. The U. S. Embassy under his direction became a center of intrigue. When Diem made concessions to meet American demands, his efforts were dismissed as inadequate.

Just a few days before the coup, Suzanne Labin, the distinguished French political philosopher, spoke with Mr. Nhu who said:

> When [Lodge] was appointed here . . . we comforted ourselves with the thought that Lodge was a 'Republican.' We thought . . . he would possess good anti-Communist feelings, and we greeted him as warmly as possible. Then little

by little, we had to face the facts; he didn't in the least possess this feeling. . . .

Lodge never stopped working against us, with the cocksureness that a representative of a colonial power might have evinced, thirty years ago, toward a protectorate. . . .

Lodge does not bother with the normal business of an ambassador, which would be to galvanize and to strengthen the friendship between our two governments. No, his only care is to intrigue against the legal government to which he has been accredited.[17]

President Diem told Madame Labin of the contrasting behavior of Lodge and other ambassadors. When military attachés of two other countries were implicated in plotting against the government, requests for their recall were promptly honored by the ambassadors involved. But when a similar request was addressed to Ambassador Lodge about four American plotters, after showing papers lost by one of the four, Lodge procrastinated. "Some weeks later, as these individuals were still in Saigon, Diem insisted on their recall. Again and again, the American Ambassador requested more time. The November coup exploded with the four plotters *still* in Saigon!"[18]

It appears from the record that Diem's extreme patience in dealing with American hostility was his undoing. He had ample reason before the coup to declare Lodge *persona non grata* and ship him back to the United States.

Perhaps that would have been a better way to end his Government. Diem knew, as did the generals, that the war against the Communists could not be prosecuted without American aid. It was improbable that he could hold the support of the Army without that aid. Moreover, it was difficult to appraise American intentions. Obviously he was being pressured to adopt measures which would jeopardize the national security and the war effort. But would the Americans support a coup? Who could believe that an American government would do anything so disastrous to the war against the Communist enemy? There was always the hope that an accommodation would be reached.

While political events in the city of Saigon were going badly, the war in the countryside was continuing to go well. In August General Paul D. Harkins, commanding U. S. forces in South Vietnam, told Marguerite Higgins, "the Viet Cong are losing because we are steadily decreasing their areas of maneuver and the terrain over which they can move at will. The fortified villages are cutting the Viet Cong lifeline to the little people whom they used to tax to get their piastres and their rice."

On October 2, 1963, the White House announced the result of a mission to South Vietnam just completed by Secretary of Defense McNamara and General Taylor. It said:

> The military program in South Vietnam has made pro-
> gress and is sound in principle, though improvements are
> being energetically sought. . . . The major part of the U.S.
> military task can be completed by the end of 1965, al-
> though there may be a continuing requirement for a limi-
> ted number of U. S. training personnel. . . . By the end of
> this year, the U. S. program for training Vietnamese
> should have progressed to the point where 1,000 U. S. mili-
> tary personnel . . . can be withdrawn. . . . The United States
> has made clear its continuing opposition to any repressive
> actions in South Vietnam. While such actions have not yet
> significantly affected the military effort, they could do so
> in the future."[19]

No doubt his awareness of favorable relations with the United States military forces helped to disarm President Diem. He knew about the plots against the Government but he knew also that none of the plots could be significant without U. S. support. He could not believe that the United States would destroy a war effort progressing so favorably.

Mr. Nhu expressed this view to Marguerite Higgins before the August 21 raids on the pagodas: "I do not think that a coup d'etat could be successful without American support. And I certainly do not suspect the Americans of plotting to overthrow us, especially at a point when the war is beginning to go better.

Still people are not always rational. And so somebody might be crazy enough to attempt a coup d'etat, especially in the present atmosphere."[20]

The American pretension about Diem's loss of popular support was of a piece with the religious persecution hoax. President Kennedy's phony solicitude was echoed by his staff. On Sept. 30, 1963, McGeorge Bundy said:

> Yet it would be folly for the United States to neglect, or to regard with indifference, political developments of recent months which raise questions about the ability of the government and people of South Viet Nam to support each other in their contest with communism. The President has made it clear that the United States is not indifferent to these events and regards them with great concern.

> The requirement upon statemanship, once again, is to seek ways of meeting both the need for effective prosecution of the struggle and the need for a workable relation between the people and the government of a friendly country.[21]

It simply is not credible that the United States government, with all its resources, was unaware of the real political situation in South Vietnam in the summer of 1963. The C.I.A. could hardly have been so far off the mark as to misjudge the causes, quality and significance of Buddhist militancy.

There can be no doubt that socialist ideologues in the Kennedy Administration combined with kindred souls in the news media to misrepresent the Buddhist rioting to the American people. To these men, overthrow of the Diem Government was warranted, regardless of its effect on the war.

Even so, to believe that these underlings in government forced a policy upon the President and his cabinet is to think upside-down. It is more reasonable to suppose that they were following a policy which had been approved by the policymakers of the Kennedy Administration. John and Robert Kennedy were not men to let control of major policy out of their own hands.

We must therefore look upon the American program to get
rid of President Diem as a deliberate design and explain it in
terms of the Kennedy policy. We saw that policy in effect in
Laos in 1962 where it compelled the submission of a friendly
government to a Communist coalition; where it withdrew from
the country while North Vietnam remained, in violation of the
treaty provisions, as recently as October 1962.

Although the military situation was favorable in South Vietnam in 1963, success had cost dearly in money and in men. The
American Military Mission had been increased by January 1963
to 12,000 men. American casualties were rising. There was no
early ending of the struggle in prospect.

These considerations were reflected in the Mansfield report
to the Senate at the close of February 1963. Although the report
did not recommend a change of policy, it raised doubts about
the course being followed, doubts which probably illustrated
judgments being made in the State Department and in the Senate Foreign Relations Committee.

Apparently the confidential recommendations of Senator
Mansfield to President Kennedy went far beyond the written
report. According to Kenneth O'Donnell of the White House
staff, Senator Mansfield visited the President at Palm Beach
during December, 1962: "Mansfield emphatically advised, first,
a curb on sending more military reinforcements to South Vietnam and, then a withdrawal of U.S. forces from the country's
civil war, a suggestion that startled the President. . . . He said
to me later when we talked about the discussion, 'I got angry
with Mike for disagreeing with our policy so completely, and
then I got angry with myself because I found myself agreeing
with him'. . . .

"In the spring of 1963, Mike Mansfield again criticized our
military involvement in Vietnam, this time in front of the congressional leadership at a White House breakfast, much to the
President's annoyance and embarrassment." Kennedy called
Mansfield to his office for a private discussion. "The President
told Mansfield that he had been having serious second thoughts
about Mansfield's argument and that he now agreed with the

Senator's thinking on the need for a complete military withdrawal from Vietnam."

The temporary military advantage in South Vietnam might even be dangerous if it should attract Red China to intervene in the war, the report suggested. Then, the President would find himself in the land war in Asia which he feared.

There can be no doubt that Britain was pressing these fears in order to restrain the United States. In the minds of the men counseling the President, these fears were never absent. It would not be difficult to persuade John and Robert Kennedy that the interminable war then in prospect could be ended only by establishing a coalition government in South Vietnam.

But everyone knew that President Diem would never accept Communists into his Government. Therefore, Diem had to go. After his overthrow, a new government could negotiate with Hanoi for the establishment of a coalition government in the South. American forces, no longer needed, could then be withdrawn. Thus, peace would be restored by betraying an ally.

When did this change in U.S. policy occur? We can be sure that the change would promptly be known in Moscow. Could knowledge of the change have prompted the May 8 riot in Hue which sparked the Buddhist offensive in a land hitherto without religious strife? How else can we explain the confidence with which the Buddhist leaders sought the overthrow of the government? Were they assured of U. S. protection?

In late July Father Patrick O'Connor reported from Saigon, appraising Buddhist intentions:

> Ostensibly, the agitation is to enforce "five demands," the first of which concerns flag-flying and to obtain religious freedom, the absence of which is not apparent. But now some of the leaders are admitting in private that the real goal is political: to topple the government."[22]

Was this new policy explicit in the appointment of Henry Cabot Lodge as Ambassador to South Vietnam? Was this the great mission which attracted him to the service of a Democratic President? Would he end the war and restore peace?

In August, Marguerite Higgins confirmed that the overthrow of President Diem was indeed the purpose of the Buddhist subversives. She observed also the confidence with which they expected continuing support from Washington.

We have noted the undeviating hostility of Ambassador Lodge to the Diem Government. He was not a man who had come to mend the distress.

From these events, we conclude that the balance of judgment favoring coalition government in South Vietnam was established in Washington in April 1963. It was probably the result of extended discussion at the highest level. Soviet agents learned of the decision, and the Buddhist rioting followed.

While the timing may be in question, the decision for coalition government is not. Kenneth O'Donnell confirmed the presidential purpose when he wrote, "The President was not averse to the idea of changing the government for a practical and useful purpose. One day when he was talking with Dave Powers and me about pulling out of Vietnam, we asked him how he could manage a military withdrawal without losing American prestige in Southeast Asia.

" 'Easy,' he said. 'Put a government in there that will ask us to leave.' "

After the coup, foreign observers remarked that the American claims of replacing Ngo Dinh Diem in order to improve the war effort were sham. No successor government could be as effective as Diem had been, and the American Government knew that.

When, on January 31, 1964 the Minh Junta which overthrew President Diem was in turn overthrown, it was accused of planning to neutralize South Vietnam, the very mission assigned to it by the United States.

History, too, confirmed the Kennedy purpose. By the time of the 1968 election, Robert Kennedy had moved from veiled suggestion to open advocacy of coalition government. His opponent, Senator Eugene McCarthy, was advocating the same course. Vice President Humphrey could not at that time bring himself to advocate "letting the fox into the chicken coop," but he has since done so. The men around President Kennedy were simply incapable of conceiving any other way of ending the war.

On a national television program on March 8, 1970 Senator Mike Mansfield, a Kennedy policymaker in 1963, said: "I have said for a long time that the only answer in South Vietnam is a coalition government because, as far as the Viet Cong are concerned, they are South Vietnamese and they are made up of different political complexions. And as far as the present Thieu-Ky government is concerned, they happen to be North Vietnamese."[23]

So power took its inexorable course, and South Vietnamese generals who had been taught American respect for civilian government were confronted with a choice of rebellion or loss of American support. General Duong Van Minh, who had been military adviser to the President, said that the curtailment of U. S. aid was decisive in forcing the generals to act against the government.

The attack on the Presidential Palace was launched by General Ton That Dinh on November 1, 1963. President Diem telephoned Ambassador Lodge to ask U. S. policy on the insurrection. Lodge replied, "I'd like to get you safely out of the country."[24]

The attacking forces gave the President until 8 A. M. on the second to surrender. During the night Diem and Nhu escaped from the Palace to the home of a friend in Cholon. They had received offers of asylum from friendly ambassadors, but the Ngo's were not men who would take refuge from their own people in a foreign embassy.

On the morning of the second they went to St. Francis Xavier Catholic Church, made their confessions and received Communion. It was All Souls Day, the day set aside by Catholics to pray for the dead. They prayed.

They sent notice of their presence to the Military Junta. Military vehicles arrived to take them to headquarters. They were handcuffed and pushed into a vehicle. En route to headquarters they were shot, executed by Major Nguyen Van Nhung, aide-de-camp to General Duong Van Minh, Chairman of the Military Junta—until the day before military adviser to President Diem.

Was General Minh cowardly or wise? Did he lack the stomach to face the man who had honored him and whom he had betrayed? Or did he know that while Diem lived the people would not accept any other leader? General Minh later said to Marguerite Higgins: "Diem could not be allowed to live because he was too much respected among simple, gullible people in the countryside, especially the Catholics and the refugees."

Tran Van Huong, former Mayor of Saigon and Prime Minister (1964-65) said of the coup:

> The top generals who decided to murder President Diem and his brother were scared to death. The generals knew very well that having no talent, nor moral virtues, and no popular support whatsoever, they could not prevent a spectacular comeback of the President and Mr. Nhu if they were alive.[25]

The deep tragedy of this betrayal is written in the characters of the actors. Ngo Dinh Diem and his brother Nhu were in basic human qualities of intelligence, morality, integrity and wisdom far superior to the Kennedy policy-makers who destroyed them. American policy reflected not only moral weakness and inconstancy but grossly defective perceptions of the vital issues. This was the ancient tragedy of virtue slaughtered by power.

Ngo Dinh Diem was one of the truly great men of this Twentieth Century. In wisdom, in moral fibre, in great achievement against seemingly overwhelming odds, his leadership and patriotism were of the highest order. In comparison, the talents of policymaking Americans in both Executive and Legislative branches of government were mediocre.

When he accepted the premiership of Vietnam in 1954, Ngo Dinh Diem said to this people: "Follow me if I advance! Kill me if I retreat! Avenge me if I die!"[26]

His death has been avenged by an inexorable law of nature in the killing and wounding of a quarter of a million of the flower of our American youth. There is a price on appeasement. The American people are paying for the quality of the leadership they elected.

XIV

JOHNSON
FACES
CHAOS

IN THE AFTERMATH OF THE OVERTHROW OF PRESI-
dent Diem, the american press maintained for a while the pretense that the war would now be prosecuted more effectively.
But that deception could not long face the facts.

In an address to the National Security Industrial Association
on March 26, 1964, Secretary of Defense McNamara described
what happened:

> There were two changes of government within three
> months. The fabric of government was torn. The political
> control structure extending from Saigon down into the
> hamlets virtually disappeared. Of the 41 incumbent prov-
> ince chiefs on November 1, 35 were replaced. Nine prov-
> inces had three chiefs in three months, one province had
> four. Scores of lesser officials were replaced. Almost all
> major military commands changed hands twice. The
> confidence of the peasants was inevitably shaken by the
> disruptions of leadership and the loss of physical security.
> Army and paramilitary desertion rates increased, and the

morale of the hamlet militia—the "Minutemen"—fell. In many areas, power vacuums developed, causing confusion among the people, and a rising rate of rural disorders.

The Vietcong fully exploited the resultant organizational turmoil and regained the initiative in the struggle. For example, in the second week following the November coup, Vietcong incidents more than tripled from 316, peaking at 1021 per week while government casualties rose from 367 to 928. Many overextended hamlets have been overturned or severely damaged. The January change of government produced a similar reaction.[1]

Treason had done its work. The government was rent from top to bottom. The conspirators did not know whom they could trust. Within 90 days another coup overthrew the Minh junta. General Nguyen Khanh, leader of the coup, proclaimed, "The armed forces have decided to rise up and continue to carry out the national revolution to satisfy the aspirations of all the people. They are determined to sweep away the Communists and the Vietnamese traitors who advocate neutrality."

The generals who foolishly thought they could replace President Diem to keep the Americans happy, and then have government go on as usual, discovered their mistake. In alarm they saw the whole fabric of their winning strategy disintegrate. They discovered that the United States wanted not to win the war, but to get out of it by imposing a coalition government on the country.

A coalition government? That had never been mentioned in the complaints against President Diem. That meant putting Communists into the cabinet. That meant surrender, because everyone knew Ho Chi Minh would stop at nothing less. That meant the men who had fought communism for so many years would be the first victims of the Communist purge. No, thank you. They wanted none of that American plan.

The Khanh revolt on January 31, 1964 was virtually without dissent. Major Nguyen Van Nhung, who had shot Diem and Nhu, committed suicide in his own home, the sole casualty of the new revolution. He would never tell whose order he had obeyed.

Meanwhile, President Kennedy had been assassinated, only twenty days after the death of Diem and Nhu. There was turmoil in the United States, too, as President Lyndon Baines Johnson assumed the powers of office.

The emotional impact of the assassination bound President Johnson to adhere to the aims and programs of his predecessor. But would he not in time turn away from the Kennedy policies? It had been reported that Lyndon Johnson opposed the plan to overthrow the Diem government. Would he return to the earlier policy of opposing aggression?

In his domestic legislation, Lyndon Johnson outperformed the most ardent liberals. He worked with black radicals and the news media to raise emotional storms about civil rights and to enact punitive legislation against the South such as the country had not seen since Reconstruction. Surely this would make him acceptable to the liberals. He never could see the difference between the socialism of ADA and Big Daddy.

In foreign affairs, he placed himself squarely in the hands of the Kennedy men—Dean Rusk, McGeorge Bundy, Walt Rostow and J. William Fulbright. He talked with old friends in the Senate, men like Richard Russell of Georgia and John Stennis of Mississippi, but only superficially. They never had any perceptible influence on his policy because they would not oppose him openly. They went along quietly with Presidential policy.

The Khanh revolt took policy out of Johnson's hands. Coalition government was dead. After forcing the ouster of Diem under pretense of winning the war, the United States could not now oppose a Khanh government dedicated to winning the war. The appearance of cooperation had to be maintained.

General Khanh was not equal to the crisis. He might have been a fine military leader, but he lacked the vision or the courage to handle the political problem. Pressed by the United States to re-establish civilian government and to allow demonstrations against the government, General Khanh never could restore public order.

In the end, the Armed Forces Council had to retire General Khanh and appoint Air Vice Marshal Nguyen Cao Ky as Premier before the Buddhist resistance was squarely faced. Ky summarily ended Buddhist politicking and sent the bonzes back to their pagodas. Public order was then restored.

In the military junta which seized power on November 1, 1963, General Duong Van Minh was Chairman. Former Vice President Nguyen Ngoc Tho became Premier of a new government established on November fourth. Other cabinet ministers included Major General Tran Van Don, Defense; Pham Dang Lam, Foreign Affairs; and Ton That Dinh, Security. The United States recognized the new government on November 7 and resumed the aid programs which had been suspended.

The spectacle of American policy smashing the elected government of South Vietnam filled Prince Norodom Sihanouk with apprehension. He dismissed the American Military Mission which had been training the Cambodian military forces, terminated United States aid and went to Peiping to make his peace with the Communists. The price was Communist access to Cambodia for new bases from which to assault South Vietnam. In consequence, the Communist sanctuaries in Laos were extended to Cambodia, a new line of communications from the port of Sihanoukville was opened and the power of the Communist assault on South Vietnam was multiplied.

Within South Vietnam, the war intensified as Communist forces took the offensive. Internal strife also mounted as the militant Buddhists, filled with success, incited attacks against loyal elements of the population. The zealous hunt to rid the country of pro-Diem elements in government provided cover for internal vendetta. In the northern provinces where radical Buddhist strength was greatest, there was collusion with the Vietcong as Buddhist leaders provided protection.

Tri Quang, who had served in the Viet Minh and had been arrested by the French, and whose brother served in the Hanoi government, was working hand in glove with the Vietcong. With the assistance of Vietcong cadres, often disguised in the robes of Buddhist bonzes, he exploited the innocence of bona fide religious personnel to obtain "voluntary" suicide victims. He gave religious cover to Communist attacks on government.

The alliance of Tri Quang with the Communists was to become more apparent as he exploited his new power in the year following Diem's overthrow. On October 15, 1964 Thich Huyen Quang, a secretary of the United Buddhist Church, complained:

> On August 20 and 26 Communist Vietcong forced people of the four villages of Phu Yen to carry Buddhist flags and block with their own bodies the passage of M-113 armored personnel carriers of the Vietnamese Army. On other occasions when Communist agents were arrested, the Vietcong threatened Buddhist monks and compelled the pagodas to demand the release of the Communists by insisting that they were Buddhists subjected to religious persecution.
>
> In four villages occupied by the Vietcong, the Communists outfitted known Vietcong sympathizers in Buddhist robes and insisted that they be given refuge in the pagodas. If the senior monks in the pagoda refused their demand the Communists took the monks away and put Vietcong agents—dressed as monks—in their place.
>
> On one occasion the Vietcong themselves burned a historic pagoda, only recently renovated, and then forced local Buddhist leaders to call out the provincial Buddhist Association to complain about the "outrage" against Buddhists, which they blamed on Catholic government agents.[2]

In 1964, Premier Tran Van Huong was to say:

> Thich Tri Quang is very clever. One has to be very careful with him. He acts like a Communist. He talks like a Communist. The things he does help the Communists. But you Americans want absolute proof. And evidence is not the same as absolute proof. We can prove that Thich Tri Quang held a recent meeting with Vietcong leaders near Cap Saint Jacques [November 1-4th]. But Thich Tri Quang is capable of saying that he was down there trying to con-

vert the Communists to Buddhism—and some people would believe him.[3]

In January 1964 President de Gaulle of France recognized Communist China. He declared that Communist China was a reality to be reckoned with in any Asian settlement and he urged the neutralization of Southeast Asia. In reality, President de Gaulle had read into the overthrow of President Diem an American intention to withdraw from South Vietnam; and he had moved to protect French interests in the only way available to French diplomacy.

On taking power, General Khanh deposed and arrested General Duong Van Minh; Premier Nguyen Ngoc Tho; Major Generals Tran Van Don and Le Van Kim; Mai Huu Xuan, National Police Chief; Major General Ton That Dinh, Interior Minister; and Brigadier General Nguyen Van Vy, Deputy Chief of Staff. He then appointed Phan Huy Quat Foreign Minister.

General Khanh called for national unity in the war against the Communists. He inaugurated programs to rebuild military and hamlet strengths so deeply ravaged by the November coup and its aftermath. Under continuing United States pressure to restore civilian government, he increased civilian participation in his government and then tried to establish a civilian administration. Throughout his tenure he strove to win the approval of the Buddhist political clique.

Ngo Dinh Can, a brother of Diem and a former governor of Thua Thien Province in Central Vietnam, had come to Saigon from Hue after the November coup, under U. S. protection, and had then been delivered to the Military Junta by Ambassador Lodge. Mr. Can was convicted and sentenced to death on April 22 and was executed on May ninth. General Khanh dared not disregard Thich Tri Quang's opposition to reprieve.

General Paul D. Harkins departed for the United States on June 20 and was succeeded by his deputy, General William C. Westmoreland. On June 29, Lodge announced his resignation as Ambassador to return to the United States to help the effort to deny the Republican Presidential nomination to Senator Barry

Goldwater. General Maxwell D. Taylor was designated to succeed Lodge as Ambassador.

On August 2 and 4, 1964 the U. S. Navy reported attacks on its destroyers in the Gulf of Tonkin. President Johnson responded on the fourth by announcing U. S. retaliation against North Vietnamese torpedo boat bases and supporting installations. He asked and received from the Senate a declaration of support which has come to be known as the Gulf of Tonkin Resolution.

On August 7, General Khanh declared a national emergency to combat increasing Communist insurgency following the Tonkin Gulf incident. On August 16, Gen. Khanh became President under a new constitution approved by the Military Revolutionary Council; but he resigned on August 25, after widespread rioting protesting his assumption of emergency powers. The Revolutionary Council repealed the constitution and retained the Khanh regime in office pending the establishment of a new government.

Generals Khanh, Minh and Tran Thien Khiem then formed a triumvirate to replace the Council. They called for a national convention in two months to elect a national leader and the organization of a permanent government through national elections in 1965.

On September 13, Brigadier Generals Lam Van Phat and Duong Van Duc led an abortive revolution against the Khanh Government. These officers opposed Buddhist influence in political affairs. Their coup collapsed when it was opposed by ground and air forces at Tan Son Nhut Airfield. The United States declared its support to the Khanh Government but dissatisfaction in the Army and in the country persisted.

On September 26, a seventeen-member High National Council of civilian leaders was formed with Phan Khac Suu as chairman. It was to write a provisional constitution, convene a constitutional convention and serve as an interim legislature.

On October 20 the Council proclaimed a new draft constitution, and on October 24 elected its chairman Phan Khac Suu as Chief of State. On October 30, Suu designated Tran Van Huong, a former Mayor of Saigon, as Premier. The new government, with its seventeen-member cabinet, was installed on November fourth.

Premier Huong inaugurated a vigorous and independent government. He was bitterly criticized by both Buddhist and Catholic factions over the composition of his cabinet but he resolutely refused to be intimidated by the factions. On Nov. 22, Buddhist militants led violent riots against the Huong Government. Against Huong's appeals for cooperation, the opposition continued its violent course.

On December 18 senior military officers organized an Armed Forces Council, with General Khanh as chairman, to coordinate the war effort. On December 19, younger dissidents of this group, with Air Commodore Nguyen Cao Ky as spokesman, ousted the High National Council and arrested seven of its members along with 50 Buddhists.

The United States opposed this attack on civilian government, insisted on restoring the Huong government and suspended aid. On December 22, the State Department declared that "a duly constituted government, exercising full power on the basis of national unity and without improper interference from any group, is the essential condition for the prosecution of the effort to defeat the Vietcong."[4] General Khanh bitterly criticized U. S. pressures, stating that Ambassador Taylor's "attitude during the past 48 hours . . . and his activity have been beyond imagination as far as an ambassador is concerned."[5]

On January 9 an agreement for the restoration of civilian government was announced by Huong, Suu and Khanh. Huong retained his post as Premier. The arrested Council members and Buddhists were released. On January 20, four members of the cabinet were replaced by military leaders: Air Vice Marshal Nguyen Cao Ky, Major Generals Tran Van Minh and Nguyen Van Thieu, and Brigadier General Linh Quang Vien.

Premier Huong continued to encounter the hostility of Buddhist activists. Violent demonstrations occurred in Hue and other cities. On January 27, Huong was deposed by the Armed Forces Council for failing to meet the civil crisis. General Khanh assumed the powers of government.

On February 16 the Armed Council appointed Dr. Phan Huy Quat Premier and reappointed Phan Khac Suu Chief of State. General Thieu served as Deputy Premier.

On February 17 the Armed Forces Council announced the appointment of a new twenty-member National Legislative Council to replace the defunct High National Council.

On February 19-20 an attempted coup to oust General Khanh as commander of the Armed Forces failed. But the Armed Forces Council then dismissed General Khanh for inadequate leadership. General Thieu was elected to head the Council.

In May, Catholic opposition to Premier Quat mounted. He was charged with persecution of anti-Communist Catholic leaders and failing to oppose the Vietcong. On June 12 Quat resigned and the Armed Forces established a military government with Air Vice Marshal Ky as Premier.

Thus, a year of political strife and turmoil was associated with General Khanh's leadership. Perhaps through undue deference to his American mentors he never cracked down on the Buddhists. These militants were fundamentally opposed to the war effort and striving to reach an accommodation with the North.

Meanwhile, President Johnson had taken a stance in firm support of the independence of South Vietnam. He expressed willingness to neutralize all of Vietnam as President de Gaulle had proposed but he saw no prospect of Communist concurrence in such a program.

Unfortunately, President Johnson left the prosecution of the war in the hands of the State Department. His failure to declare war on North Vietnam or even to allow South Vietnam to do so had handicapped the White House more than it had Hanoi. United States policy continued to be dominated by the illusion that some mythical government would gain the voluntary cooperation of all the factions in prosecuting the war. As we have seen, Thich Tri Quang and his militant Buddhists opposed the war effort. Forcing successive governments to accommodate Buddhist rioting was perhaps necessary after Tri Quang's service in overthrowing President Diem, but it was destructive of national unity and damaging to the war effort.

During 1964 there was a steady increase in U. S. participation in the war. Instead of the promised reduction of U. S. forces, there was an increase of U. S. forces to 23,000 men.

U. S. participation in the fighting also increased. U. S. airmen, while nominally instructing South Vietnamese flyers, were actually providing air support to the Army of Vietnam. United States men killed in action increased to 140 in 1964 as compared with 76 in 1963.

South Vietnamese casualties also increased as the Vietcong sought to exploit the weakness of the government after the overthrow of Diem. During 1964, South Vietnamese Army and local defense forces were increased in strength by 117,000 to 514,000, while Vietcong forces under arms increased to about 100,000.

During this election year the President received little constructive advice from the opposition. Candidate Goldwater spoke of winning the war but Republican leaders in the Congress declined to challenge the President. They had no alternative to offer.

With his usual skill Lyndon Johnson arranged for a cabal of liberal Democrats to attack his policy and demand withdrawal from Vietnam. These attacks brought Republican Senators to the defense of the President—which was just where Lyndon Johnson wanted them.

Richard M. Nixon, former Vice President and defeated candidate for the Presidency, returned from a trip to Asia in April 1964. He proposed extending the war into North Vietnam and Laos. He told the New York Chamber of Commerce that ". . . enemy can no longer have privileged sanctuary."[6] He told the American Society of Newspaper Editors that the South Vietnamese Army should engage in "hot pursuit" of enemy forces in Laos and North Vietnam.[7] In a piece published in the *Reader's Digest* in August 1964 Mr. Nixon repeated his call for an end to sanctuary. Senator Barry Goldwater, the Republican candidate, spoke boldly of winning the war but the Democrats, aided by sympathetic news media, skillfully misrepresented his views as irresponsible and dangerous. The election endorsement of President Johnson was overwhelming.

The Tonkin Gulf Resolution and his election victory put President Johnson in a strong leadership position. Most Americans believed the war should be won quickly. A small but growing minority was clamoring for withdrawal, charging that military victory was not possible. Military victory was indeed not possible under the restraints which policy had placed on operations. However, now that Lyndon Johnson was President in his own right and not as a legatee of John Kennedy, he was in a position to adopt policy which would end the war quickly.

The issue was simple and clear. Would the United States continue to tolerate North Vietnamese attacks against an ally while prohibiting South Vietnam from striking back? Would Lyndon Johnson have the good sense and courage to say to Moscow: "If your satellite attacks my ally, my ally will strike back and destroy your satellite." How else could "wars of liberation" be deterred?

It never happened. President Johnson remained throughout his term the intellectual captive of Rusk and Rostow and Harriman, fearful of conflict with the Soviet Union or Red China, incapable equally of winning the war or of accepting defeat.

Because the whole ethic of the Diem Government had been oriented to winning the war, the United States was obliged to maintain that posture. It pledged support to the Khanh Government and increased aid even as the national situation deteriorated. But when General Nguyen Khanh proclaimed on July 19, 1964 that he would carry the war to the North to liberate the Vietnamese enslaved by communism, Ambassador Taylor told Khanh that it was not U. S. policy to carry the war beyond South Vietnam's borders. Air Vice Marshal Ky said his planes were ready to bomb the North. General Khanh said, "We are already victims of North Vietnamese aggression. . . . Any response from us would be a counterattack."[8]

Ho Chi Minh declared that he had powerful friends. Red China and the Soviet Union warned the United States against expanding the war. President Johnson denied that the United States had any plans to expand the war.

No doubt the war at that time seemed secondary to Lyndon Johnson. He was preoccupied with the domestic legislation he would send to Congress, with civil rights strife, with the Voting Rights Act of 1965. He had general support for his war policy so he let it roll along with only occasional attention.

Under his neglect, the war was worsening. The North was moving its fighting units into the battle. Where formerly the Vietcong attacked in small bands they now launched major offenses with battalions or even regiments.

Under Kennedy promises to reduce the war, Johnson was loath to increase the scale of conflict. He would provide just enough support to keep the South from losing. Secretary McNamara was using up old, obsolete equipment, sacrificing lives to save money.

That approach to war was of course demoralizing to South Vietnam. It gave countenance to Vietcong claims that the Americans would in time tire of fighting and go home. Americans in the war zone, too, were disheartened by the conditions under which they had to fight. Their complaints began to reach the news media as widows revealed the frustrations of their soldier husbands.

By the close of 1964 the Vietcong had formed and committed a division to action. At the same time intelligence sources reported the departure of three North Vietnam regiments for the South. Infiltration during the year had amounted to 12,000 men. It was apparent that the North was determined to cap its expanding warfare in the South with a victory campaign.

XV

THE GREAT PEACE GAMBIT

★   ★   ★

A CURIOUS PARADOX WAS OBSERVED IN 1965. PRESI-
dent Johnson conducted one of the most intensive and far-
reaching peace searches in history while he steadily enlarged
the war in Vietnam. His peace pleading did not add credibil-
ity to his military measures. His military build-up seemed to be-
lie his commitment to peace. But the schizophrenic quality
of his policy was never comprehended by Lyndon Johnson. Perhaps a collection of conflicting notions should not be called
a policy.

At the close of 1964 rising Communist military strength in
South Vietnam begot a new Vietcong confidence. War which
theretofore had been directed at the Vietnamese people and
their armed forces was now openly directed at the Americans.
In November a band of Vietcong raiders invaded Bien Hoa Airfield, north of Saigon. They destroyed or damaged 27 U. S.
planes and killed five Americans and two Vietnamese. Ambassador Maxwell Taylor recommended air strikes against the
North in reprisal.

In December, a terrorist attack on the Brink Hotel, an American billet in Saigon, killed two Americans and wounded more than one hundred.

When the Vietcong again struck on February 7, 1965, at American forces on the Camp Holloway Airbase at Pleiku, killing or wounding 134 Americans and destroying or damaging 25 aircraft, the U. S. struck back. On that very day, U. S. carrier-based planes attacked the military base at Donghoi in North Vietnam. On February 8, South Vietnamese planes with an American jet escort bombed the North Vietnamese communications center at Vinhlinh. These raids opened the air war against North Vietnam which was to become a subject of continuing controversy.

The air raids raised a storm of criticism throughout the Communist world. On February 9, and again on March 4, mobs stormed the United States Embassy in Moscow. Similar demonstrations were staged in other Communist capitals. North Vietnam proclaimed that attacks on United States installations in South Vietnam would be continued. Soviet spokesmen declared that an American invasion of North Vietnam would not be tolerated. Peking muttered vague imprecations.

In the Free World, too, there was criticism, not alone from the Communist fronts but also from the "peacemakers" concerned about the increased dimensions of war. Liberals who had watched complacently and without protest the increasing scale of the North Vietnamese aggression throughout 1964 spoke out against the American counterattack. On April 2 Canadian Prime Minister Lester B. Pearson suggested that a pause in the U. S. bombing would give Hanoi a chance to moderate its stand and open the door for a peace conference.

President Johnson sent out peace feelers but obtained no response from the other side. Secretary Rusk said a halt in the bombing "would only encourage the aggressor and dishearten our friends who bear the brunt of the battle."

The bombing had served not only as retaliation for attacks on U. S. installations in the South but also as a vital morale booster for the disheartened South Vietnamese military forces. Here was a sign of both U. S. power and U. S. commitment.

Although the bombing inflicted substantial damage on North
Vietnam's military installations, it did not appreciably slow the
build-up of Communist arms in South Vietnam. That war continued relentlessly. General William C. Westmoreland, Commander of U. S. Forces in South Vietnam, described events as
follows:

> By late spring of 1965 the South Vietnamese Army was
> losing almost one infantry battalion a week to enemy ac-
> tion. Additionally, the enemy was gaining control of at
> least one district capital town each week. It was my esti-
> mate that the Government of Vietnam could not survive
> this mounting enemy military and political offensive for
> more than six months unless the United States chose to
> increase its military commitment. Substantial numbers of
> ground combat forces were required.
>
> The evidence strongly suggests that in 1965 the enemy
> intended to cut South Vietnam in half along a line from
> Pleiku in the highlands to Qui Nhon on the central coast.
> The initial commitments of North Vietnamese Army
> forces was in this area and the threat was real and im-
> mediate.[1]

In March, the Ninth Marine Expeditionary Brigade from
Okinawa was deployed at Danang to give protection to the important air base at that point. The Vietcong attacks continued.
Later in the month a truck loaded with explosives was detonated in front of the United States Embassy in Saigon. In May,
the 173rd Airborne Brigade from Okinawa was deployed as
security at the Bien Hoa and Vung Tau Airfields. In June, the
First Battalion of the Royal Australian Regiment joined the
force at Vung Tau. U. S. Marine forces began the preparation
of a base at Chu Lai.

Beginning in July, major United States Army and Marine
ground combat forces were deployed in Vietnam. The III Marine Amphibious Force moved into the Chu Lai base. In August,
the Marines inflicted a crushing defeat on the Vietcong Second
Regiment which had been driven into the sea on the Batangan

peninsula. Brigades of the First Infantry Division and the 101st Airborne Division arrived at Long Binh and Camranh Bay to cover the logistic build-up.

In September the First Cavalry Division (Airmobile) arrived in Qui Nhon and moved to its new base at An Khe. The First Brigade of the 101st Airborne Division cleared the An Khe area and Route 19 in preparation for the First Cavalry Division arrival.

In October the Korean Capital (Tiger) Division and the Korean Second Marine (Dragon) Brigade arrived in Vietnam. Both units soon established fine combat records.

In November the First Cavalry Division moved to clear Pleiku Province of enemy forces. At mid-month it developed a major battle in the Ia Drang Valley near the Cambodia border. ARVN and 1st Cavalry Division forces killed an estimated 1800 enemy in this battle, not without heavy cost to our side.

On Christmas, both sides observed a 30-hour truce. Then the Vietcong and North Vietnamese forces resumed their attacks.

While this emergency reinforcement of military forces in the South was being made, the air war against North Vietnam was also being intensified. In early February 1965 air strikes had been launched against NVA barracks north of the Demilitarized Zone in retaliation for Vietcong attacks on U. S. installations at Pleiku and Qui Nhon. On March 2 the first Rolling Thunder strikes against North Vietnam were made under conditions strictly controlled by Washington. These strikes opened the air campaign which was to cause heavy losses to the Communists and mental anguish in the United States. For three years it remained the target of war complaints, whether because it hurt the Communists so badly or because the daily reports of air strikes made it so visible.

The first air strikes brought a quick response from North Vietnam. MIG jet fighters and IL-28 light bombers were moved down to North Vietnamese airfields, presumably from Red China where North Vietnam pilots were in training. By the end of 1965, the North Vietnam air force included 75 MIG jet fighters and eight IL-28 bombers.

North Vietnam responded also with a fast build-up of its air defense system. During 1965 some 60 SAM missile sites were built, AAA and automatic weapons systems were strongly reinforced, and radar systems were installed.

Rolling Thunder operations began on a small scale with modest bomb loads and strict controls of targets. In 1965, all strikes were to be made south of the Twentieth Parallel unless specially authorized. Thus the major industrial and population centers were excluded from target systems. The chief targets were military installations and communications in the southern provinces of North Vietnam.

The ambivalent notions of the Johnson Administration about the war, even at this early stage of the American reinforcement, are illustrated in a memorandum of Townsend Hoopes, then serving as an assistant to the Assistant Secretary of Defense for International Security Affairs. Never before had an American President led such reluctant warriors at headquarters!

During the bombing pause of Christmas 1965, Mr. Hoopes wrote:

> The continued suspension of bombing in the North seems sensible and prudent because it will help the psychological climate in the neutral world, and even in those countries allied to us for other reasons (NATO); it should give Moscow a plausible excuse for attempting to moderate Hanoi's views; and it may, if continued long enough, enable Hanoi to resist the Chinese policy of no concessions.
>
> I am drawn to the idea of limiting U. S. military objectives in Vietnam to the holding and pacification of certain defined cities and parts which can be made secure at about the present level of U. S.-South Vietnamese effort.
>
> We should develop greater patience, and not allow ourselves to escalate the war even if, as seems probable, nothing very tangible develops from the President's present peace overtures.[2]

It was mid-1966 before the more critical target systems were opened for attack—and then only oil storage depots and bridges were put on target lists. By that time, North Vietnam had done much to disperse its fuel supplies and to minimize bomb damage.

The plan of the Rolling Thunder program was to build up a steadily increasing weight of air attack against the enemy with a view to improving his interest in negotiations. The plan was never executed. Changing political factors influenced controls from Washington so that the air campaign tended to be sporadic. The President would authorize an intensification of the bombing and would then reduce the attack for reasons unrelated to the effectiveness of the air war.

During 1966 the target system was extended north of the Twentieth Parallel but the industrial areas of Hanoi and Haiphong and a zone along the Chinese border were excluded from it. The weight of U. S. strikes had increased substantially; but so had the anti-aircraft defenses of the enemy, so that our losses also mounted.

During 1967, important targets in the Hanoi-Haiphong industrial complex were made available and were destroyed or disabled. Railroad marshalling yards and repair facilities previously excluded from attack were heavily damaged, as were bridges and power plants.

Adverse weather conditions and target controls from Washington limited operations so that the steadily increasing pressures sought were never achieved. Nevertheless a formidable toll of industrial plants and communications facilities was taken during the year.

In 1968, a special campaign to interdict the movement of supplies away from the Port of Haiphong was undertaken until the bombing curtailment of April 1 ended the project. Thereafter bombing was again limited to military installations in the Southern Provinces until October 31, when all bombing of North Vietnam was stopped.

Much misinformation and misjudgment of the air war has been promulgated by malicious detractors as well as by ill-informed observers. Some of the misjudgment comes from ignorance about the function of air power.

Interdiction of military movement is a percentage operation. Air attack can hamper and restrict ground movement but cannot stop it. This relationship was most strikingly illustrated in Korea where the enemy maintained a million men on the battle line for two years, in occasional offensive combat, and the United States Air Force could not with conventional weapons cut the supply lines. The air force did damage and harass enemy supply lines, and no army would want to be in the field without that support. The air arm is of course most effective in a war of movement when our ground attack drives the enemy out of his deep entrenchments and exposes him to air attack.

The air war against North Vietnam was greatly reduced in effectiveness because of the way it was mismanaged from Washington. When enemy installations were extremely vulnerable to air attack, Washington would not allow attacks against them. Only after enemy defenses were built up were targets opened to attack, and then on a piecemeal basis so that the enemy never sustained the shock of massive, severe damage. He could repair or restore one facility before another was attacked.

For the critical observer in the United States, the rate of infiltration of NVA forces to the South somehow became an index of air war effectiveness. This infiltration increased from 12,500 in 1964 to 26,000 in 1965, to 58,000 in 1966, to 101,000 in 1967, to 250,000 in 1968. From such figures, public opponents of the war effort launched their irrelevant conclusions that the bombing was ineffectual.

The build-up in the South was a function of enemy purpose and determination. You could block trails, destroy vehicles and kill soldiers from the air but you could not stop the movement. But killing men and destroying equipment is a part of war, better done by planes than by the bodies of our fighting men on the ground—*when* the plane can be used efficiently. The argument that bombing should be stopped because infiltration was increasing is a non-sequitur. The increased infiltration was reason for increasing the interdiction.

Official estimates that half a million men were diverted from other work to defend and repair vital facilities suggest the magnitude of the air operation. The bombing was also an important morale factor because it made every part of the enemy territory subject to attack.

To the extent that the air war was limited in effect, it was a part of the general mismanagement of the war. Amateur theories about the application of force ruled the roost in Washington.

On the home front, 1965 was a year of mounting confusion. When President Johnson began bombing the North in February, he had the general support of both Democratic and Republican politicians. But as the war continued with no sign of relenting by the enemy, the voices of appeasement began to emerge in the United States. These voices had of course been audible in varying degree as the fortunes of war had varied.

Senator Mike Mansfield, the Majority Leader, said in January that neutralization of Southeast Asia "perhaps would offer some hope for the future. . . . Expansion will not resolve the problem. It is more likely to enlarge it, and in the end we may find ourselves engaged all over Asia in full-scale war."[3] The Administration was trying to sustain public support of the war effort without being forced by public pressures to defeat the enemy. At that stage, it was concerned about demands for victory.

On April 18 Senator J. William Fulbright said that if a truce could not otherwise be reached "there might be some value in stopping the bombings temporarily."[4] On the 23rd, Senator George Aiken of Vermont urged a halt in bombing because the raids "will not put the North Vietnamese in a mood to negotiate."[5] Fulbright had loosed his shock troops against the bombing of North Vietnam.

From May 13 to May 18, President Johnson suspended bombing the North, with due notice to Hanoi of his readiness to negotiate. There was no response from Hanoi.

Senator Everett McKinley Dirksen, the Minority Leader, supported the President's course. He opposed negotiations with the Viet Cong. The Republican Policy Committee opposed negotiations with the North while infiltration into the South continued. In September, former Vice President Richard Nixon spoke from Saigon: "There is only one basis for negotiations on South Vietnam, and that is for a Communist withdrawal of their forces and for the Communists to agree to quit infringing on the independence and territorial integrity of South Vietnam. Anything less than that would be defeat or retreat for the United States and for the forces of freedom in Asia."[6]

Long before the President began bombing North Vietnam he had been urged to do so. He had been criticized for allowing sanctuary to the enemy. As the bombing continued without deterrent effect on the North Vietnamese aggression, complaints arose about Administration limitations on the bombing. Word came back from Vietnam that our attacks were being wasted on unremunerative targets where damage could easily be repaired by the enemy. Vital enemy installations which would cripple the war effort were excluded from the bombing attacks.

In November, Chairman L. Mendel Rivers of the House Armed Services Committee called on the President to begin bombing the port of Haiphong and the Haiphong-Hanoi industrial complex. President Johnson, however, steadfastly refused to bomb these key installations or to close the port of Haiphong by blockade. These actions would have employed the air and sea power in which we had marked superiority, but someone had apparently persuaded the President that he should not use them.

When the President authorized the bombing program he limited it to selected military targets which would not hurt the enemy very much. He seemed to be hoping that some moderate damage would induce Hanoi to negotiate. Hanoi wouldn't, and so Lyndon Johnson was left with a major war on his hands.

In theory, President Johnson would increase pressure to give Hanoi an interest in peace, while holding open the door to negotiation. But his plan was based on the kind of responses

Lyndon Johnson would make if *he* were Ho Chi Minh—not on what the real Ho Chi Minh would do. The Johnson program never came close to testing the endurance of Ho Chi Minh. Johnson never really understood the enemy psychology and purpose.

His utter inability to take the action required to end the war became Johnson's undoing. He committed his country to endless, costly warfare as long as the enemy chose to continue fighting. In this posture, he duplicated precisely the attitude which President Truman had taken in Korea. Because a chief purpose of Soviet strategy was to bleed the United States, the Johnson policy accommodated Soviet aims. The war would continue.

It is one thing to go to the defense of an ally assaulted by Communist aggression and to repel that aggression. It is another matter to enter an interminable war of attrition where you spend at thirty times the Soviet rate, where your youth are killed and wounded while Soviet youth are not, and then to make it plain that you have no capacity to end the war! How could any leader expect to keep the confidence of his people in so misconceived a policy?

Americans believed in opposing Communist aggression. They believed in meeting our obligations in Southeast Asia. But they never agreed to endless warfare in which our side refused either to defeat the enemy or to repel aggression. That kind of behavior was entirely foreign to our ethic and our experience.

The Johnson policy steadily lost public support. As casualties mounted and prospects of peace receded, criticism intensified. At first there was only the Far Left, which voiced the Soviet line. Then the liberal chorus rose, the voices of those who had persuaded President Kennedy to neutralize South Vietnam. These critics felt justified in their earlier decision as they saw the casualties mount. They could still see no other way to end the war than by surrender. Let Ho Chi Minh have the country but stop killing our young men, they said.

The clamor soon spread to the campuses of America where liberalism was enthroned. There the agony was acute in the minds of men utterly ignorant about war. Their sole policy was to hate it and to attack these who waged it. Lyndon Johnson was a likely target.

Students joined in the worldwide demonstrations against American bombing of North Vietnam. Campus liberals took the view that the United States was an aggressor and must be condemned. Sit-ins and teach-ins were organized to arouse opposition to the bombing.

In April 1965 a national march on Washington, D. C. was conducted to protest the war. In May, a national teach-in was held in Washington, D. C. In all-day debate, professors and government officials discussed the war and United States policy. The debate was broadcast on television and carried back to many of the campuses of the country.

The attack on United States policy was limited to the voice of the Left. Administration opponents alleged that the war was an exercise of capitalistic imperialism, that indigenous revolutions could not and should not be suppressed, that the government of South Vietnam was a corrupt puppet of the United States, that the Vietcong were patriots fighting for freedom from oppression, that the United States was obsessed with the spectre of communism, that a Communist South Vietnam would be independent of Peking and Moscow, that the United States should cease bombing the North, that the United States should withdraw from Vietnam.

Defenders of Administration policy alleged that the Vietcong were not indigenous to South Vietnam but represented aggression from the North, that there was a clear case of Communist aggression against a free neighbor, that U. S. support of South Vietnam was moral and necessary, that withdrawal would surrender our allies to mass extermination by the Communist victors, that the United States sought no enlargement of the war but was exploring avenues to peace.

These views reflected the general character of the debate which raged throughout 1965. They define the character of the American illness.

The war offered three general options: (1) To withdraw, (2) To stay and defend, and (3) To take the offensive and defeat the aggressor. Only the first two options were debated. The third alternative was not considered. Had the defeat of Barry Goldwater's Presidential candidacy in 1964 somehow persuaded the American people that victory in Vietnam was not possible? Or had his defeat confirmed the confidence of our news media in excluding such "dangerous" ideas from public discussion?

The narrow range of discussion in the teach-ins reflected the similar limits of discussion in the national news media. A proposal to take the offensive and defeat North Vietnam would have been rejected out of hand by Administration supporters and by their critics in the teach-ins. The same view had been inculcated in the American public by television news reporting from the war zone. It was a curious affliction which had killed the concept of victory in the world's most powerful state.

This tunnel vision of the war inevitably produced the frustrations which followed. To offer the people two intolerable alternatives is to induce paralysis. The Administration proposal of endless war was indefensible. It could rationally be argued that endless warfare was worse for the people of South Vietnam than Communist domination. But the alternative to Administration policy—to quit and withdraw—was also unacceptable. The damage to the position of the United States and to its worldwide system of alliance would be devastating. And besides, war is *not* worse than Communist domination—it is vastly better. The people at war say so.

The range of discussion was set by frightened men. Intimidated by false representations that a decisive defeat of aggression would precipitate world war, these men foreclosed the only option which could restore peace. Idle fears of conflict with Red China or the Soviet Union froze their mental processes. Holding the power to deter aggression, they weakly invited it. Fearful that the good sense of the people would compel them to take the option they shunned, these men had to exclude that option from the public view.

Senator Fulbright spoke for these frightened men when he addressed the Senate on June 15, 1965: "A complete military victory in Vietnam, though theoretically attainable, can in fact be attained only at a cost far exceeding the requirements of our interest and our honor." He added that U. S. policy should remain one of "determination to end the war at the earliest possible time by a negotiated settlement involving major concessions by both sides."[7] In these words, the Senator stated two false premises: first, that a military victory would be costly; and second, that Hanoi would make major concessions to negotiate a settlement of the war. In five years, Hanoi has made *no* concessions.

When a politician desperately needs peace but has forfeited his capacity to win it, he becomes frantic. So it was with President Lyndon Johnson in 1965. The mounting opposition to the American presence in Vietnam intensified his need for peace. Riotous demonstrations were being held across the country. Students were burning their draft cards. Two young men burned themselves to death.

On April 12, 1965, Radio Hanoi broadcast its conditions for restoring peace in South Vietnam, as follows:[8]

   a. U. S. must withdraw all military forces and weapons from South Vietnam and cease all activity against North Vietnam.
   b. Pending reunification, north and south zones of country must strictly observe provisions of 1954 Geneva Treaty prohibiting foreign alliances and foreign assistance.
   c. South Vietnamese must settle their internal affairs in accordance with the program of the National Liberation Front of South Vietnam.
   d. Peaceful reunification of the two zones to be arranged by people of North and South without foreign interference.

These demands constituted an ultimatum for surrender by the United States and South Vietnam. They have been reiterated many times and have never been withdrawn or mode-

rated by North Vietnamese spokesmen. There have been inti-
mations that replacement of the Thieu Government in South
Vietnam with an NLF-dominated coalition government would
be a satisfactory method of meeting the conditions.

Some Americans had suggested that the United Nations
might do the peacemaking in Vietnam. These people did not
know or they ignored the truth that the United Nations cannot
resolve disputes between the great powers. Where the Soviet
Union was supporting the aggression against South Vietnam,
United Nations interference would have received an instant
veto.

Secretary General U Thant could act only against the United
States, because it would brook such hostile action and had
never used its veto. He showed his position on February 24, 1965
when he told reporters:

> I have been conducting private discussions on this ques-
> tion of Vietnam for a long time, as you all know. . . . The
> political and diplomatic method of discussions and
> negotiations alone can create conditions which will en-
> able the United States to withdraw gracefully from that
> part of the world.[9]

But even U Thant could not persuade President Johnson to
impose a coalition government on South Vietnam, so the
United Nations efforts remained ineffectual.

In mid-March, seventeen "non-aligned" nations meeting in
Belgrade, Yugoslavia appealed to the nations involved in the
Vietnam war to achieve a political solution. The United States
received the appeal cordially but there was no response from
Hanoi.

On April 7, 1965, in an address at Johns Hopkins University, President Johnson stated his position: The North was
waging blatant aggression against the South. The United
States was fulfilling its obligations to defend an ally. If the
North would cease its war of aggression against the South, the

United States would cease bombing the North.

On April 17, Hanoi rejected the seventeen-nation appeal for peace, rejecting at the same time any United Nations interference in Vietnam.

Efforts by the British, French and Canadian governments to obtain assistance in promoting peace talks were bluntly discouraged. Britain sought Soviet cooperation in reconvening the Geneva conference of 1954, of which the two nations had been co-chairmen, but the Soviet Union demanded that the United States first withdraw from Vietnam.

A special mission of the British Commonwealth powers to assist in a peace settlement was rejected by Peking before the mission could begin work.

Prime Minister Lal Bahadur Shastri of India worked out a peace proposal with Moscow but saw his plan blasted by Peking.

As time passed, appeals to President Johnson for another bombing halt became more pressing. On October 24, Senator Fulbright urged that U. S. air strikes against North Vietnam be halted for a longer period than the May suspension to encourage peace talks. Without any indication whatsoever that a bombing halt would encourage peace talks, distracted American politicians nevertheless urged a new unilateral truce. Their escapist psychology could think of nothing else to do.

Nor could the President think of anything else to do. In December, he launched his great diplomatic offensive for peace. He extended a Christmas Day battlefield cease-fire by stopping the bombing of North Vietnam in an indefinite suspension which actually ran to 37 days. On December 27, he sent Vice President Humphrey to Tokyo, Manila, Seoul and Taipei; United Nations Ambassador Arthur J. Goldberg to the Vatican, to Rome, Paris and London; Ambassador Averell Harriman to Cairo, Belgrade, Teheran, Moscow, New Delhi, Canberra, Bangkok and Saigon; Special Assistant McGeorge Bundy to Ottawa; Assistant Secretary of State G. Mennen Williams to Africa; and Assistant Secretary of State Thomas Mann to Latin America. These Ambassadors were to give the powers consulted a clear picture of the American commitment to peace and to enlist their help in obtaining the cooperation of the other side.

On January 7, 1966 the State Department issued a press release summarizing the United States official position on Vietnam, as follows:

The following statements are on the public record about the elements which the United States believes can go into peace in Southeast Asia:

1. The Geneva Agreements of 1954 and 1962 are an adequate basis for peace in Southeast Asia;

2. We would welcome a conference on Southeast Asia or any part thereof;

3. We would welcome negotiations "without pre-conditions" as the 17 nations put it;

4. We would welcome "unconditional discussions" as President Johnson put it;

5. A cessation of hostilities could be the first order of business at a conference or could be the subject of preliminary discussions;

6. Hanoi's four points could be discussed along with other points which others might wish to propose;

7. We want no United States bases in Southeast Asia;

8. We do not desire to retain United States troops in South Vietnam after peace is assured;

9. We support free elections in South Vietnam to give the South Vietnamese a government of their own choice;

10. The question of reunification of Vietnam should be determined by the Vietnamese through their own free decision;

11. The countries of Southeast Asia can be non-aligned or neutral if that be their option;

12. We would much prefer to use our resources for the economic reconstruction of Southeast Asia than in war. If there is peace, North Vietnam could participate in a regional effort to which we would be prepared to contribute at least one billion dollars;

13. The President has said, "The Vietcong would not have difficulty being represented if for a moment Hanoi decided she wanted to cease aggression. I don't think that would be an insurmountable problem."

14. We have said publicly and privately that we could

stop the bombing of North Vietnam as a step toward peace
although there has not been the slightest hint or suggestion from the other side as to what they would do if the
bombing stopped.[10]

During January, 1966, President Johnson was under continuing pressure from prominent Senators and Congressmen to extend the suspension of bombing North Vietnam. Despite the
cost to our fighting men in the big build-up of enemy forces
during this period, President Johnson extended the bombing
halt to the end of January.

On January 28, Ho Chi Minh's reply to some of the states
urging peace negotiations was broadcast by Hanoi. He condemned the U. S. presence in South Vietnam and the President's peace plan as an attempt to defend that presence. He
reiterated the conditions for a cease-fire talk: The United
States to get out of South Vietnam, recognize the National Liberation Front, accept the N.L.F. program for South Vietnam
and accept the four points previously stated by Hanoi. It was
apparent that the Great Peace Gambit had failed.

Someday an authority on aberrant behavior may give a more
scientific explanation of the behavior of American policymakers in this period. For the present we must be content with our
common knowledge gleaned from history.

How could apparently sane men cling to premises so obviously in conflict with their knowledge of the enemy aims and
character? How could they persist in futile endeavors, year
after year, failure after failure? How could they fail to comprehend and use their superiority of military power to deter
aggression?

In British minds there was a clear and profitable objective to
be achieved. But in American minds there was only a compound of ignorance and fear which paralyzed reason.

XVI

TURNING
THE
TIDE

★ ★ ★

AS NOTED IN THE PRIOR CHAPTER, GENERAL WEST-moreland found himself in mid-1965 with a rapidly deteriorating military situation in South Vietnam. The enemy was building combat superiority in the South which might enable him to cut South Vietnam in two.

General Westmoreland's first measures had to be defensive in character, to stop the threatened enemy offensive and to secure the base areas from which the new American effort could be projected. By the end of 1965, United States forces in South Vietnam had been increased to about 184,000. Deployment of U. S. Army and Marine units had checked the North Vietnam offensive. There were big battles to be fought but the time had passed when the enemy might have struck a decisive blow against the South.

Just as the enemy had built up his assault on South Vietnam from small hit-and-run guerrilla attacks through small-unit conventional warfare to regimental and division operations, the task of General Westmoreland was to force the enemy back through that sequence. By destroying the enemy's larger formations, our side would make it possible for the regional and district forces to restore their control of local security.

The superior arms and equipment of the United States forces dictated their employment in the offensives against the enemy while the South Vietnamese continued to provide local security. This was a general division of forces, but South Vietnamese troops, too, were engaged in many of the big battles fought in their combat areas.

As additional ground combat units arrived in South Vietnam, they were posted to protect vital areas and to get combat experience which would prepare them for future offensives. The First and 25th Infantry Divisions were deployed north and west of Saigon. The First U. S. Marine Division was assigned in the northern provinces south of the Demilitarized Zone. The ROK Ninth Infantry Division was placed in the critical area near Qui Nhon.

The first battles were fought in or near these areas as the newly-arrived forces attacked enemy forces nearby. After the Chu Lai and Ia Drang battles in 1965, other major unit engagements followed in 1966. In January, elements of the U. S. 101st Airborne Division, the ROK Second Marine Brigade and the ARVN 47th Regiment attacked the NVA 95th Regiment in the Tuy Hoa Valley and secured a rich rice harvest. In February, two NVA divisions threatened invasion across the Demilitarized Zone. U. S. forces were moved into the Northern provinces to stop the offensive. In June the First Brigade of the 101st Airborne Division and cooperating ARVN units fought their way into Dak To in bitter fighting. In June and July, offensives into War Zone "C" west of Saigon drove the enemy out of the area into his sanctuary in Cambodia. In August, elements of the 25th Infantry Division made the first American move into the Delta, south of Saigon. In October, the Vietcong Ninth Division and the NVA 101st Regiment attacked the U. S. Special Forces camp at Sui Da in Tay Ninh Province. Elements of the Fourth and 25th U. S. Infantry Divisions and the 173rd Airborne Brigade together with allied forces entered the battle and repulsed the attack in the biggest battle of the war. More than 22,000 allied forces were committed to the action. More than 1100 enemy were killed and large quantities of munitions were captured.

By the close of the year, U. S. forces had increased to 385,000. Australian and Korean forces had been augmented. Other allied forces, including a 2000-man civic action team from the Philippines, had joined the war effort. Enemy combat strength was estimated at 280,000.

Although the enemy still retained a formidable combat capacity, his chief attacks had been blunted and our offensives had invaded his key strongholds in the South. The action had demonstrated that NVA units could not hold ground in South Vietnam against the superior firepower of the U. S. forces. Moreover, though the NVA might obtain a local superiority in battle, the mobility of U. S. forces enabled General Westmoreland to reinforce the battlefield rapidly and to overcome the initial disadvantage. The enemy was increasingly limited to attacks against allied outposts at the Demilitarized Zone or along the Laotian and Cambodian borders close to his sanctuaries.

The bombing of North Vietnam had quieted much of the early criticism of President Johnson for allowing enemy sanctuary beyond the borders of South Vietnam. But this air offensive was only a minor mitigation of the sanctuary problem. The air attack could harass and handicap the flow of men and supplies from the North but it could not stop them. Only combined action with ground forces could sever the enemy's line of communications and force him back into North Vietnam.

A notable development of the air warfare was the heavy bomber support of tactical ground operations. General Westmoreland began in 1965 to use B-52 bombers from Guam against well defined and heavily protected enemy positions which had shown high resistance to tactical bombardment. The heavy bombers, with their bigger weapons and salvo impact and with the psychological effect of their sudden attack out of complete silence (they could be neither seen nor heard), were highly effective against prepared positions. They were used regularly and came to be a key element of the combat operations in South Vietnam.

As the tide turned, the Vietcong control receded and the Republic of Vietnam began to recover control of areas which had been lost after the overthrow of President Diem. A new program of pacification was needed to restore civilian government in these areas, to clear out remaining elements of the Vietcong political structure, to establish local security and to restore economic activity. The RVN government organized "Revolutionary Development Teams" for the pacification mission. In May 1966 the U. S. phase of the effort was removed from the Embassy and placed under General Westmoreland with Ambassador Robert W. Komer serving as his deputy for this program.

Pacification was a difficult program because the RVN could not provide adequate security to areas which had been cleared of Vietcong combat units. Although the allied forces had the strength to defeat any enemy combination within South Vietnam, they could not cover the whole country with positive protection. The long western border could not be sealed. The shallow depth of the country from west to east put the pacified areas within reach of sallies from the sanctuaries. Because the terrorists could enter a village and murder government sympathizers, prudent peasants would not take sides. They tried to avoid antagonizing either side, but they were most fearful of the Vietcong.

These realities have been misrepresented by critics who imagined that the military formations of the enemy could be defeated without fighting through some legerdemain of building good government: "The shooting war on the ground thus proceeded with full autonomy, subordinating by its sheer weight (and undermining by its sheer destructiveness) the political efforts aimed at pacification, reform and nation-building."[1]

The problem of pacification was illustrated by the Marines in Quang Tri Province. They had initiated an excellent program of stationing a squad of Marines in cleared villages to work with local defense forces, to provide communications and call in supporting fire when needed. Pacification of the province was making excellent headway when the NVA launched new attacks across the Demilitarized Zone. General Lewis Walt knew that if he pulled his Marines from pacification work to meet this threat, the Vietcong would return to the province and massacre the villagers who had cooperated with the pacification program. He therefore called on General Westmoreland for reinforcement. General Westmoreland withdrew combat forces from the Delta to reinforce the northern border, thereby weakening his Delta position.

Despite our over-all military superiority, the sanctuary and initiative allowed the enemy rendered pacification of the country impossible. It was possible to protect the principal population centers against all but sporadic terrorist raids. Outlying villages were more exposed to attack by regular Vietcong and NVA forces. The countryside could not be pacified while the enemy enjoyed sanctuary in Laos and Cambodia.

During 1966, President Johnson continued his peace campaign. After the collapse of his January effort, he made no change of policy but simply announced that he would continue his search for peace.

On February 7, President Johnson met in Honolulu with General Thieu and Premier Ky of South Vietnam, Ambassador Lodge, General Westmoreland and other members of the Presidential staff. He reaffirmed his commitment to the independence and security of South Vietnam. "If we allow the Communists to win in Viet Nam," he said, "it will become easier and more appetizing for them to take over other countries in other parts of the world. We will have to fight again some place else—at what cost, no one knows. That is why it is vitally important to every American family that we stop the Communists in South Vietnam."[2] At the same time Chief of State Thieu and Premier Ky committed their government to a program of revolutionary development, social justice and democracy. Emphasis was given to new programs for pacification and economic development.

At Manila in October 1966, the President met with representatives of South Vietnam and other allied powers—Korea, Thailand, Australia, the Philippines and New Zealand—to reaffirm his commitment to peace. The allies pledged to withdraw their forces as North Vietnam withdrew its forces from the South and ceased infiltration, and as the level of violence subsided. The allies would complete their withdrawal "not later than six months after the above conditions have been fulfilled."[3] But this effort, too, elicited nothing but denunciation from Hanoi.

In 1966, President Johnson faced a growing estrangement of the left wing of his party. Senator Fulbright, who had been unhappy about bombing North Vietnam and about American intervention in the Dominican Republic, opened in February 1966 televised public hearings of the Senate Foreign Relations Committee on the war in Vietnam. Administration spokesmen were exposed to the barbs of the unhappy warriors who infested the committee. Other witnesses were called to voice left-wing criticism of United States policy, but spokesmen for military victory were excluded from the roll of "experts."

Senator Fulbright seemed at the time to be enamored with the "enclave theory" expounded by retired Lieutenant General James Gavin, former Ambassador to France, then serving as Chairman of the Board of Arthur D. Little Associates, a consulting firm holding lucrative contracts in foreign operations. General Gavin argued that protecting all of Vietnam was too costly; that the United States should defend a series of enclaves in populated base areas; that it should wage war in the outlying territory but not attempt to secure it.

Some years earlier, General Gavin had been an articulate advocate of army firepower and mobility. It was therefore something of a spectacle to see him advocating Seventeenth Century concepts of defense in an age when Soviet missiles could pound his enclaves to shreds. Such were the inroads of the peacemakers on military strategy.

But the Gavin theory also had political disabilities. Once the outlying areas had been conceded to the aggressors, there could be no hope of retaining them in any peace settlement. Thus the prospect of any agreement except complete surrender would be prejudiced.

Also, in February, following the Senate hearings on Vietnam, Senator Robert F. Kennedy of New York came out openly for a coalition government in South Vietnam. This astute politician decided that this was the time to enlarge his attack on the Johnson policy and stake out a position with the left wing of the party. In a press conference on February 19, Senator Kennedy said:

> Whatever the exact status of the National Liberation Front—puppet or partly independent—any negotiated settlement must accept the fact that there are discontented elements in South Vietnam, Communist and non-Communist, who desire to change the existing political and economic system of the country. . . . To admit them to a share of power and responsibility . . . is at the heart of the hope for a negotiated settlement. It is not the easy way or the sure way; nor can the manner or the degree of participation now be described with any precision.[4]

The Kennedy surrender plan received warm praise from the Democratic Left but severe criticism from Johnson Administration aides. The most colorful comment came from Vice President Hubert Humphrey, who was then in Wellington, New Zealand making a tour of Asia and associating for a change with some courageous people. The Vice President noted the history of coalition governments as "letting a fox in a chicken coop; soon there wouldn't be any chickens left." He described the Kennedy proposal as "a prescription for the ills of South Vietnam which includes a dose of arsenic."[5]

Premier Ky of South Vietnam commented sagely, "I think now is too soon to begin the [Presidential] campaign. It is not good if you use the destiny of 20 million people as an issue. . . ."[6]

But Senator Kennedy knew that much work had to be done to deny a second term to an incumbent president.

Within the Senate Foreign Relations Committee, the Chairman and Senators Morse, McGovern and Church offered bills to restrain the prosecution of the war effort. All failed. The Congress as a whole remained strongly committed to the Johnson war policy. Congressmen didn't like the policy but they had nothing better to offer. Many marched with the President to defeat in mid-term elections. Although the Democrats retained control of House and Senate, they suffered a major setback in the November elections.

1966 had indeed been a curious year of a curious war. On the fighting front, the enemy's best forces had been met and had been stopped, if not defeated. The despair of 1965 had been dispelled and the allied forces looked forward with confidence to certain victory. True, our casualties had risen swiftly with the commitment of large forces to battle, but the enemy's casualties were far greater, and he was giving ground.

On the home front, confidence in American policy was waning. Even as morale on the battlefront improved, morale at home deteriorated. The constant pounding of the news media on themes that the war could not be won and that we must make the concessions necessary to negotiate peace were weakening American resolution. Although the politicians continued to vote war appropriations and give lip service to our fighting men, few could be found to subscribe openly to the Johnson policy. In the springtime Democratic politicians were saying privately, "If the President doesn't settle this damned war, we'll be in trouble in November." But they had no idea how the President could end the war. A candidate could endorse coalition government but a President could not.

XVII

THE
BIG
BATTLES

THE OPERATIONS PLAN FOR 1967 CALLED FOR THE ARVN to concentrate on pacification and on security of the populated areas while U. S. forces moved into the highlands, the border areas and the Delta to search out and destroy enemy bases and forces. This was a logical coordination of mission with the special capabilities of the forces. The American units with their superior firepower and mobility were well designed for the offensive mission. Moreover, their firepower could be used more effectively in the unpopulated border areas than in smaller battles in the populated areas.

There has been much short-sighted criticism of this offensive strategy as involving more fighting and higher casualties than the security of South Vietnam required. That criticism is largely misconceived. By knocking out the major Vietcong and NVA units in South Vietnam, the United States won for South Vietnam and for its own forces a security which it could never have achieved in passive defense of the populated areas. The search-and-destroy operation in this way served in time to reduce our casualties below what they would otherwise have been.

There was one serious limitation on this offensive strategy. Because of the enemy sanctuaries across the border in Cambodia and Laos, because of the shallow depth of our positions and because of the political desire to deny occupation of SVN territory close to the border to the NVA, our forces fought under serious handicaps of time and space. They were constantly exposed to surprise attack by an enemy operating from a secure sanctuary along a front too great to be securely posted.

This handicap was imposed by the political decision which allowed sanctuary to the enemy. General Westmoreland had to achieve his sound purpose of beating the enemy in South Vietnam with an eye to the hazards of his own exposure to the enemy.

It has also been suggested by some critics that the increased scale of warfare in 1965-69 was a consequence of American impetuosity. This theory asserts that the bombing of the North caused the NVA to retaliate by invading the South and that NVA escalation was thereafter a response to American escalation. The record exposes the erroneous quality of this judgment.

The Vietcong buildup and the commitment of NVA regiments in the South were part of an entirely orthodox "war of liberation" against the South. The infiltration into the South from North Vietnam amounted to 12,500 in 1964, the year before the bombing began. Vietcong attacks on U. S. installations were intended to demoralize the Americans and send them home. The surprise and shock of the Communist world when President Johnson bombed the North were unconcealed. Soviet strategists had judged from his peace talk that the President would not take such action.

In the subsequent fighting, both sides strove for mastery, but the superior American power could not be denied. The North still possessed in sanctuary a decisive advantage which no military strategy could overcome. This was the factor which enabled Ho Chi Minh to look with equanimity to a long war of attrition.

Throughout 1967, the war for Vietnam raged as both sides increased the scale of battle. During the year, U. S. forces were increased to 486,000 and the South Vietnamese forces were increased to 685,000. Enemy strength at the close of the year was estimated at 280,000. Major battles were fought during 1967 at Con Thien and Khe Sanh in the North; at Dak To, Duc Pho and Pleiku in the II Corps area; at Bu Dop, Loc Ninh, War Zone C and the Iron Triangle west of Saigon; and at Konh O Mon Canal in the Delta.

In January and February, attacks into the Iron Triangle and War Zone C, respectively, smashed enemy resistance, captured munitions and valuable intelligence and destroyed long-established enemy bases. Heavy fighting in the Con Thien and Khe Sanh areas opened in March and continued throughout the year. In mid-November a concentration of four NVA regiments in the Dak To area were attacked and shattered. In December, the South Vietnamese 21st Infantry division trapped and smashed elements of two enemy battalions in the Delta.

On July 15, the enemy made initial use of his 122 mm. rockets, firing fifty at the Danang airbase, destroying ten aircraft and damaging forty-one.

As the year closed, the big battles continued, with regiments of enemy forces assaulting periodically the chief allied outposts in the northern and western provinces of South Vietnam. The enemy could not hold ground but he could use it for assault whenever he could bring superior force to bear. Operation from his sanctuaries gave him the capacity to sustain offensive combat.

While the battles of 1967 made significant progress in destroying enemy bases and decimating enemy forces in South Vietnam, even more significant progress was made in providing stable government in South Vietnam. More than two years of internal weakness and strife had been ended in 1966 and sound plans had been laid for the restoration of constitutional government in 1967.

When Premier Phan Huy Quat resigned on June 12, 1965, he ended the period of weak, ineffectual government which had

followed the overthrow of President Diem. The country had
been brought to the verge of collapse. The Vietcong had moved
from guerrilla to open warfare. North Vietnamese regiments
were moving South to deliver the coup de grace. President
Johnson had begun bombing the North and had committed
U. S. combat forces to the war in Vietnam. Something had to be
done to restore unity and strength to local government.

At this point the military leaders created a new military government with General Thieu as Chief of State, Air Vice Marshal Ky as Premier, a 14-man executive council and a
10-member leadership committee. Premier Ky said the war was
going badly and that his government would take measures to
end the political turmoil, economic collapse, war profiteering
and injustice then rampant in the country. He extended martial law, imposed price controls and made heavy cuts in government salaries.

It seemed that at long last the Johnson Administration had
recognized the impracticality of maintaining any stable government in Vietnam while riotous factions were allowed to stir
mass demonstrations against responsible authorities. In June,
the Ky government decreed the death penalty for Vietcong terrorists, corrupt officials, speculators and black marketeers.
Executions were to be carried out without trial if there was
tangible proof of guilt. Now at last the measures of President
Diem to preserve public order, so roundly condemned by Washington in 1963, seemed mild by comparison.

On July 8, the White House announced that General Maxwell
D. Taylor had resigned as Ambassador to South Vietnam and
that Henry Cabot Lodge would return to that post. Ambassador
Lodge arrived in Saigon. Perhaps President Johnson got a sub-
tle satisfaction out of sending Ambassador Lodge back to South
Vietnam to view the suppression of the Buddhist insurrection.

The new austerities of the Ky Government were not popular.
Protest meetings were held in Hue, a center of anti-government Buddhist strength. Buddhist leaders condemned the military dictatorship and called for the restoration of civilian rule.

Buddhist demonstrations in I Corps area continued with the

apparent support of the I Corps commander, Lt. General Nguyen Chanh Thi. They reached crisis proportions in March 7, 1966 when student demonstrations challenged the authorities in Hue and Danang. When the Leadership Committee removed General Thi from his command, mass protest resumed. Only when Premier Ky used military force to quell the armed Buddhist faction and arrested its leaders, including Thich Tri Quang, was the rebellion put down. With the government taking a firm stand against the Tri Quang faction, senior and more responsible members of the Buddhist hierarchy resumed control of Buddhist policy. Political agitation subsided.

With political stability restored, Premier Ky then proceeded with the business of recreating constitutional government. In September, 81 percent of the country's eligible voters elected a 117-member Constituent Assembly to draft a new constitution. The high voter response evidenced the returning confidence of the people that the war was going well and that the government would ultimately prevail over the Vietcong. It also evidenced confidence in Chairman Thieu and Premier Ky before they went to join President Johnson at the Manila Conference in October.

On March 15, 1967, the White House announced that Ambassador Ellsworth Bunker would replace Ambassador Lodge.

On March 18, the Constituent Assembly voted unanimous approval of the new Constitution. In September, the people elected General Thieu as President of the Republic and Air Vice Marshal Ky as Vice President. At the same time they elected members of the upper house of the National Assembly.

In October, the people elected members of the lower house of the National Assembly. On October 31, President Thieu and Vice President Ky were inaugurated and the military directorate was dissolved. The Constituent Assembly also dissolved as the National Assembly assumed the national legislative responsibility.

As 1967 closed, the Republic of Vietnam had a legitimate government validated by the people for the first time in the

four years since the overthrow of President Diem. Although the
new government had been created by civilian leaders working
through the Constituent Assembly, their work had been made
possible by a military dictatorship which suppressed the factions and restored public order.

In the perspective of four years of tragic disorder and raging
war, the Kennedy error in overthrowing President Diem could
be seen more clearly. But we should also see the courage and
tenacity of the people of South Vietnam. With all the agony of
war imposed upon them, they steadfastly refused to compromise their freedom and independence by accepting a coalition
government.

Again, as in 1966, as the war situation improved in South
Vietnam morale in the United States deteriorated. The attacks
of the vocal Left increased in ferocity and unreason, ably assisted by generous television coverage. By blaming the war for
wasting resources needed for the poverty program, the peace-
at-any-price crowd brought leaders of the civil rights movement into their action programs. In November, a mass march
in Washington to protest the war was addressed by Mrs. Martin
Luther King, Jr.

President Johnson continued to retain the support of labor
leaders, businessmen, intellectuals and the Congress for his
war policy, but this support received scant news coverage.

As the peace movement grew, its capacity to monopolize the
front page also grew. Student protests became more radical and
violent as the war gave a new focus to rebellion. Campus litera-
ture seemed in large part to come straight out of Hanoi. American students—and faculty—were duped by the most outrageous
falsification of current and recent history. Strangely, the intellectual community had a more tenuous perception of the
march of events than did the ordinary workingman.

XVIII

THE
TET
ASSAULT

★ ★ ★

VIEWED FROM THE VANTAGE-POINT OF NORTH VIET-
nam, the Tet assault of 1968 came three years too late. If General Giap had thrown his forces into South Vietnam at the close
of 1964 or early in 1965, when the damage done by the overthrow of the Diem government was at its peak, he might have
achieved a decisive victory before American forces could intervene. In 1968 it was too late for such a victory. Viewed in its
effect on the war in South Vietnam, the assault was a colossal
failure. As strategy, it could be redeemed only by its effect on
the United States government. Perhaps that was its true aim.

Hanoi strategists saw in the restoration of constitutional government in the South and the growing American military
strength their own inevitable defeat. They would have to give
up the conventional war and return to guerrilla warfare, at
some loss of face. While they still had the power to do so, they
would deal a serious blow to South Vietnam and to American
prestige.

It appears that General Giap seriously overestimated his capability. His task forces seemed to have orders to capture and hold the cities they attacked. He should have realized that he could not hold these positions against the superior allied forces. True, in defending urban strongholds the Communist forces could inflict massive property damage on the cities. But that gain could hardly compensate for the loss of his elite warriors.

If General Giap had inflicted a sharp and devastating blow against the cities and had then withdrawn his forces before superior forces could be brought against them, he would have achieved a great victory. But in leaving his forces to be beaten by the South Vietnamese and American units, he raised the morale of the defending forces and people. In the final outcome, this was the crucial factor in South Vietnam.

Except for this basic flaw in the Giap strategy, the Tet operation was conceived and executed with masterful competence. The assault was a radical departure from the general trend of the war and it therefore achieved surprise. It used the cover of the New Year holiday to assemble forces in the heartland of South Vietnam. It struck with ferocity against an unprepared victim and achieved early success.

In preparation for the assault, General Giap intensified his operations against the allied Khe Sanh base in the northwest corner of South Vietnam. He had learned in 1967 that General Westmoreland would fight for this base, which covered Route 19 access to the rear of allied forces at the Demilitarized Zone. He knew also that the Khe Sanh position was vulnerable.

The NVA assault on Khe Sanh opened in mid-January. Assaulting troops had been told that this was to be the new Dienbienphu in which an American garrison would be surrounded and defeated; prisoners communicated the information to the Americans.

General Westmoreland reinforced the regimental garrison with two additional battalions but depended primarily on supporting air and artillery fires for defense and on air supply to the garrison. This battle was clearly the focus of his concern in January.

As if to distract American attention from the impending attack, North Korea on January 23, 1968 seized the U.S.S. *Pueblo,* an intelligence ship operating in international waters off the Korean coast, and took ship and crew into the port of Wonsan. The ship was accused of violating Korean national waters. The United States denied the charge and protested the seizure at Panmunjon—to no avail. After a year of humiliating begging— including a false confession—by the United States, the crew was released.

The Czechoslovak Communist General Jan Segna was later to relate that Moscow had long planned such a coup. In May 1967 General Segna had met with Soviet Marshal Grechko at a villa in Prague. The Marshal said, "It is absolutely impudent the way the Americans sail their damn ships around as if they owned the water. Their espionage ships come right up to our shores to spy on our communications. But I can tell you this: we have decided to humble the Americans. Just as we humiliated them in the air by shooting down the U-2, we are going to humiliate them at sea by grabbing one of these ships."[1] On January 24, 1968, the Soviet representative at Warsaw Pact Headquarters confirmed that the Soviet plan, using North Korean operators, had achieved a magnificent success.

But if Lyndon Johnson thought he had trouble in the *Pueblo,* he was destined to be overwhelmed by the Tet Assault.

In accordance with practice established in prior years, the Vietcong declared a Tet truce to last from January 27 to February third. As the people moved on their holiday travels, the Vietcong and NVA forces, dressed in civilian attire, moved to their assigned stations in the cities. At the same time or by previous arrangement, weapons, ammunition and supplies for the assault were delivered to the assembly points. In the early morning of January 31, some 84,000 Vietcong and NVA soldiers struck in Saigon, Quang Tri, Hue, Danang, Nha Trang, Qui Nhon, Kontum City, Ban Me Thuot, Can Tho, Ben Tre and more than 100 other cities and hamlets. The named cities were penetrated in strength. The enemy held Hue until February twenty-fifth.

In Saigon the attackers breached a wall of the United States

Embassy compound and entered the administration building, but they were all killed or captured. Others attacked the Presidential Palace and were driven off by police. The police bore the brunt of the attack in Saigon but they were quickly reinforced by ARVN and American combat battalions.

At Hue, supporting NVA forces struck from the Ashau Valley to capture the city and fight a bitter battle to hold it. They lost about 8000 killed in the battle of Hue. U. S. and South Vietnamese losses exceeded five hundred. While they held the city the Communists executed about 3,000 of the city's citizens judged hostile to the Vietcong cause.

At Hue and in other cities, the underground cadres of the Vietcong surfaced to join the attack and to assist the invading forces. These cadres were killed in the ensuing battles or escaped with the defeated forces. The event gave the people a view of the extensive underground of traitors in their midst. In Hue, the cadre included all ranks of society.

In the total assault, 84,000 Vietcong and North Vietnam soldiers were committed: of these 32,000 were killed and 5,800 were captured. By the end of February, enemy killed had risen to 45,000.

As defensive elements of the local forces moved to protect the cities and government centers, rural areas were exposed to attack. Fighting in some localities continued for weeks. The devastation wrought by the assault was extensive. In Hue alone, 116,000 civilians were made homeless.

But the final result of the assault was the defeat and rout of the attacking forces. Vietcong and NVA troops had achieved surprise and shock action, but they had lost the battle.

If an aim of the assault was to demoralize civilian resistance, it had an opposite effect. Before Tet, while the big battles were being fought in the outlying war zones and remote outposts, civilians had survived in security disturbed only by occasional terrorist attacks. Many people had continued to be skeptical and uncommitted, waiting to see which side would ultimately prevail. But when Tet brought the war into their homes, it became easy to decide which side they were on. Instead of being intimidated by the attack, the people rallied to the government in defense of their own homes.

This involvement of the people in the war was one of the most important fruits of the Tet assault. Hue, which had been a center of skepticism and neutralism, became the most anti-Communist city in the country. The enemy had been unmasked.

Where recruiting for the regional and local defense forces had been slow because people were reluctant to identify themselves with the government, new commitments were made. Recruiting and arming these forces went up sharply. The local defense forces became aggressive in seeking out Vietcong units and gave a good account of themselves in battle.

If the Tet assault was designed to topple the newly-created constitutional government, it had an opposite effect. In the battle, the government showed its capacity to respond to crisis. Its cool and competent reaction brought it new support from the people. Here was a government which could provide national leadership.

In all these effects the Tet assault was a disaster for the North, a triumph for the South. From that point forward, the government and the people had a firm confidence in their ability to defeat the aggression.

But in the United States, Tet had an opposite effect. Opinion-makers called it a defeat for our cause, a victory for Ho Chi Minh. They counted not the annihilation of the enemy but the increase in our casualties. Just when our government had been reporting the damaged war potential of the enemy, he had launched a heavy blow. He had confirmed the fears of the "peacemakers" that we faced a long war and increased their determination to end it by surrender.

Men who had only counseled the President privately against his war policy began to speak out. Senator Eugene McCarthy of Minnesota, with a youth corps for peace, won a sweeping victory in the New Hampshire Democratic primary, which the President had not entered. Senator Kennedy was being urged by party liberals to come out in opposition to the President.

The public dismay at the Tet casualties was heightened by a false report, leaked by one of President Johnson's civilian experts, that General Westmoreland had asked for 200,000 more U. S. troops. *There* was a leak calculated to discourage support of the war effort!

When General Wheeler visited Saigon after Tet, General Westmoreland did not ask for any troops at all. He had the situation well in hand. When General Wheeler offered a brigade which was available, General Westmoreland accepted it.

The two generals did discuss contingency plans for such eventualities as Chinese intervention and prepare estimates of troop requirements for various cases. It is possible but improbable that the civilian concerned did not know the difference between a contingency plan and a request for reinforcements.

The Administration acted as though it had sustained an irreparable defeat. The President transferred Secretary of Defense Robert McNamara to the World Bank and nominated lawyer Clark Clifford to the Defense post. He directed Clifford and Rusk to make a complete review of war policy.

Clifford assembled a top-level special study group to review war policy. When he asked the group what must be done to win the war, he was told that the war could not be won. The conferees pointed out that the President had prohibited a blockade of Haiphong, bombing of vital installations in North Vietnam and entering the sanctuaries in Laos and Cambodia. Under these rules the war could not be won. According to Mr. Clifford, all the conferees agreed that these rules were prudent and desirable. The conferees included Generals Maxwell D. Taylor and Earle G. Wheeler.

It does seem strange that military leaders meeting with a new secretary seeking a solution to the President's dilemma would not tell him that these rules were improvident and disabling and that they should be changed.

Secretary Clifford accepted the advice given. From that point, the only way out for the United States was to build up the ARVN forces to take over the battle and then to withdraw U. S. troops. General Westmoreland had started a program to re-arm the ARVN units. Secretary Cifford proposed to accelerate that program.

Finally, President Johnson was overcome by the frustrations of the policy he had espoused. He was unwilling to surrender South Vietnam but he could see no politically tolerable alternative. The powerful left wing of his party had virtually renounced his leadership. On March 31, 1968, President Johnson announced that he would not be a candidate for re-election. In order to devote himself exclusively to the pursuit of peace in his remaining months in office, he would stand aside from the internal political contest.

The President also announced the cessation of bombing North Vietnam north of the Twentieth Parallel, later dropped to the Nineteenth Parallel. This decision freed the industrial and supply centers of the enemy from attack and limited our planes to chasing convoys on the Ho Chi Minh Trail.

Washington made the Tet offensive a great victory—which it was not of itself—when it stopped the air war against the North. It was especially tragic that the United States made this great gift to the enemy without getting at least the release of our men held prisoner in the North.

The President hoped this generous concession would induce Hanoi to send representatives to a peace conference. Apparently he had an understanding of some kind with Hanoi because representatives did meet to discuss the possibility. After a month of wrangling about the site of peace talks, the Conference opened in Paris on May 10, 1968.

Meetings without further progress continued to address the question of South Vietnamese and NLF participation through the summer and fall of 1968. Then, on October 31, on the eve of the Presidential election, President Johnson announced the complete cessation of bombing North Vietnam and called for meaningful negotiations at Paris. But President Thieu knew American politics too well to be caught in such a trap. He denounced the unilateral bombing halt, said he had not approved it and refused to call for peace talks. No doubt this quick reaction exposed the cynical quality of this final Johnson peace gambit. The President seemed to have no comprehension of war except as it affected domestic politics.

Lyndon Johnson fancied himself to be a man of action. But no man was ever a more complete captive of his advisers. By controlling the information and opinion reaching the President, they controlled the President. In a significant commentary on these last critical months of his Administration, he revealed that it was Dean Rusk and not Clark Clifford who persuaded him to lift the bombing of North Vietnam and hope for reciprocal action.

Townsend Hoopes, who was involved in high policymaking, testified to the Presidential isolation from disturbing ideas: "By this time (1967) Rostow had become the channel through which President Johnson received almost all written communications on foreign affairs; he had, moreover, a large hand in determining whom, outside the closed circle of advisers, the President would see or not see."[2]

Apparently President Johnson would not have agreed with President Kennedy's appraisal of Rostow: "Walt is a fountain of ideas; perhaps one in ten of them is absolutely brilliant. Unfortunately, six or seven are not merely unsound, but dangerously so."[3]

It is too bad that Lyndon Johnson had never had time to read history. He might have been interested in the lament of the Roman Emperor Diocletian:

> How often is it in the interest of four or five ministers to combine together to deceive their sovereign. Secluded from mankind by his exalted dignity, the truth is concealed from his knowledge; he can see only with their eyes, he hears nothing but their misrepresentations. He confers the most important offices upon vice and weakness and disgraces the most virtuous and deserving among his subjects. .:. By such infamous arts, the best and wisest princes are sold to the venal corruption of their courtiers.[4]

In May, seemingly to influence the convening peace conference in Paris, another "Little Tet" offensive was launched. The assault was largely aborted by the aggressive tactics of allied troops, which prevented enemy forces from reaching assembly areas. Only a few squads reached Saigon. A battalion which reached theTan Son Nhut Airfield was wiped out by the defending forces. Another attack made in August was even less effective. In June, General Westmoreland was recalled to the United States to serve as Army Chief of Staff. He was succeeded by his deputy, General Creighton W. Abrams.

General Abrams gave new emphasis to aggressive spoiling of enemy mobilization by detecting and attacking the supply bases being built to sustain planned operations. Discouragement of North Vietnamese forces with the conduct of the war, with heavy losses and with the use of raw replacements led after Tet to increasing defections. From these defectors, excellent intelligence about enemy bases and planned operations were obtained to sustain the Abrams program. In consequence, the military prospect in Vietnam brightened even as the political outlook of the Johnson Administration grew ever more cloudy. The peace conference had produced nothing from North Vietnam to warrant the unilateral concessions which the United States had already made. Three years earlier a more determined Lyndon Johnson had said of the bombing of North Vietnam:

> We do this in order to slow down aggression.
> We do this to increase the confidence of the brave people of South Vietnam who have bravely borne this brutal battle for so many years with so many casualties.
> And we do this to convince the leaders of North Vietnam —and all who seek to share their conquest—of a simple fact:
> We will not be defeated.
> We will not grow tired.
> We will not withdraw, either openly or under the cloak of a meaningless agreement.[5]

Lyndon Johnson did grow tired. His ministers could not show him how to end the dreadful and costly war. He withdrew under the cover of a meaningless agreement.

XIX

THE NIXON POLICY

AFTER HIS DEFEAT FOR THE PRESIDENCY IN 1960 AND for the governorship of California in 1962, Richard Nixon moved to a new law practice in New York City. He maintained his activity as a leader of the Republican Party, speaking frequently at major gatherings of the party, supporting party candidates. He also traveled to foreign countries and talked with political leaders of friendly countries. He wrote about world problems and about American policy.

In his known counsel to Presidents Kennedy and Johnson, Richard Nixon was an advocate of resolute opposition to Communist aggression. In his judgment of the Vietnam war, given in 1964,[1] he clearly identified the critical factor of sanctuary and urged a change of policy. His criticism of the incumbent Democratic administrations was constructive.

And yet, in the political campaign of 1968, when he was again a candidate for the Presidency, there was no such offer of clear policy. In accepting the Republican nomination, Richard Nixon spoke in vague platitudes about stirring and fearless leadership, as politicians do. On the hustings he spoke generally about the sad state of the nation and promised the leadership which the country needed to end the war. He refused, however, to make any criticism of Administration war policy, pleading that dissent at home might jeopardize the delicate peace negotiations in Paris.

The plea was of course specious. A criticism of the Johnson policy would hurt the Administration's negotiating position in Paris only if it urged a weaker position. But we must suppose that a Nixon policy would have been stronger than the Johnson policy and would therefore have strengthened the Administration position in Paris. That kind of policy could only have had a beneficial effect on the peace talks. Why then did Richard Nixon fail to speak to the people about the most critical issue confronting the nation? Did he fear that he might defeat himself by driving the Soviet Union to make peace with Lyndon Johnson? Did he conclude that public dissatisfaction was playing into his hands anyway and he should not jeopardize his advantage by engaging in debate? Or did he fear the kind of clobbering which the powerful news media had visited upon Senator Goldwater four years earlier for daring to advocate winning the war?

Richard Nixon seemed to be badly shaken after his official briefing at the White House by President Johnson. At the time, he expressed abject agreement with the President's policy.

Curiously, candidate George Wallace took a similar tack after his briefing by President Johnson. Though he had earlier spoken out strongly for using our military power to win the war, Governor Wallace thereafter was remarkably reticent about war policy.

Had President Johnson somehow communicated his own overpowering and unreasoning fear of nuclear war to the two candidates who stood for stronger policy? What could the Presidential advisers say in a briefing which would strike fear into the heart of a man as experienced in foreign policy as Richard Nixon or as committed to military victory as George Wallace? These are the mysteries of a foreign policy which hides the real wellsprings of action from the people in the vain illusion that entrenched bureaucrats are better qualified to resolve the crises.

During the election campaign, Richard Nixon assembled an impressive panel of advisers on military policy, to include such knowledgeable men as Admiral Arthur Radford and General Nathan F. Twining, former Chairmen of the Joint Chiefs of Staff. But after his election, Richard Nixon cut himself off from these advisers. He brought to the White House as his special assistant for National Security Henry Kissinger, a foreign policy adviser to Governor Nelson Rockefeller of New York during the Governor's ill-starred campaign for the Republican Presidential nomination. Townsend Hoopes was later to claim that he had been, "along with Henry Kissinger, a principal draftsman of the 1958 'Rockefeller Report,' which constituted perhaps the pioneering effort to develop the concept of graduated deterrence and flexible military response." If any military fancy has ever been thoroughly discredited, this is it.

He retained a legion of holdovers from the Democratic Administration. He brought into other policymaking offices men who had supported Hubert Humphrey in the Presidential campaign or Republican liberals who had been cool to the Nixon candidacy. Why?

President Nixon faced a Congress controlled by the Democratic Party. Was he trying to join his opposition because he couldn't lick them? Was he trying to ease into just a slight change from the policies which the people had repudiated? Was this the old political game of left and right in which you stand as close as possible to your opponent in order to enlarge your share of the spectrum? In 36 years of political success, Democrats had never followed the rule. They had moved steadily away from the positions which Republicans had staked out, always leftward. Maybe the leftward move of Republicanism was the rule of a party born to lose.

These were some of the many questions raised by the Nixon behavior before he took office. He had said nothing about Vietnam except to underwrite the Johnson policy. But his chosen assistant for national security had written profusely on foreign policy. His view on the Paris negotiations had just been published in *Foreign Affairs.* Professor Henry Kissinger was an orthodox Harvard intellectual, more realistic than McGeorge Bundy and Walt Rostow in some respects but bearing essentially the same illusions about the real world.

For example, in his *Foreign Affairs* essay, Henry Kissinger suggested that the peace talks could be speeded up by dividing them into two sections: in one, the United States would talk with Hanoi about mutual troop withdrawal, while in the other Hanoi would talk with Saigon about Vietnamese political problems. The real problem was of course that Hanoi had no intention of discussing either question with either party. The differences were substantive, not procedural. Only a Harvard professor could exorcise the substantive obstacles by devising a more logical procedure. President Nixon's representatives tried the gambit at Paris and of course failed. The differences at Paris were nothing that could be resolved by talk.

Some of the Nixon believers argued that the President had taken a soft line for political reasons but that he would himself control the vital decisions in both foreign and domestic policy. No doubt he would try—but what kind of decisions would he make? Every President is broadened or narrowed by the advice —and the information—which he receives.

We are learning only now how severely President Johnson's perspective on foreign policy was circumscribed by his coterie of advisers. There is no reason to believe that President Nixon's men are wiser or more perceptive than the men they replaced. The President seems even more isolated than Lyndon Johnson was from challenges to his policies.

Further misgivings about the President's policy direction were raised by his dealings with the Congress. When Senator Kuchel, the Minority Whip, was defeated for re-election, the White House urged the election of the junior candidate, Senator Hugh Scott of Pennsylvania, and the obedient Republican conservatives complied. When Senator Everett McKinley Dirksen, the Minority Leader, died, the White House encouraged the candidacy of Senator Baker of Tennessee, a weak candidate who of course lost to Senator Scott.

Americans for Constitutional Action found that in the first session of the Nixon Congress, the House member who most consistently supported the Nixon programs was Peter Frelinghuysen of New Jersey with an ACA rating of 20 percent; and the member who most opposed the Nixon programs was H. R. Gross of Iowa, with an ACA rating of 100 percent. The Nixon programs were aimed at the Frelinghuysens.

These and other straws suggested that the President might take a very different course on Vietnam from the one he espoused with such clarity in 1964. Which way would he go?

In his Inaugural Address President Nixon made no direct reference to the war but he voiced his philosophy in these words:

> After a period of confrontation, we are entering a period of negotiation. . . . Those who would be our adversaries, we invite to a peaceful competition—not in conquering territory or extending dominion but in enriching the life of men.

The philosophy is indistinguishable from that voiced by Presidents Kennedy and Johnson.

At his press conference on Jan. 27, the President said:

> We have been quite specific with regard to some steps that can be taken now on Vietnam. Rather than submitting a laundry list of various proposals, we have laid down those things which we believe the other side should agree to and can agree to: the restoration of the demilitarized zone as set forth in the Geneva Conference of 1954; mutual withdrawal, guaranteed withdrawal, of forces by both sides; the exchange of prisoners. All of these are matters that we think can be precisely considered and on which progress can be made.

Why Mr. Nixon thought he could make progress on these issues when the Johnson Administration had failed is obscure. Was he refusing to face up to the real nature and purpose of the enemy? He made no progress.

At his news conference on March 4, the President was asked about the recent Communist offensive in Vietnam which included rocket shelling of cities. Did it breach the understanding reached in our suspension of bombing North Vietnam? He replied:

> I think that, therefore, we must now analyze the offensive in terms of the understanding of October 31st. That understanding was to the effect that continued shelling of or attacks on the cities—the major cities of South Vietnam— would be inconsistent with talks toward peace which would be productive in Paris.
>
> Now we are examining this particular offensive, examining it very carefully, to see whether its magnitude is in violation of that understanding. . . . I do not want to discount by this analysis the seriousness of these attacks, because the American casualty rate, I note, has doubled during the period of these attacks. . . . We have not moved in precipitate fashion, but the fact that we have shown patience and forbearance should not be considered as a sign of weakness. We will not tolerate a continuation of a violation of an understanding. But more than that, we will not tolerate attacks which result in heavier casualties to our men at a time that we are honestly trying to seek peace at the conference table in Paris. An appropriate response to these attacks will be made if they continue.

Obviously, the time for an appropriate response had come and gone and the President had not made it. Soviet strategists had tested him and found him as fearful as Lyndon Johnson.

On March 14, in response to further questioning about the Communist offensive in Vietnam, President Nixon said, "It will be my policy as President to issue a warning only once, and I will not repeat it now. Anything in the future that is done will be done. There will be no additional warning." Nothing was done.

On March 25, the President addressed the National Association of Broadcasters:

> I will tell you, looking toward the future, I think we are going to achieve that objective of a peace that will be one that will not be just for the year or two years but for the foreseeable future in the Pacific and in the world—that kind of peace. So I can tell you that it is our conviction and our belief that it is through private talks with the North Vietnamese and others involved that real progress toward peace will be made.

Was the President really so far removed from reality? This was patent utopianism.

As a candidate for the Presidency, Richard Nixon had spoken over CBS radio on Oct. 24, 1968:

> The Vietnam war ... has been painstakingly nurtured year after year by a new policy of "gradualism" until it has become the longest and one of the bloodiest, most costly military ventures in our history.
>
> With these mistakes, respect abroad for America has plummeted, to the point where a fourth-rate military power, North Korea, felt free, impudently, to seize the U.S.S. *Pueblo* on the high seas. Today, ten months later, the ship is still in their hands. The crew is still held captive. It is an incredible humiliation of the United States.

On April 14, a Navy four-engine, propeller-driven reconnaissance plane with 31 men aboard was shot down by North Korea over international waters in the Sea of Japan. The plane and all aboard were lost. The United States entered a protest at Panmunjom and announced that future flights would have fighter escorts. That was all.

On May 14, President Nixon made a nationally-televised address to the nation about Vietnam. He said in part:

We have ruled out attempting to impose a purely military solution on the battlefield.

We have also ruled out either a one-sided withdrawal from Vietnam or the acceptance in Paris of terms that would amount to a disguised defeat. . . . We must recognize that peace in Vietnam cannot be achieved overnight. A war which has raged for so many years will require detailed negotiations and cannot be settled at a single stroke.

To implement these principles, I reaffirm now our willingness to withdraw our forces on a specified timetable. We ask only that North Vietnam withdraw its forces from South Vietnam, Cambodia and Laos into North Vietnam, also in accordance with a timetable.

In his first 100 days in office, President Nixon was repeating the futile gestures of his predecessors and getting the same response. Like them, he persisted in rhetoric which seemed more designed to calm the American people than to influence the enemy.

It was most significant that he had renounced a military solution. President Eisenhower had not done that in Korea. And it was against President Nixon's philosophy to foreclose options which might be needed to get a peace settlement. *Who* among his supporters could have prevailed on the President to make such a declaration? Or had it been Prime Minister Wilson of Britain?

At commencement exercises of the Air Force Academy on June 4, the President again voiced his utopian concept of peacemaking:

And I believe this above all: that this nation shall continue to be a source of world leadership, a source of freedom's strength, in creating a just world order that will bring an end to war. . . . We want to be remembered not as the generation that suffered in war but as the generation that was tempered in its fire for a great purpose: to make the kind of peace that the next generation will be able to keep.

Mr. Nixon did not seem to grasp the reality that if he would just win his wars, the next generation would be able to take care of itself.

At Midway Island on June 8, Presidents Nixon and Thieu jointly announced that a reduction of 25,000 in the U. S. combat forces in Vietnam would be made by the end of August. Both praised the progress made by ARVN in preparing to assume added combat responsibility.

From Saigon on July 11, President Thieu offered new elections in South Vietnam, under an election commission with NFL representation, with all candidates given equal opportunity to campaign and with international supervision. Inasmuch as the 1954 Geneva Protocol provided for free elections in both North and South, President Thieu's offer was a serious surrender of position. True, he had nothing to fear from the results of such an election. He had obviously been persuaded by President Nixon that this gratuitous offer would add world prestige to his government.

On July 24, after welcoming from the deck of the U.S.S. *Hornet* the returning Apollo 11 astronauts, President Nixon flew to Guam. Before starting a world trip which would take him to the Philippines, Indonesia, Thailand, Vietnam, India, Pakistan, Romania and England, he enunciated what was to become known as the Nixon Doctrine. He reiterated the American commitment to our treaties but said that the U. S. would henceforth be in support of our allies, who must carry the responsibility for their own defense. In the course of his travels, this new pronouncement was well received by our allies.

In Bucharest, President Nixon received a tumultuous welcome from the oppressed people, who used this rare opportunity to express their hope in America as the symbol of freedom. On his return to the United States, President Nixon said:

> Another thought that occurs to me is with regard to the visit to Bucharest. This was the most moving experience that I have had in traveling to over 60 countries in the

world, not that all the other countries were not also extremely exciting and interesting and receptive; but here in this country, in which we have an entirely different political philosophy from our own, people were out by the hundreds of thousands—not ordered by their Government, but cheering and shouting; not against anybody, but simply showing their affection and friendship for the people of the United States.

This means to me one simple thing: that differences in political philosophy cannot permanently divide the people of the world. This has a great meaning for the future. It means that we can live in peace with other nations who may have different political philosophies.

The President had misjudged the significance of his Bucharest reception. The people had through his presence a rare opportunity to tell the world that they subscribed to the American philosophy of freedom and not to the Communist philosophy of their masters. To treat these people as though they subscribed to the Communist philosophy was to rebuff their hope of freedom.

At the United Nations on Sept. 18, President Nixon said,

For centuries, peace was the absence of war, stability was the absence of change. But in today's world, there can be no stability without change—so that peace becomes a continuing process of creative evolution. It is no longer enough to restrain war. Peace must also embrace progress —both in satisfying man's material needs and in fulfilling his spiritual needs.

I believe our relations with the Soviet Union can be conducted in a spirit of mutual respect, recognizing our differences and also our right to differ, recognizing our divergent interests and also our common interests, recognizing the interests of our respective allies as well as our own.

These views of President Nixon were of a kind with, but even more utopian than, those of his predecessors. The West had displayed this attitude for 36 years but the Soviet Union had *never* made it mutual. What made Mr. Nixon suppose he could change the Soviet attitude?

On November 3, the President again addressed the nation via radio and television on the subject of Vietnam. He reviewed the history of our involvement in Vietnam. He pointed out that precipitate withdrawal could lead to the massacre of one million South Vietnamese: "We saw a prelude to what would happen in South Vietnam when the Communists entered the city of Hue last year. During their brief rule there, there was a bloody regime of terror in which 3,000 civilians were clubbed, shot to death, and buried in mass graves." He told of his public and private efforts to open peace negotiations and how all had been repulsed: "No progress whatever has been made except agreement on the shape of the bargaining table."

The President restated his new foreign policy, emphasizing the responsibility of our allies, which he had voiced originally at Guam on July 25. In words ringing with the misconceived criticism of Sir Robert Thompson, the President said: "We Americans are a do-it-yourself people. Instead of teaching someone else to do a job, we like to do it ourselves. And this trait has been carried over into our foreign policy." (A greater misrepresentation of the paralysis and indecision of American foreign policy in recent decades could hardly be conceived.) The President ascribed the reduced scale of American participation in the Vietnam fighting to his new policy.

The President offered a program for the future:

> We have adopted a plan which we have worked out in cooperation with the South Vietnamese for the complete withdrawal of all U. S. combat ground forces and their replacements by South Vietnamese forces on an orderly scheduled timetable.

He warned the enemy:

> Hanoi could make no greater mistake than to assume that an increase in violence will be to its advantage. If I conclude that increased enemy action jeopardizes our re-

maining forces in Vietnam, I shall not hesitate to take strong and effective measures to deal with that situation.

This is not a threat. This is a statement of policy which as Commander in Chief of our Armed Forces I am making in meeting my responsibility for the protection of American fighting men wherever they may be.

The President summarized his conclusion as follows:

My fellow Americans, I am sure you recognize from what I have said that we really only have two choices open to us if we want to end this war:

I can order an immediate, precipitate withdrawal of all Americans from Vietnam without regard to the effects of that action.

Or we can persist in our search for a just peace, through a negotiated settlement if possible or through continued implementation of our plan for Vietnamization if necessary—a plan in which we will withdraw all of our forces from Vietnam on a schedule in accordance with our program, as the South Vietnamese become strong enough to defend their own freedom.

I have chosen the second course.

The President appealed for national unity in support of his policy.

In this address to the nation, President Nixon seemed to have set his course in Vietnam. Although he would continue to meet the enemy in Paris, he now recognized that the other side did not have an interest in peace. He would proceed with the Vietnamization of the war.

But what could Vietnamization achieve? Who could believe that substituting 200,000 Vietnamese for 200,000 Americans in South Vietnam would change the balance of power or enable South Vietnam to end the war? Was the President really quitting? Was he transferring the burden of casualties to our small ally in order to reduce criticism in the United States? How could he ever achieve his goal of a stable peace by withdrawing U. S. forces from the battlefield before the enemy aggression had been repulsed?

The Nixon policy of Vietnamization courted the disaster which had overtaken the Johnson policy. The American people would be disposed to give the new President time to work out a solution to the war—but how much time? As weeks rolled on and the toll of casualties continued, it could be expected that the peace-at-any-price faction would recover its voice and attack the President.

So it happened. Softly at first and then with increasing stridency, the Democratic Left mounted its attack. In March, 1970, Senator Edmund S. Muskie, reportedly the front-runner for the Democratic Presidential nomination in 1972, took the rostrum of the National Press Club to denounce Vietnamization as a plan for prolonging the war.

At a testimonial dinner in Massachusetts in April, Senator Edward M. Kennedy said: "Vietnamization is a misguided and inhuman policy, constructed only to avoid the hard political realities that could have been faced by a new President and faced, I am convinced, with broad national support." He continued, "Vietnamization has nothing to do with peace. It is a policy of continued war with a lessening of tensions here in the United States. It is based on the hope of military success in a struggle that knows no such solution." The Senator said that at the current rate of troop withdrawal, "we will still be involved in the war for three more years."[2]

Richard Nixon had been fortunate in succeeding to the Presidency after the big battles of the preceding years, culminating in the Tet Offensive, had smashed the enemy forces and compelled retreat. He was fortunate to have in South Vietnam a good government with good leadership and a people with new confidence in their capacity to defend their freedom. The Vietnamization program which had been started by President Johnson was due to bear fruit. In substance, President Nixon was following the Johnson policy, though with much improved relations with South Vietnam and our other Asian allies.

The shock of this policy lay in Richard Nixon's rejection of a military solution. In narrowing his choice to two distasteful alternatives, he had rejected the option which could have brought the war to an early conclusion.

President Eisenhower had illustrated that option when he took office. He faced an endless war of attrition in which two years of negotiations had made no progress. He recognized instantly that the differences could not be resolved by negotiation —that the enemy would consider a truce only when the truce was more advantageous to him than continuation of the war. President Eisenhower notified Peking through India that he would not continue the war of attrition. If he could not get a prompt cease-fire, he would take the offensive and beat the enemy. The enemy preferred a truce. That is how the fighting in Korea was ended. And Richard Nixon was there!

Someone persuaded Richard Nixon that the Vietnam war is different. There are indeed many differences. There is no established front in Vietnam. Taking the offensive in Korea did not necessarily mean breaching the Manchurian sanctuary, but in Vietnam it would require invasion of Laos at least. Whereas Eisenhower had an overwhelming nuclear superiority over the Communist powers, Nixon had only parity. And while the American people in 1953 were dismayed by the long war, they were informed and exasperated by the discussion following the removal of General MacArthur. They were mobilized for action by the aggressiveness of Senator Joseph McCarthy. With Vietnam, in contrast, the racial conflict and poverty programs of the Johnson Administration had divided the people and weakened their resolution. The Nixon staff argued that it was now too late to do what Mr. Nixon had advocated in 1964.

But the more things change, the more they are the same. Truman's failure was one of leadership, not of circumstance. We have in Vietnam a greater superiority of military force than we ever had in Korea. It would be much easier to whip the enemy. Nuclear parity is enough cover for repelling aggression. And the division of the people was a consequence of poor leadership—something Richard Nixon was called to change, not to continue. No action on his part could have done more to unify the country than to win a quick military victory in Vietnam. Like Eisenhower facing Korea, Richard Nixon had a magnificent opportunity to win the confidence of the American people. He backed away from it.

How was President Nixon moved to renounce military action and to embrace Vietnamization? We have a partial answer in his progress report to the nation made over radio and television on Dec. 15, 1969. On that occasion the President said:

> First let me share with you how I reached this conclusion. In making decisions, I believe a President should listen not only to those who tell him what he wants to hear but to those who tell him what he needs to hear. It is most important to get independent judgments from individuals who are expert on the factors to be considered, but who are not directly involved in the operations themselves. This is particularly essential when the lives of American men are involved.
>
> Several months ago I read a book by Sir Robert Thompson, a British expert who was one of the major architects of the victory over the Communist guerrillas who attempted to take over Malaya in the 1950s. In his book which was published just as this Administration took office, he was pessimistic about the conduct of the war in Vietnam—he particularly noted the failure to prepare the South Vietnamese to take over the responsibilities for their own defense.
>
> On Oct. 7, I met with Sir Robert and asked him to go to Vietnam and to give me a first hand, candid, and completely independent report on the situation there. After five weeks of intensive investigation he gave me his report on December third.
>
> His full report, which makes several very constructive recommendations, must remain confidential since it bears on the security of our men. But let me read to you from his summary of his findings:
>
> "I was very impressed by the improvement in the military and political situation in Vietnam as compared with all previous visits and especially in the security situation, both in Saigon and in the rural areas.
>
> "A winning position in the sense of obtaining a just peace (whether negotiated or not) and of maintaining an

independent, non-Communist South Vietnam has been achieved but we are not yet through. We are in a psychological period where the greatest need is confidence, a steady application of the 'do-it-yourself' concept with continuing U. S. support in the background will increase the confidence already shown by many South Vietnam leaders."

The report, which I would describe as cautiously optimistic, is in line with my own attitude and with reports I have received from other observers and from our own civilian and military leaders in Vietnam.

Two months after Thompson's visit to Vietnam, this writer confirmed at first hand the security and confidence which he reported. But as the reader of this book will understand, these were dividends flowing from the establishment of the Thieu-Ky leadership in 1965, from the smashing of the major NVA assaults in 1966 and 1967, from the upsurge of civilian morale following the Tet assaults of 1968. How had President Nixon come to associate these dividends with Thompson's book?

The fact is that Thompson told President Nixon not what he should hear but what he wanted to hear. He wrote that the war could be won without expansion of its territorial limits by reducing the scale of conventional war and by concentrating on counterinsurgent warfare to root out the Vietcong infrastructure from the countryside. That is the way the job was done in Malaya.

Thompson said we must not invade the sanctuaries because that action would enlarge the territory to be pacified and would make the task more difficult.

He said we must reduce the scale of conventional warfare. To support his contention that this is possible, he alleged that expansion of the war was caused by American aggressiveness and impatience, and that North Vietnam merely moved to counteract the American buildup. This thesis reverses the roles of aggressor and defender, as does the propaganda of the Left, and misrepresents the course of the war.

And finally, Thompson said that by counter-subversive work

the Vietcong could be rooted out and the country could be made secure.

Thompson termed this his "long haul, low cost" strategy which would bring costs within limits which the United States could sustain indefinitely, and which the Communists therefore could not defeat.[3]

The disability of Sir Robert's plan was that it wouldn't work. Let us consider why it wouldn't work and then weigh the consequences of trying it.

At the close of 1969, it was in the interest of Hanoi to see the Americans go. When the American combat forces were gone, the NVA would have only to deal with the less powerful ARVN units. Then it could strike again as it did in 1965. The NVA, not the United States, controlled the scale of conventional warfare.

Moreover, it was impossible to pacify the country while the enemy was allowed sanctuary across the border in Cambodia and Laos. As we have seen in years of warfare, it was impossible to protect the people of South Vietnam against assault by enemy units operating from the sanctuaries. South Vietnam, with its long and vulnerable western border, is quite unlike Malaya, where the area to be pacified could be readily isolated from outside intrusion.

Because of these inadequacies, the true prospect offered by the Thompson strategy was this: the war of attrition would continue for two years more while our combat forces were being replaced by ARVN units. Somewhere near the end of this process, the NVA would strike in force both to show that they had driven out the Americans and to inflict a major defeat on the ARVN.

The United States would then be able to intercede only with air and sea power. The incapacity of these elements to affect the ground battle decisively was demonstrated in 1965. Disillusionment of the American people with this repeated failure would probably lead the President to let South Vietnam go to the Communists.

This was not a strategy which should commend itself to an American President striving to establish a durable peace. But it was a strategy entirely consonant with British interests in Asia. It preserved the sanctuaries which are so essential to the Communist war of liberation. It rationalized an American withdrawal from Asia before the Communist aggression which drew our response has been defeated. This strategy could be of inestimable value to Red China, the Soviet Union and Hanoi.

In the spring of 1970, the Nixon program of Vietnamization approached a crucial stage. The President was under heavy pressure to continue and accelerate U.S. troop withdrawals. North Vietnam was building up its forces in Laos and Cambodia. The capacity of South Vietnam to resist a new enemy offensive after the departure of United States combat forces was in doubt.

On March 18, 1970, while Prince Sihanouk was absent from Cambodia, Premier Lon Nol led the government in removing Sihanouk as Chief of State. Premier Lon Nol then asked North Vietnam to remove its military forces from Cambodia. Instead of doing so, the North Vietnamese forces moved out from their positions to attack the government of Lon Nol. The Cambodian Army, too weak to offer effective resistance, fell back.

On April 20, 1970, President Nixon announced the planned withdrawal of 150,000 additional combat troops from Vietnam in the next year. He noted the increased enemy activity in Laos and Cambodia and the threat of North Vietnamese forces to the government of Cambodia, but he gave no indication of action against these threats. He warned the enemy against any action which would threaten the safety of U.S. forces in South Vietnam.

On April 30, 1970, President Nixon announced that U. S. and South Vietnamese forces were invading the sanctuaries in Cambodia. He said that the operation would be limited in time and space for U.S. troops. Action would be taken only against the established enemy bases and U.S. forces would be withdrawn by the end of June when the monsoon rains could be expected to handicap operations.

The attack on the Cambodian sanctuaries aroused the ire of American peace demonstrators who had been quieted by the continuing withdrawal of American troops. President Nixon explained that knocking out the enemy sanctuaries was necessary to maintain the continuing withdrawal of U.S. forces; but the peace demonstrators weren't listening. They saw only an expansion of the war.

When campus rioting led to the deaths of four students at Kent State University, campus opposition to the war rose to new heights of intensity. A student march on Washington was organized. Students visited Congressmen and Senators on Capitol Hill. Senator Fulbright reported out of the Senate Foreign Relations Committee the Cooper-Church amendment to limit the expenditure of funds for U.S. troops in Cambodia. Senators McGovern and Hatfield proposed an amendment to require withdrawal of all U.S. forces from Vietnam by mid-1971. Former Secretary of Defense Clark Clifford condemned the movement into Cambodia as reckless and dangerous. McGeorge Bundy blamed the President for not consulting Congress before attacking the sanctuaries.

The employment of U.S. forces was of limited scope and effect. It sustained South Vietnamese forces in their first major offensive operation. It destroyed the established North Vietnamese bases in Cambodia. But the chief importance of the action was in breaking the rule of sanctuary. President Nixon ended the rule which for a decade had wasted men and resources and reputation in imbecilic warmaking.

The President had taken the first constructive action of the war. He had not consulted Britain. He had not consulted the policymakers who had managed a no-win war for a decade. He simply did what had to be done to continue the American withdrawal while assuring the security of South Vietnam.

The Nixon initiative opened up a new perspective on the war, a perspective largely lost on the country's intellectuals. Developing cooperation among South Vietnam, Cambodia and Thailand augured the defeat of the North Vietnamese invaders and an end to Communist aggression in Southeast Asia, with only moral and logistical support from the United States.

The North Vietnamese positions in Cambodia and Laos were

extremely vulnerable to attack, strung out as they were along the border and with supply lines coming in from the flanks. If the supply lines were cut, the positions would become untenable. Some of the North Vietnamese forces might survive for a while as guerrillas, supported by Cambodian Communists, but no significant military capability could be sustained after the supply lines were severed.

On June 30, 1970, President Nixon issued a statement announcing the termination of the Cambodian operation, the withdrawal of U.S. troops according to plan and the results achieved by the venture. He described the April move of the North Vietnamese to overthrow the government of Lon Nol and the threat which that move posed to the U.S. position in South Vietnam. He appealed again for a negotiated settlement.

On July 1st, the President gave a live radio-television interview to representatives of the three major networks. He announced the appointment of Ambassador David Bruce to head the U.S. Mission at the Paris Peace Talks. He said that his government had no intention of sending U.S. troops back into Cambodia.

An early benefit of the campaign in Cambodia was the virtual ending of the war in the southern provinces of South Vietnam. North Vietnamese and Viet Cong forces had either to withdraw into Cambodia to protect their bases and lines of communication or to go underground. Without the sustenance from sanctuaries, they could no longer wage war in South Vietnam.

The war continued apace in the northern provinces, sustained from enemy bases in southern Laos. U.S. casualties decreased with the withdrawal of U.S. forces from combat but South Vietnamese casualties increased in like amount. The killing was not diminished.

In midsummer, the prospect for clearing the North Vietnamese from Cambodia was good but the prospect for military action in Laos was obscure. Would President Nixon support a move by South Vietnam and Thailand to sever the Communist supply lines in southern Laos, generally along the 17th parallel? Would he support an operation of Thai troops to recover the

Plaines des Jarres and deny that important base of operations to the Communist invaders? No U.S. troops would be needed for these operations, but the withdrawal syndrome had gained such impetus in the United States that it might jeopardize essential moral and logistical support of these allied operations.

The clarity of Mr. Nixon's vision and the tenacity of his purpose would be tested in the months to follow.

In a news conference at Los Angeles on July 20, 1970, the President expressed optimism about the peace talks in Paris. He reiterated the unity of the United States and South Vietnam governments in rejecting an imposed coalition government but accepting the decision of the people expressed in a free election. But by August 29, when the President gave an interview to newsmen of the Columbia Broadcasting System, his expectations of success in Paris had cooled. Xuan Thuy, the senior North Vietnamese representative, had not yet returned to Paris.

On October 7, 1970, after returning from a trip to Europe, the President addressed the nation over radio and television to propose a new peace plan for Indochina. His plan had five points:

1st, An immediate cease-fire in place.

2nd, A general peace conference on Indochina, building on the Geneva conferences of 1954 and 1961–2, to settle the war not only in Vietnam but in Laos and Cambodia.

3rd, A timetable for the withdrawal of all U.S. troops, to be negotiated.

4th, A political settlement reflecting the will of the Vietnamese people.

5th, An immediate and unconditional release of all prisoners of war.

The proposal was promptly condemned by the Communist powers. It soon dropped from public discussion.

On October 23, 1970, President Nixon addressed the 25th Anniversary Session of the United Nations General Assembly on the subject: "The World Interest: A Generation of Peace." He reviewed the history of U.S.-Soviet relations during World War II and in the ensuing Cold War. He reiterated his call for an era of negotiation, for competition in peacemaking—not warmaking, for disarmament and for commitment to economic development. He pledged a continuing American commitment to peace and called again for a cease-fire in Indochina.

On November 21, 1970, after an unarmed U.S. reconnaissance plane had been shot down over North Vietnam in the preceding week, U.S. planes bombed enemy installations and assembly areas below the 19th parallel. At the same time, a helicopter-borne commando raid with air cover was launched to rescue American prisoners from the Son Tay compound, twenty miles west of Hanoi. U.S. prisoners had been moved from the camp. North Vietnamese prisoners were taken for intelligence purposes. The strike and withdrawal were made with only one American wounded.

The resumption of bombing and the commando raid raised a new clamor of protest from those Americans who never criticize escalation of the war by North Vietnam. But the attempt to rescue American prisoners won popular approval, even though it failed.

As President Nixon neared the end of his second year in office, peace seemed more remote than ever. He had reduced U.S. combat and U.S. casualties; but the Nixon totals were passing 13,000 Americans killed in action and 95,000 wounded in action. He had sharply increased the rate of Vietnamese casualties. He had no plausible plan for ending the war in Indochina. U.S. allies still faced the prospect of war without end—or surrender.

The administration was showing disillusionment with the Paris peace talks. In November, when it was suggested before the House Foreign Affairs Committee that the bombing of North Vietnam might jeopardize the talks, Secretary of State Rogers replied that it would not. "No progress has been made in Paris," he said. "It is as simple as that."

In an interview with television newscasters on Jan. 4, 1971, President Nixon praised his Vietnamization program and refused to consider the possibility that South Vietnam might be unable to defend itself after the departure of U.S. combat forces. He expressed confidence that the Soviet Union wanted peace and disarmament in order to lessen its armaments burden and that his policy of negotiation—not confrontation—would ultimately be productive.

It appeared that the Nixon Administration was continuing all the mistakes of the Johnson Administration—putting unrealistic hopes in negotiation with the Soviet Union, misleading the American people with utopian hopes of peace, dallying with negotiation while the Soviet Union continued its rapid build-up of strategic nuclear weaponry. Domestic political pressures seemed to preclude any facing up to the true powers and purposes of the enemy.

XX

STRATEGIC
APPRAISAL

★ ★ ★

IN OUR REVIEW OF RECENT HISTORY WE HAVE NOTED
the course of United States policy and some of the misjudgments which have embroiled us in war in Vietnam. In the light
of the record, let us now consider what a sound course of policy
might have been if the United States had not been inhibited by
its fears and illusions and by the influence of Britain.

Let us enter the scene in 1954 when Dwight Eisenhower did,
with the Geneva Conference having divided Vietnam against
our better judgment. South Vietnam was in dire peril, but it
found in Ngo Dinh Diem a leader worthy of the hour, a patriot
who would save his country. On that front, we had at least a
temporary stability.

But Vietnam was only one of our points of conflict with the
Communist powers. In Korea, in Germany, all around the
world, we faced that Iron Curtain which Winston Churchill had
so aptly described.

The nature of that confrontation had been described 100
years earlier by Karl Marx. It had been re-stated and elaborated
by Lenin 35 years earlier. Stalin had adhered religiously to the
revolutionary ethic. The purpose of communism was to destroy
freedom wherever it existed.

This was not a war of the kind which Western Europe had known for centuries. Those struggles had been largely for power among people who shared a common culture. You might change sovereigns or be incorporated in the domain of a foreign potentate, but life went on, little changed by the political struggles.

Communism was not concerned merely with power. It was committed to destroying the whole fabric of Western culture— religion, ethics and custom. There was no common ground on which the conflicting forces could be reconciled. That is how the Communists saw the confrontation.

In the beginning, the West also saw the conflict clearly. In 1920, Secretary of State Bainbridge Colby stated the reasons why the United States had refused to recognize the Soviet Union. His reasons were cogent and ample.

The Colby judgment of the Bolshevist system governed United States policy until 1933. Then President Franklin D. Roosevelt, newly in office, extended recognition to the Soviet Union. He acted upon a theory which had received growing support in the country, that it was better to bring the Soviet Union into the family of nations and influence it through normal international intercourse than to continue the policy of ostracism. Besides, some American businessmen foresaw opportunities for profit in trade with the Soviet Union.

This was an important change of direction for the United States and for the Free World. It was an attempt to end the war which the Bolshevists had declared; and to this purpose a condition of recognition was that the Soviet Union renounce its commitment to subvert and overthrow the United States government. We have seen in subsequent revelation of the penetration of Soviet agents into the United States government during the 1930's that Stalin honored, not his pledge to the United States, but his pledge to world revolution.

Nevertheless, in 1933 recognition seemed like a reasonable gambit. The way was paved, it is true, by *New York Times* and other reporters whose dispatches from Moscow were propaganda pieces for the Stalinist tyranny. If the American people had understood what was really happening, there might have been no recognition. But even if the wickedness of the regime had been fully comprehended, the Christian spirit would have influenced many Americans to extend a helping hand in hope of moderating the tyranny.

Prudence should have caused us to enter upon this experiment with some circumspection. Some standards should have been established for measuring the effect of the new policy. If we expected to change Soviet political behavior, how soon should beneficial effects be observable? What tenets of the obnoxious Bolshevist dogma should we expect them to shed and when?

It would clearly be suicidal to welcome such an enemy into the heart of our society if he were to persist in his purpose of destroying us. If the theory didn't work, if the Bolshevists didn't change, what should we then do?

But this became a political question, not a scientific question. Politicians are borne on waves of public fancy. The proposition that the Bolshevists could be changed by association with our superior culture was no longer a theory; it was a dogma, not to be questioned. Thenceforth old concepts of international morality and responsibility were dead. We would maintain diplomatic relations even with our enemies.

What did happen? We have had 38 years of diplomatic relations with the Soviet Union. Has the Soviet government abandoned any of the immoral precepts prescribed by Lenin and which Secretary Colby condemned? Not one! It still subscribes to and practices resort to every lie, deception, subterfuge and subversion which will help to speed our destruction. It is the United States which has abandoned its standards of international morality and has dragged down the whole Free World with it. The Communist powers are granted free rein to enter and subvert our society while we are excluded from their society.

If arrangements were reciprocal, if we were free to preach freedom to their citizens, the Bolshevists would be destroyed by their own people. As Secretary Colby noted, they know that the

destruction of freedom in all the world is essential to the survival of Bolshevism in Russia.

Who can believe that the continuation of diplomatic relationships under these conditions is to our benefit? We are committing suicide.

The new dogma of diplomatic recognition has introduced a
paralyzing rigidity into our international policy. There is no
good reason why recognition should not be used as a tool of
policy. It should be extended when favorable agreement can be
reached, withdrawn when unsatisfactory relations develop.
For example, when Premier Khrushchev at Paris in 1960 so
arrogantly and capriciously assailed President Eisenhower
over the U-2 flights, flights which had to his knowledge been
made for years preceding, it would have been most appropriate
for President Eisenhower to have recalled our Ambassador
from Moscow.

President Roosevelt made the ending of subversion in the
United States a condition of recognition. There is sound reason
now to require all Communist governments to cease their attacks on the United States as a condition of recognition. It is
hard to see how any self-respecting nation can ask less.

There is an urgent need for the United States to define as a
matter of policy the conditions which it requires of nations
with which it maintains diplomatic relations. It would thereby
set a standard to be used by other Free World powers and would
exert a pressure for change in the Communist countries.

In the absence of such enlightened self-interest the United
States has simply submitted to the Communist assault. It saved
the Soviet Union from defeat by Hitler without in the least
altering Stalin's determination to destroy the United States. It
opened trade channels which Stalin used selectively to build
his own power. It worked actively but unwittingly for its own
destruction.

This concept that the United States can by association and
good will alter the Soviet design of conquest is of course *mad.*
All human history attests that the ambition of a conqueror is
never deflected by the good will of the victim. Conquerors are

stopped only by unconquerable resistance mounted before the conqueror has the power to prevail.

And yet, this mad hypothesis has for thirty-eight years remained the cornerstone of American foreign policy. It is the heart of recognition, the heart of our wartime alliance, the heart of Yalta, the heart of detente.

The great German philosopher of war, Karl von Clausewitz, wrote: "In war, the first and the greatest of all strategic questions is to decide the kind of war you are in." Any analysis of United States strategy must begin with recognition that we have not made this judgment. We are in an epic war which the Bolshevists have been waging since 1918, and we do not even know we are in it. Our leaders have persisted in the illusion that we are at peace with the Soviet Union. But Soviet leaders do not share that illusion. They know they are at war with the United States.

Having so badly misjudged the war we are in, it follows that our efforts to promote international peace and concord are misconceived and misdirected. When we turned away from reality, our minds had to embrace a host of other misconceptions which would be consistent with our mad hypothesis. Thence came the mythology that restraint in the use of power serves the cause of peace, that a treaty or other agreement could restrain Soviet rapacity. The sequence of our behavior in Vietnam derives inevitably from this basic misjudgment about the war we are in.

This basic misjudgment of our position in the world has not of course blinded us entirely to the existence of conflict. President Truman turned from praising "Uncle Joe" to a flat refusal to have any negotiation at all with the Soviet Union. But because of our basic misjudgment, we have regarded every setback as a temporary aberration and returned like a man on drugs to the cultivation of Soviet goodwill.

Our presidents from Eisenhower to Johnson have condemned Soviet aggression, but they have all persisted in the illusion that somehow they could overcome it through negotiation. Thus, there has been no continuity of policy. Emergency adjustment to crisis has been made as events required.

In Southeast Asia after 1954, Ho Chi Minh ruled a Communist state with a population of about 20 million. At that time, the non-Communist states of South Vietnam, Laos, Cambodia and Thailand ruled a combined population of about 60 million. The capacity of the free nations to defend themselves should not have been in question.

However, when North Vietnam invaded Laos in 1959 the United States did not support local action to resist the aggression. President Eisenhower had been immobilized intellectually by the Khrushchev peace offensive. He could not oppose Soviet aggression in Laos without (he thought) jeopardizing his negotiations with the Soviet premier. Thus, the Soviet stratagem paralyzed allied opposition to the aggression in Laos.

When President Kennedy took office, the general strategic situation had deteriorated. North Vietnam had overrun northeastern Laos and was operating from an air base in the Plaines des Jarres. But Thailand, South Vietnam, Cambodia and Laos still had overwhelming superiority. They could drive the North Vietnamese out of Laos. The problem of policy was to bring this power to bear against the Communist aggression. But, strangely, that was not to be the judgment of United States policy. Our leaders bemused themselves with plans to introduce American troops into Laos. Why would policy take such a turn when ample Thai and South Vietnamese troops were available for the task?

What really happened is that British representations raised the spectre of war with Communist China and our strategists obediently wrestled with that irrelevancy. If you begin with an assumption that any resistance to North Vietnamese aggression will bring Chinese intervention, you are already defeated.

But how could our leaders accept that premise? Our allies could protect their own interests in Southeast Asia if we deterred Chinese intervention with the threat of our vastly superior military power. How could Britain so confuse this strategic reality and paralyze our diplomacy? We actually neutralized Laos and provided Ho Chi Minh the corridor through eastern Laos which he needed for the attack on South Vietnam.

As the North Vietnamese attack on Laos mounted in 1962, we compounded our error by denying South Vietnam its clear right in international law to counterattack the North Vietnamese aggressors operating from Laos. President Kennedy allowed the Communists the sanctuary which they required for the success of their aggression. If he had simply told Thailand and South Vietnam to defend themselves, there would have been no sanctuary and no war in Vietnam. American policy made the war.

These basic errors of United States policy persisted throughout the Johnson Administration. In these years American policy so weakened South Vietnam that it was on the verge of collapse. Instead of adjusting policy to the realities of power, President Johnson persisted in blind adherence to the intolerable handicaps imposed by irrational fear. All the while, Thailand and South Vietnam had the capacity to cut off the North Vietnamese line of communications through Laos and end the war. That strategy was publicly advocated by General John K. Waters in December 1966, after his retirement as commander of U. S. Army Forces in the Pacific; but this defensive response was beyond the scope of action which British policy could tolerate or Presidential policymakers dare to use. The United States persisted blindly in the most wasteful, futile, unnecessary war which any great power has ever fought.

In requiring our allies to provide the first line of defense for their own security, President Nixon has returned to some basic wisdom. But that shedding of responsibility onto our allies must be accompanied by a shedding of authority also. Our allies must recover the freedom of action which will make their defense effective. They must be free to strike at and destroy aggression, in accordance with international law. Our alliance must mean that we support them in such action, not that we restrain them. It would be the ultimate arrogance and injustice if President Nixon, having forced upon South Vietnam the responsibility for its own defense, then forbade it to destroy the North Vietnamese forces in Laos and Cambodia.

We have reason to know that our allies, while suffering the stricture of United States policy, have understood the decisive disabilities imposed by that policy. President Diem had proposed in 1961 the seizure of key Vietcong bases in Laos. The strategy proposed by General Waters had doubtless been discussed with Vietnamese leaders as to feasibility. All the leaders of South Vietnam have wanted to carry the war back to the North.

In December 1968, General Cao Van Vien, Chief of the ARVN Joint Staff, addressed a meeting of the World Anti-Communist League in Saigon. He proposed that Thailand and South Vietnam should collaborate in establishing a defensive position across southern Laos in prolongation of the Demilitarized Zone to the Thai Border. That action would cut off the NVA forces in southern Laos and in Cambodia. It would protect Cambodia and Thailand from Communist aggression south of the defense line. It would give South Vietnam a shorter and more defensible position against NVA attack. In fact, that simple maneuver would virtually end the war. This had been the Waters plan.

That strategy would leave Northern Laos open to NVA occupation. But this need only be a starting strategy. Whether to clear Laos of North Vietnamese invaders could be left for subsequent decision by the nations concerned.

When we view the theatre of war in this light, when we note the superior power of the free nations available for their own defense, it becomes clear that this war should never have been. If the United States had merely backed up its allies with munitions and moral support, they would have repelled the aggression. Surely this tragic malfeasance of American foreign policy indicates the need for drastic overhaul of our policymaking institutions.

The chief obstacle to effective action against North Vietnamese aggression was American fear of intervention by Red China. U. S. leaders, hearkening to the warnings of British representatives, concluded that a South Vietnamese counterattack against the aggressors in Laos, Cambodia or North Vietnam would bring Red China into the war.

Let us address this question. Would Red China invade Southeast Asia if North Vietnamese aggression faced defeat? The Red Chinese response would be determined not by the defeat of North Vietnam but by the attitude of the United States. The Chinese leaders, like other national leaders, must judge a course of action by the consequence for their own country.

If Chinese leaders learned that, following their intervention in Southeast Asia, the United States would not bomb China because that action might lead to world war, they would be free to intervene. The damage to China would be limited to its expeditionary force.

But if Chinese leaders learned that, following intervention, the United States would attack China, nothing in Southeast Asia could compensate China for the damage it would sustain. The United States could destroy vital facilities in China without ever putting a man ashore. It could support an invasion of China from Taiwan. It could conceivably overthrow the Communist government. If the United States stands tall in support of its alliances and warns China to stay out of Southeast Asia, China will stay out. No Communist leader would bring that kind of war on his domain.

The paralysis of fear has affected our reason. We have conjured up dire consequences of being embroiled in a land war in Asia, of fighting masses of the Chinese people, in order to justify our timidity. But these hysterical fears only confirm the myopic quality of our vision.

We can use our power to promote peace. Certainly no American proposes to make war against the Chinese people. The Communist Party is not the Chinese people: it is their oppressor. We would make war in China only on the side of the Chinese people.

American policymakers have failed to note the reality of Communist weakness and to frame policy related to it. That is why our commitment to peace has been so tragically ineffectual.

This is to say that the fears of our leaders about Chinese intervention have been idle and therefore irresponsible. They have been related to strategic concepts which were ill-conceived and crippling. As an exercise of intellectual poverty, the performance has been surpassing.

The consequences of our strategic mismanagement are not limited to the bitter toll of life, limb and resources in Vietnam. Our national stature is diminished, our self-confidence is eroded, our commitment to freedom is undermined.

Some leaders are foolishly persuaded that guerrilla warfare cannot be defeated by organized military and police forces. Others are dismayed by the cost of war and determined to retrench at whatever political cost. Others argue that we are overextended, that we cannot "police the world." They want "no more Vietnams" but they have no alternative means of defending our free allies. They are closing their minds to the Communist challenge, telling reality to go away. It is understandable that men who mistakenly believe American military power has been effectively employed in Vietnam would be driven to such palpably unreasonable conclusions.

It is true that the United States cannot and should not suffer the drain of blood and resources expended in the war in Vietnam. It should be equally apparent, though it has not been, that no other power can compel us to suffer this wasting war. Only we can do this to ourselves.

The Soviet Union or Red China cannot impose a "war of liberation" on the Free World unless the United States is disposed to suffer that action without decisive response. The Free World can repel every such aggression, with small expenditure of its own resources and heavy loss to the aggressors. Aggression is deterred by making the consequences unacceptable to the would-be aggressor.

If we really expect to preserve our country and foster freedom in the world, we must so change our policy as to make costs tolerable to us and intolerable to the Communist side. The economy of war requires us to conserve our resources and destroy enemy resources. We have been following an opposite strategy.

It is first necessary to realize that we and our allies can preserve the integrity of our realm against Communist attack. We are not called upon to keep troops in Europe or Asia or anyplace else outside the United States. We need only make it clear to friend and foe that we shall support our alliance commitments.

Our allies must provide for their own defense to the extent that they are able. We have an interest in keeping Britain free, but that interest is secondary and subordinate to the British interest in the same purpose. If Britain prefers to risk Communist conquest rather than defend itself, and loses, our world will be diminished but not fatally so. We can still preserve our freedom.

We must assure each ally that we and other allies stand ready to support its defense of freedom. We must build in our alliances absolute confidence in our capacity and will to defend the Free World. When we of the Free World adopt this posture, armed Communist aggression will cease.

We cannot state this case without recognizing that we have been here before. After the loss of North Vietnam in 1954, the embarrassed Eisenhower Administration set out to preclude any more such losses. Secretary Dulles negotiated a series of regional agreements to mobilize and coordinate the defenses of the Free World.

Unfortunately, perception of the problem of security died with Secretary Dulles. He did maintain peace while he lived. But then President Eisenhower, squired by Prime Minister Macmillan, fell into the Soviet peace trap which came to be known as the Spirit of Camp David. President Eisenhower foolishly thought that *he* could negotiate detente.

The insistent voice of British policy induced this relapse into wishful thinking. British sophistry persuaded our leaders that higher aims of world peace required us to treat our treaties as scraps of paper.

It should be noted that Britain does not practice in defense of its own interests the kind of appeasement it urges on the United States where the interests of other allies are concerned. In Hong Kong, Britain rules as long as Britain remains. There is no coalition government. In Kuwait in 1958, when the revolutionary regime in Iraq threatened to seize the Sheikdom, British Tommies were rushed to the defense.

Nor do the Israelis practice the kind of passive defense which the United States has imposed on South Vietnam. They have defied U. S. restraints and carried the war to Arab territory. Why would counterattack provoke Chinese intervention in Vietnam but not Soviet intervention in the Middle East? The Soviet losses in Egypt and Syria were great.

General Minoru Genda, retired former Chief of Japan's Air Self Defense Force and a sitting member of the Japanese Diet, said of the war in Vietnam: "I feel basic U. S. policy in Asia is correct. But I don't agree with your military policy and tactics in Vietnam. . . . War should be short. Force should be used swiftly, like an arrow shot from a strong bow. I do not approve of Russia's attack on Czechoslovakia, but, militarily, they did well. It was all over in a few days, just like the Israeli-Arab war. But the Vietnam war has dragged on for so long it is now very hard to end."[1]

There is an irreconcilable conflict between our quest for detente and the reality of Communist power and purpose. If we continue to deny the latter and pursue the former, we destroy ourselves. The alternative of recognizing the latter and abandoning the former does not, as some allege, mean war. It means rather a more realistic and effective commitment to peace. Peace is not served by self-deception. It is served by facing up to the realities of life and using our power for peace.

In criticizing detente policy, we take no view that the Communist regimes are permanent and unchangeable. On the contrary, we consider them to be transient and highly vulnerable. Nor do we hold that these regimes cannot be influenced by our behavior; they are very sensitive to our behavior.

We simply find that neither in theory nor in fact is our detente policy fashioned to cause in these regimes the kinds of change we say we seek. Rather, detente policy serves to sustain the regimes, to meliorate their internal crises, to confirm their appraisal of bourgeois weakness and to reinforce their ambitions of conquest.

Only our passionate and blind adherence to misconceived notions of peacemaking keeps the nation bound to a detente policy so opposed to our aims and our interests. We must recognize that negotiation is a political fraud against the American people; that only a policy of honest confrontation with the Communist powers can really serve the cause of peace. We can expose and discredit the Nineteenth-Century concepts of a new social order which Communists continue to foist on the world. We can force these governments to be more responsive to the will of their peoples. We can dismantle the whole Communist tyranny. But we can do none of this while we persist in our illusions about achieving peace through detente.

We have in the Free World the kind of social and political organization which all peoples desire. We have the diversity of cultures which freedom nourishes. We have the advanced science of the new age. We have the productive organization of society which banishes want and minimizes human insecurity. But we have been so addled by the bombast of a pretentious Marxism, by the interventions of British self-interest and by irrational fears of nuclear war that we have lost faith in freedom.

The problem before the United States today is to mobilize Free World strength in support of a policy and a strategy which will tip the scales of conflict in favor of freedom. Fifty years of retreat must be ended and a new era of liberation must be inaugurated. The United States has the power and the authority to lead such a change of Free World strategy. It is only in the context of such change that the tragic waste of past policy, in Southeast Asia and in all the world, can be ended.

There are some basic requirements of the new strategy:

1. A realistic appraisal of Communist power and purpose must be given to all free peoples as the foundation for their comprehension of the war they are in. When official deception of the public is ended, sound policy will follow.

2. A purpose to overthrow the Communist tyrannies by internal revolution and to liberate the enslaved peoples must ani-

mate Free World political action. Our commitment to freedom must be confident and unequivocal.

3. The Free World must maintain ample military defenses to deter military adventures by the Communist powers. Because of the decisive superiority of Free World industrial resources, the necessary military posture can be maintained without strain when its essentiality for peace is understood.

4. United States military forces must be withdrawn from Europe, Japan, Korea and Southeast Asia within three years. Present deployment of these forces is wasteful and unnecessary except in Southeast Asia, where an adjustment can be made within the time period. The time period allows for necessary build-up of local forces where replacement is required.

5. The United States must maintain an invulnerable strategic nuclear capability to deter Communist blackmail. This is America's special contribution to the Free World alliance. There must be no talk of parity. Superiority is essential.

6. When each country of the Free World vigorously preserves its own security, with confidence in the collaboration of neighbors and in the determination of the United States to deter Red Chinese or Soviet intervention, the danger of war will be lifted and political action will become decisive.

7. In Southeast Asia, South Vietnam and Thailand must warn North Vietnam to withdraw to its borders or to suffer defeat. If North Vietnam persists in its aggression, its military forces must be decisively defeated and North Vietnam must be liberated from Communist rule. With the United States deterring Red Chinese or Soviet intervention, the allies are assured of a quick victory.

8. The military forces of the Republic of China and the Republic of Korea will remain poised in their homelands. They constitute an element of the deterrent to Red Chinese intervention in Southeast Asia while at the same time offering potent encouragement to revolution in Red China and in North Korea.

9. When the war in Southeast Asia has been ended, the Free World will concentrate on economic and political warfare to expose the criminal character and behavior of Communist

regimes and to encourage revolutions for freedom in the Communist countries.

10. When the Communist regimes are overthrown, world disarmament will occur because the need for armament will have been removed. A system of international law subscribed to by all nations will be established for the settlement of international disputes.

These planks of a new policy and a new strategy are derived from objective appraisal of the war we are in. They represent no hostility to the Russian and Chinese peoples—rather, they represent a genuine offer of friendship. They represent no design to change Communist governments against the will of the people governed, but only with and through the people governed.

Militarily, the policy represents no purpose of waging war but only of deterring Communist aggression while a program of political action for freedom takes effect. The power of this policy rests not in military hardware but in the universal human desire for peace and freedom.

This program would end the fighting in Vietnam quickly with a sharp repulse to the Communist aggression. It would then confront the Communist leaders with a solid front of states dedicated to freedom and well-defended against attack. With the United States possessing a predominant nuclear power and our allies alert in self-defense, the opportunities for Communist aggression would be minimized.

The political offensive for freedom would revive that devotion to and confidence in government of, by and for the people which animated the Atlantic world in the opening decades of the nineteenth century. Refugees from the Communist tyranny would be honored. Freedom fighters behind the Iron Curtain would be assisted. The iniquity of the Communist tyranny would be condemned in every forum and the inevitability of its collapse would be universally predicted. With faith and courage, men can make tyranny unbearable, so that the tyrant must either bow to the people's will or be destroyed.

Unlike the policy of detente, which dissembles reality and

projects wishful thinking, and which builds a steadily-worsening confrontation of nuclear power between Communist and free worlds, this policy projects realism and the dismantling of nuclear confrontation. It puts conflict in the political spectrum, where it should be—between tyranny and freedom, where it is. Because its goal is freedom, not destruction, it is open to any change of government which brings freedom to the people, whether through melioration of existing regimes or through revolution.

Moreover, this policy projects the faith of the American people, honestly and openly, and their goodwill toward all mankind.

There can be no doubt that the Free World has the resources to make this strategy effective. A question arises only about the quality of Free World leadership. Where will it find a Churchill or a Roosevelt capable of arousing the people to a perception of danger and fortifying their determination to destroy the Communist tyrannies?

Can the American people be united behind such a policy of opposing tyranny and spreading freedom? Or are they so paralyzed by the prevailing peace psychosis that initiatives for freedom seem too fraught with danger?

There is reason to believe that the American people understand the disastrous consequences of appeasing Communist aggression. They are not cowed by Communist bluster as their leaders are. They will welcome a political leadership which faces up to the reality of conflict instead of practicing a mean and cowardly self-deception.

The real obstacle to the adoption of constructive new foreign policy lies not with our people but with the two-party system. The two parties are so wedded to the detente policy and so fearful of change that the prospect of either party providing the required political leadership is remote.

The last successful third party movement was that of the Republican Party. The issue was slavery and secession— "whether," as Lincoln said, "that nation or any nation so conceived and so dedicated, can long endure." Third parties can be successful only when a great issue is at stake and when existing parties refuse to face that issue.

Just as the Democratic and Whig parties failed to face up to the issue of slavery in the last century, so today the Republican and Democratic parties are refusing to face up to the reality of the Communist threat to our survival. Whether this country will awaken in time to a comprehension of the war it is in is a vastly more serious issue than the question of slavery.

The times require a new political alignment dedicated to national action on the specific issue of national survival. There can be no doubt that a political party which dedicates itself prudently and rationally to informing the country about the Communist menace and arousing the country to "a new birth of freedom" will receive the support of the American people.

The inertia of old political parties argues that the task must be assumed by a new political party. In the climate of internal division and "peace at any price" which the existing parties have wrought in America today, we cannot expect the product of one of these parties to believe that the American people would rally in support of an aggressive foreign policy. Rather, our two-party system seems capable of temporizing the country into inferiority and finally into surrender.

America must find new leadership capable of seeing through the present turmoil to the true basis of national unity and possessing the moral courage to lead the people to that new ground. Whether such leadership will be given will be decisive for our national survival.

XXI

THE MILITARY FACTOR

IT IS NOTEWORTHY THAT IN RECOUNTING THIS HIS-
tory of the Vietnam war, I have hardly alluded to our military
leaders. They have apparently had little influence in making
national policy. They have acceded without public protest to a
disastrous strategic course which threatens to destroy our
Republic. How could this be?

The military services have in recent decades undergone a
drastic transformation. Standards of professional conduct
which before World War II were firmly established have since
that war been abandoned. Instead of conceiving a responsibility for the military security of the nation, for the lives of men
committed to battle, for the economy of national resources,
military leaders now conceive only an obligation to obey the
ruling political administration. They have shed all traces of
moral responsibility by blaming political leaders for the course
of policy.

Before World War II, the Army and Navy had set high standards of professional leadership. The general concept of the

military role was that when the politicians and the diplomats got the country into war, the military job was to win the war and restore the peace as quickly as possible. Speed was essential to avoid the mounting losses and waste of a long war.

This setting bred a great deal of independence. In war, certain things had to be done to win. It was the job of the professional to know what to do and to do it. It was not to be expected that the Secretary of War or the Secretary of Navy would be qualified to make these professional judgments. The President would turn to military leaders for these decisions.

With the advent of the New Deal and the growing politicalization of the Federal Government, the military services were not immune. In time of peace, politicians were not greatly concerned with military affairs, but the mobilization of the Civilian Conservation Corps illustrated a new involvement of the military in political service. During the war, some men like Patton, Krueger, Bradley, Ridgway, and Douglas MacArthur gained fame for their consummate professional competence. Some generals were of the new political breed, chosen largely for their capacity to get along with political leaders.

In this period it was notable that Franklin D. Roosevelt, the master politician of the day, never conceived himself to be a master of strategy. He had Admiral William D. Leahy ever at his side in the White House for daily consultation on the course of the war. He maintained close personal contact with the Joint Chiefs of Staff. Franklin D. Roosevelt had been Assistant Secretary of the Navy in World War I and in that role had worked easily in the traditional relationships with military leaders. He never thought to change those relationships.

After the war new trends in policymaking levels developed. A plan for three services—Army, Navy and Air Force—serving under one military department, National Defense, in which the Secretary would be assisted by a Chief of Staff of the Defense Forces, was blocked in Congress. A third service, the United States Air Forces, was created and a new Department of the Air Force was organized. But all three of the military departments were dropped to sub-Cabinet rank. The Chairman of the Joint

Chiefs of Staff and a small staff for policymaking would serve the Secretary of Defense.

This was the new organization created by the National Security Act of 1947. It is worthy of note that the United States has shown no adequate strategic conception of its proper role in world conflict since the inception of this organization. In China, in Korea, in Berlin, in Cuba, in Vietnam, our country has accepted defeat after defeat when it had all the power needed to preserve its interests.

What this organization has done is to break down military responsibility and perception with committee rule. The Joint Chiefs of Staff organization has proven to be an inept device for providing military policy for the country because it is incapable of reaching objective conclusions on vital issues.

Military advice to the President has been largely concealed in classified records. Some testimony is revealed occasionally by those who received it. The response to the 1961 Communist aggression in Laos gives us some perception of Joint Chiefs of Staff advice.

President Eisenhower, as he was about to leave the White House, discussed the problem with the Chairman of the Joint Chiefs of Staff:

> On January 2, General Lemnitzer reported that if we had to intervene, the current plan called for our forces to hold the two main cities (Vientiane and Luang Prabang), leaving the protection of the countryside to the Laotians.
> "It's my conviction," I interposed, "that if we ever have to resort to force, there's just one thing to do: clear up the problem completely." We should not allow a situation to develop, costly in blood and treasure, without achieving our objectives.[1]

By April, the situation had worsened. On April 26, Washington received reports that the Pathet Lao were attacking in force. On the 27th, the National Security Council met. Schlesinger reported:

Walt Rostow had told me that it was the worst White House meeting he attended in the entire Kennedy Administration.

Rostow and the Laos task force, supported by Harriman who was now on an inspection trip in Laos, still urged a limited commitment of American troops to the Mekong Valley. But the Joint Chiefs, chastened by the Bay of Pigs, declined to guarantee the success of the operation, even with the 60,000 men they had recommended a month before. The participants in the meeting found it hard to make out what the Chiefs were trying to say.[2]

According to Schlesinger, the Joint Chiefs continued to obstruct military action to defend Laos. He wrote:

At one National Security Council meeting General Lemnitzer outlined the processes by which each American action would provoke a Chinese counter-action, provoking in turn an even more drastic American response. He concluded: "If we are given the right to use nuclear weapons, we can guarantee victory." The President sat glumly rubbing his upper molar, saying nothing.[3]

It is indeed incomprehensible that military leaders would talk in such terms about the aggression of North Vietnam in Laos, and measures required to defeat it. Who had filled them with such nonsense? Had years of British tutelage reduced Americans to this? The Chiefs were passing the buck upstairs and refusing to accept responsibility for professional judgment.

The denouement came with a visit of General Lemnitzer to Laos, where he joined Ambassador Harriman. He then endorsed the more limited commitment. He had escaped from the "tank" in which the Joint Chiefs do their shadow-boxing.

The organization has served also to divorce the military leadership from policymaking. The addled thinking about "civilian control" which went into the National Security Act is exposed in the resulting structure. The Chairman of the Joint Chiefs of Staff, who is or should be above all else a policymaker, is not a member of the National Security Council. He is called to attend when the policymakers need his advice. Of course they don't know when they need his advice because he is not there to tell them.

In consequence of this organization and some related trends in military leadership, the President, unless he has a personal rapport with the military leadership, tends more and more to be isolated from it. Thus Lyndon Johnson, who lacked that rapport, met regularly for discussion of the war with Secretary Rusk, Secretary McNamara and Special Assistant Walt Rostow. Sometimes the Chairman of the Joint Chiefs of Staff would join the group. The President made the mistake of thinking he was getting from Secretary McNamara the thinking of the military leaders. That thinking could have been brought out only in give-and-take with the military leaders over the broad range of questions about the war. There is no indication as yet that President Johnson ever had that kind of advice from anyone. His civilian assistants couldn't give it and his military staff didn't.

The disabilities of this new organization were serious but limited until the Administration of President Kennedy. Until that time, the Secretaries of Defense were men of some competence in the business world who had learned to use people in solving problems. These men were frustrated by the conflicts of the professional services which they were loath to resolve. Secretary Charles E. Wilson used Admiral Radford as a Chief of Staff and told him to resolve the professional differences. Where the Secretaries failed, Congress resolved the issues on an ad hoc basis through the appropriation process. Congress decided who got the money.

The National Security Act of 1947 flattered Congress by continuing three operating military departments. Because the Joint Chiefs were limited to policymaking, the Joint Staff lacked a capability of coordinating the administrative work of the three service departments. This task fell to Congress as the services contended for funds. But Congress found that it too was incapable of resolving the service differences. Consequently it applauded the arrival of Secretary Robert S. McNamara, a man who would "knock some heads together."

The National Security Act of 1947 had failed to provide adequate management for the Defense Department. It established three administrative departments with no provision for their coordination and direction. Gradually, in piecemeal action, the Congress gave more administrative authority to the Secretary of Defense. It enlarged the Joint Staff, and the Secretaries have further augmented that staff through management contracting. Thus, instead of setting up an efficient organization to do the job, Congress has sanctioned the growth of an administrative monstrosity which is incapable both of providing efficient management and of providing sound strategic direction for the country.

If there was one man who could create a greater monstrosity than anyone else, it was Robert Strange McNamara. He was in essential character and experience an auditor, not a manager. He did not have the mind for organizing and directing great enterprises. His mind was filled with details of method and efficiency and procedure which are the concerns of auditors. He was frightfully miscast as Secretary of Defense, a portfolio of grand policymaking responsibility. In seven years of service, he never learned what war is all about.

Secretary McNamara brought to his office some disabling concepts about war. He conceived, for example, that if the military establishment would furnish him all the facts bearing on a problem, he would be able to weigh the facts and solve the problem. He seemed unaware of the nature of professional judgment. I would be glad to remove the Secretary's appendix under his most detailed instruction, but I am sure he would rather have a surgeon do the job without the McNamara guidance.

This fundamental ignorance of the problem at hand was reflected in his war management. Secretary McNamara persuaded Lyndon Johnson that the President could and should exercise detailed control of the bombing of North Vietnam. The

Secretary would develop detailed plans for Presidential approval.

Instead of giving policy direction to responsible commanders, as a President should, and depending upon them to achieve his desired objectives, President Johnson therefore became involved in details which neither he nor the Secretary of Defense should ever have known. Presidential direction introduced rigidity into the program. Commanders were not free to take advantage of the latest intelligence and varying conditions of warfare to obtain maximum effect with minimum loss. Professionals in the field who saw such waste of men and material in war became bitterly disillusioned with the national leadership.

The effects of the McNamara management were, however, most devastating in policymaking. This is the first and greatest responsibility of a Secretary of Defense; and Secretary McNamara failed it abjectly. It was his job to introduce into national policymaking realistic appreciation of the capabilities and uses of military power in serving our national interests.

Robert S. McNamara was a philosophic captive of the intellectual community. He shared the utopian illusions and fertile biases which had marked the avant garde thinking of the postwar years. Consequently he readily agreed that it was the province of the State Department to make foreign policy and of the Defense Department to execute the military phases of that policy.

This thinking of course negated the considered judgment of the National Security Act which established his office. Congress recognized that making policy by the State Department in time of peace and by the War Department in time of war had produced a critical discontinuity of national policy. It created the National Security Council to bring both departments into a continuing participation in the policymaking process. When Secretary McNamara subordinated the military perception of the national interest to the diplomatic perception, he did the country a crucial disservice. Through this default, the war in Vietnam came in fact to be run by the State Department.

Secretary McNamara was isolated even from his own staff.

One of his admirers explained his aloofness in terms of loyalty: "He observed, moreover, so strict a sense of privacy in his relationship with the President that he found it virtually impossible to report even to key subordinates what he was telling the President or what the President was saying or thinking."[4]

In truth, Robert S. McNamara was a man of severely limited talent. He could not brook the presence of smarter and wiser men. When the Chief of Naval Operations, Admiral George W. Anderson Jr., gave frank and honest testimony to Congress about the TFX contract, in accord with military practice, the Secretary induced President Kennedy to replace Admiral Anderson at the close of his first two-year tour. For similar independence, General Curtis Le May was replaced as Chief of Air Staff after three years in office. The word went out that military leaders must not give Congress any views in conflict with Administration programs.

The effect of the McNamara tenure was therefore to assemble in top military positions a panel of yes-men, completely dominated by the Secretary. Our military leadership is today made up of men who complacently view the agony of our country as they prostitute their professional integrity to the demands of a false loyalty.

In a survey of retired general officers of the Army and the Air Force made in 1969, *Human Events* asked whether a senior officer should retire rather than serve in a war which wasted the lives of his fighting men. A majority of 56 percent said he should not, against 35 percent who said that he should. The general thinking was that when higher authority has made its decision the military leader must stay on the team and continue to serve.

This dominant view is consistent with the normal practice of military command. Officers in military service must often carry out orders with which they disagree. The company commander may have preferred a different course, but when he has made his recommendation and has been overruled, he knows that the success of the battalion operation requires him to execute battalion orders.

In the military organization, that kind of response is both necessary and reasonable. The battalion commander has previously served as a company commander. He knows the company's problems and capabilities. There is professional accord.

When, however, military men serve at the top of the military structure, in direct association with civilian policymakers of the political administration, a different relationship exists. The civilian administrator is not a professional. He does not have the same grasp of tactics and strategy. In this circumstance, a soldier who allowed the civilian to overrule him on an important issue of professional judgment would render a disservice to our country. He would indeed be prostituting himself to keep a job which he had stripped of its professional integrity.

Why would he do it? Why would any man of integrity serving as a member of the Joint Chiefs of Staff cling to the office for a few additional years of service, at the cost of degrading the office, rather than sacrifice his position in order to maintain the high professional stature of the office? Would the political leaders then select a successor who would degrade the office anyway? Probably. But each man is responsible for his own decisions; and the prospect that another man will lower the standards is a poor excuse for doing so yourself.

Some would make submission a matter of loyalty. But the loyalty of soldiers is owed to the Constitution of the United States and not to any individual. Our loyalty to the Commander in Chief is bounded by the Constitutional definition of his authority. This is to say that we live not in an omnipotent state but in one bounded by law. The powers and authority of every official are limited by his office.

Moreover, every officer is by his office committed to serve the national interest. What should he do if the action of his superior constitutes a catastrophic disservice to the nation? He cannot undermine his superior with disloyal service. But he can resign his office, recover his full rights of criticism and take his dissent to the people. That is what he *must* do.

General Douglas MacArthur faced the question in 1933 while he was serving as Chief of Staff of the United States Army.

Franklin D. Roosevelt, the new President, had an economy program before the Congress which would place one-half the Army officer corps on leave without pay for six months, then put the other one-half on leave without pay for the second six months.

General MacArthur recognized that this program would destroy the officer corps. Many officers would get other jobs and would resign their commissions. Secretary of War Dern protested to the President, to no avail. General MacArthur obtained an appointment with the President and presented his case eloquently. The President was adamant that his program could not be changed. Finally General MacArthur stated that if the President persisted with this bill, he would resign his office as Chief of Staff and carry the issue to the people. He left the President's office convinced that he had lost his appeal and forfeited his office. But President Roosevelt sent word to Congress to kill the bill.

The action of General MacArthur was completely honest and loyal. President Roosevelt respected his sincerity and his courage. Moreover, he knew that General MacArthur was right about the interest of the country.

We Americans are first of all citizens of this Republic. We may accept an obligation of military service which limits our freedom to debate national policy, but that service must always be in furtherance of our duty to our country. Military discipline must never become an excuse for disservice to our country. The military leader who is called to administer policies he knows to be inimical to the country's interest must decide his course of action. Does the national interest require him to retire, recover his right of open political action and oppose the bad policy?

General MacArthur decided in time of peace that the threat to the officer corps and thence to the national security required him to oppose the President. How could military leaders now accept the disastrous policies which embroiled the United States in a bloody, costly war of attrition under rules assuring sacrifice without end? Why did no military leader challenge a course so disastrous to the United States and carry the issue to the people? If one had had the courage to do so, he might have persuaded the President to a better course of policy.

Every policymaker must answer that question for himself. I can only record what I find in the course of history.

A military leadership may, to a degree, maintain higher standards of integrity and patriotism than the political leadership. But the degree is limited in time and quality. Politicians will advance military leaders who accommodate the political interests. In time the military ethic must follow the political ethic.

In the United States, the process of decay is far advanced. Professional standards have been eroded by rationalization of the prevailing political propaganda. Military leaders are preaching that restraint in the use of power serves peace, that there is no such thing as victory in the nuclear age, that breaching the Laotian sanctuary would bring Red Chinese intervention in Vietnam. While military leaders hold their offices, they cannot publicly oppose the prevailing political policies, but they have no obligation to promote them.

The critical point of political confrontation was illustrated by President Kennedy's relationship with the Joint Chiefs of Staff. When John Kennedy took office, he told the Joint Chiefs that he wanted their over-all judgments on issues—not judgments limited to the military aspects of issues. When the test ban treaty was before the Senate in 1963, the Joint Chiefs, who had opposed the treaty, recommended Senate approval *because the political advantages more than offset the military disadvantages.*

Had the Joint Chiefs set themselves up as judges of political questions? Certainly not. They could only take that judgment from the President. By departing from their proper base of military judgment, they became captives of the President. They had to approve every Presidential program regardless of military consequences because the President said the political advantages outweighed the military disadvantages!

This was colossal error, a terrible disservice to the country.

The Joint Chiefs of Staff are obligated in law to advise the Congress as well as the President. When they allow themselves to be seduced by the President, they betray their duty to the Congress and the people. Clearly, the Joint Chiefs of Staff should speak boldly on military questions and be silent on political questions.

General Maxwell D. Taylor, Chairman, spoke for the Joint Chiefs of Staff on the test ban treaty. He played a significant role in the military decisions of the 1960's.

General Taylor had been unhappy in his service as Army Chief of Staff to President Eisenhower. Eisenhower was the top Army man in government. He paid scant attention to the Taylor protests. After retirement, General Taylor wrote *The Uncertain Trumpet,* reciting his disappointment with the denigration of Army needs by the Eisenhower Administration.

General Taylor had close ties to the Kennedy Administration. After the Bay of Pigs debacle, he joined the White House staff as a Presidential assistant. With Robert F. Kennedy, he made a special review of the Bay of Pigs operation for the President. In 1962, he succeeded General Lemmitzer as Chairman of the Joint Chiefs of Staff. From 1964 to 1965, he served as United States Ambassador to the Republic of Vietnam. When he returned to the United States, he served as a Presidential adviser and became President of the Institute for Defense Analysis. In 1969, President Nixon appointed General Taylor as Chairman of the President's Foreign Intelligence Advisory Board. General Taylor's influence on military policy since the Bay of Pigs disaster is on the record.

In an address to the Air War College in February, 1968, General Taylor gave his views on the future role of the military in serving national policy. He conveyed a picture of changing times in which the armed forces are happily loosed from their former "isolation ... from the realities of life in time of peace," in which civilians will exercise increasing control over the employment of military forces, in which these leaders will be increasingly paralyzed by fear of World War III, in which the use of force to restrain aggression will be severely restricted and in which the prospect of detente with the Soviet Union will improve.[5]

General Taylor thought that civilian government was making greater use of military advice in reaching decisions. He cited President Kennedy's instruction of May 27, 1961 to the Joint Chiefs of Staff to give him appraisals of political as well as military aspects of foreign policy issues. He cited also President Johnson's Memorandum 341 of March 1966 which charged the Secretary of State, as agent of the President, with the direction of interdepartmental committees to be established in Washington. On the Senior Group, chaired by the Under Secretary of State, the Chairman of the Joint Chiefs of Staff was a member.

It seems incredibly naive of General Taylor not to realize that both these measures *stifle* the military voice in policymaking. President Kennedy silenced military advice to the Congress by subjecting it to his political judgment. The Chairman of the Joint Chiefs of Staff is by law an adviser to the President and the Congress, not to the Under Secretary of State. His deputy should serve on the Senior Group.

General Taylor was succeeded as Chairman of the Joint Chiefs of Staff by General Earle G. Wheeler, a Taylor protege who had served as Army Chief of Staff. In April 1970, General Wheeler described for a National Security Seminar at Pensacola, Florida, the standard used by the Joint Chiefs of Staff for the advice they give to the President: "If I were the President of the United States, would I be willing to undertake this course of action that my principal military advisers have recommended to me?" The General thought this test was a "surefire inducer of responsibility."

The test is of course an improper one. It confuses instead of clarifying responsibility. It involves questions of political judgment which the Joint Chiefs are neither competent nor required to make. Their responsibility is to tell the President the best military solution to the problem and let him decide whether the course is politically tolerable. When the Chiefs recommend only what *they* consider to be politically tolerable, they are probably excluding the advice the President really needs.

General Wheeler's testimony confirms what history records, the incompetence of the Joint Chiefs of Staff as a policymaking body. This military failure is deeply significant. Some citizens ascribe the reverses of the past two decades to our political leaders, assuming that these leaders failed to heed the advice of the Joint Chiefs of Staff. On the contrary, the record reveals that our Presidents have been badly advised by their military subordinates. It is doubtful that our military leaders can today devise a prudent winning strategy for our confrontation with Communist aggression.

In his political role as a Presidential adviser, or earlier, General Taylor became a faithful apostle of the new Kennedy foreign policy of retreat. He served as the bellwether of the Administration, leading the docile military establishment into the catastrophic errors of the Sixties. Early military resistance within the Defense establishment was removed. Obedient followers were advanced to key positions.

Throughout the decade, General Taylor maintained his rapport with Presidential assistants and cabinet officers. He served on a committee to reorganize the State Department Foreign Service. His thinking seemed at all times to be consonant with the State Department appraisal of the national interest. It is not therefore surprising that General Taylor and General Wheeler told Secretary Clifford in 1968 that the political limitations on the war in Vietnam were prudent.

It would be wrong, however, to regard General Taylor as more than a symbol of our time. In his accommodation of the political powers, he was following the example of Marshall, Eisenhower and Bradley. The process set in motion in 1933 had reached fruition. There would be no more MacArthurs, no more Pattons, no more Wedemeyers.

XXII

THE
TOWER OF
BABEL

WAR CANNOT BE SO MISMANAGED WITHOUT PROVOK-
ing great controversy and confusion in society. The ordinary
drive of the human mind to make sense out of policy inspires
the invention of ignorance about causes. Bizarre explanations
of events abound.

In addition, the factions of society opposed to the war find in
the debacle the fulfillment of their dire forecasts. When the
ship of state lacks intelligent direction, a thousand voices will
rise up to direct it.

Every society has its dissonant voices, but when policy is well
directed, their role is small. The people approve and support
the national leadership. When leadership falters, however, the
people seek other guidance, national unity is sundered and
false prophets arise on every hand. We have seen the process
in the United States in the Sixties.

The chief dissent over the war came from the architects of
the Kennedy foreign policy. These men, passionately committed to detente, could not endure the growing breach with the

Communist world which the war represented. They had induced President Kennedy to neutralize the country and withdraw. The success of the same tactic in Laos persuaded him
that it could be done.

President Johnson found that it could not be done. With the
Vietnamese Army adamantly opposed to neutralization, the
United States could not force that solution on the country. The
blatant and cynical operation would have brought rebellion not
only in Vietnam but in the United States. The American people
might be deceived about a politically contrived coalition government but they would not tolerate the open abandonment of
an embattled ally.

The Kennedy crowd disagreed. They would have accepted
defeat and withdrawn from the country. When, therefore,
President Johnson bombed North Vietnam, they were deeply
alarmed. When he sent American combat troops to stay the
North Vietnamese assault, they were doubly alarmed. The war
was becoming, they thought, an obstacle to progress in relations with the Soviet Union and Red China. It was also taking
funds which they wanted for domestic programs.

As the debate waxed in intensity, it became a conflict between the Johnson policy and the Kennedy dissidents. Republicans generally supported the President but were content to
observe from the sidelines the deep division in the Democratic
Party.

One of the serious disclosures of the debate was the channel-
ing of public information by the television news media. Although polls indicated strong popular support for a policy of
winning the war quickly, this view was virtually excluded from
the national networks. All debates were staged between the
Johnson defenders and the left-wing attackers of U.S. war
policy. Because both sides rejected the alternative of military
victory, the people were bombarded with propaganda asserting
or implying that the war could not be won.

In radio and television, Congress had established an anti-
monopoly policy and had encouraged the wide dispersion of
station ownership. The Federal Communications Commission

duly limited ownership; but it then allowed the major networks to establish virtual monopolies through exclusive contracting. It matters little who owns a station when a monopoly controls the programs and the advertising. That is the heart of the business. In consequence, we have television monopolies, with the connivance of the Federal Communications Commission and in defiance of the policy established by Congress, and against the public interest.

Why would the three major networks exclude, as though from an agreed policy, any presentation of the thesis that the United States could win the war in Vietnam easily and quickly, without interference from Red China or the Soviet Union? Was ignorance so general and fear so pervasive that the common action was instinctive? Or is the pretence of objective news reporting a fraud obscuring service to a common propaganda objective?

It appears that the television networks had swallowed the Kennedy thesis of detente. They were deathly afraid that the open discussion of the alternative of winning the war might persuade the public and then force the government into action which, in the Kennedy view, might start World War III. As long as public perception of the war could be limited to war without victory and withdrawal, the danger of confrontation with Red China or the Soviet Union would be minimal.

Freedom of the press is not a self-sufficient value. It springs from the essential need of the citizens of a republic to have full disclosure of all public information. Network policy, however virtuous the motives, was a negation of the network obligation to inform the people. We cannot tolerate news media monopolies which tell us only what the editors consider good for the country. In this conflict, the blatant bias of television news favoring the Kennedy war policy was a national disgrace.

Senator Fulbright became the effective Congressional leader of this faction. Senators Frank Church and Wayne Morse spoke more stridently but they only voiced the misgivings of their Chairman. In his polished, didactic manner, Senator Fulbright directed the assault. He voiced first skepticism, then dissent and finally condemnation. He exploited the readily available television cameras with personal statements and committee hearings. He professed to be interested only in peace for the American people, but he stacked his hearings with figures committed to his dissent.

In May 1961, after consulting with President Kennedy, Senator Fulbright announced that he supported the sending of U. S. combat troops to South Vietnam. He explained that the situation was different from that in Laos because the Thais and the South Vietnamese had shown a readiness and capacity to defend themselves. This was of course at a time when the chief Communist thrust was being pressed in Laos.

In September 1964, Senator Fulbright had managed the Tonkin Gulf Resolution supporting President Johnson's retaliation for the North Vietnamese attacks on our ships on the high seas.

In June of 1965, Senator Fulbright was concerned about the President's performance but still hoping to correct his policy. The Senator was upset about the bombing of North Vietnam and the intervention in the Dominican Republic (April 28). With considerable restraint he lectured the President publicly on the essentials of foreign policy.

> I am opposed to an unconditional American withdrawal from South Vietnam because such action would betray our obligation to people we have promised to defend, because it would weaken or destroy our credibility of American guarantees to other countries, and because such a withdrawal would encourage the view in Peiping and elsewhere that guerrilla wars supported from outside are a relatively safe and inexpensive way of expanding Communist power.
>
> I am no less opposed to further escalation of the war, because the bombing thus far of North Vietnam has failed to weaken the military capacity of the Vietcong in any visible way; because escalation would invite the intervention—or infiltration—on a large scale of great numbers of North Vietnamese troops; because this in turn would probably draw the United Sates into a bloody and protracted jungle war in which the strategic advantages would be

with the other side; and, finally, because the only available alternative to such a land war would then be the further expansion of the air war to such an extent as to invite either massive Chinese military intervention in many vulnerable areas of Southeast Asia or general nuclear war. . . .

There have already been pressures from various sources for expanding the war. President Johnson has resisted these pressures with steadfastness and statesmanship and remains committed to the goal of ending the war at the earliest possible time by negotiations without preconditions. In so doing, he is providing the leadership appropriate to a great nation.

The most striking characteristic of a great nation is not the mere possession of power but the wisdom and restraint and largeness of view with which power is exercised. A great nation is one which is capable of looking beyond its own view of the world, of recognizing that, however convinced it may be of the beneficence of its own role and aims, other nations may be equally persuaded of their benevolence and good intent. It is a mark of both greatness and maturity when a nation like the United States, without abandoning its convictions and commitments, is capable at the same time of acknowledging that there may be some merit and even good intent in the views and aims of its adversaries.

The Senator then recited the long history of U. S. peace efforts over the past four-and-a-half years and the repeated rebuffs received from the Communist side. He continued:

I believe that President Kennedy and President Johnson have been wise in their restraint and patience, that indeed this patience has quite possibly averted a conflict that would be disastrous for both the Communist countries and for the United States and its associates. I believe that continued restraint and continued patience, even in the face of expanded Vietcong military activities, are essential to avert a catastrophe in Southeast Asia.[1]

We should note in passing that these views of Rhodes Scholar Fulbright articulate precisely the British argument for restraint of the United States in the Far East. Had Senator Fulbright advocated similar "greatness and maturity" in viewing the self-esteem of Adolph Hitler? His implication that United States withdrawal in the face of Communist aggression had avoided "disastrous" conflict with the Communist countries was exactly untrue; but it was also the line which Britain had used to influence United States foreign policy.

Note also the casuistry of the argumentation. Senator Fulbright tells us that the Communists believe their purpose of destroying our free society is justified. Is he seeking to console us? Does the sincerity of the conqueror make our destruction more palatable? The lamb may admit the hunger of the lion but if its "largeness of view" leads it to cooperate in its own destruction, its imprudence can hardly be acclaimed.

The Fulbright thesis that, despite all prior failures, we must restrain our military power and negotiate peace with the enemy, was reinforced in a great outpouring of scholarly argument from the Left. For example, Richard J. Barnet voiced his view of American responsibility in these terms:

> The purpose of law in any social system is to provide a framework for the fulfillment of politics. The essence of politics is that members of a society do not act to the limit of their physical power. They derive security from the presence of limits—on themselves as well as others. Nowhere are such limits needed more than in the international society, which has always been in a state of varying degrees of disorder, but which now faces the prospect of unprecedented anarchy.
>
> The very changes in international relations that have convinced U. S. leaders that international law is a luxury actually make the rebuilding of a system of legal limits a necessity for survival. We need to observe legal restraints for classic moral and social reasons: to encourage others to behave in the same way. If, as is more than likely, Russia and China see the U. S. as the principal threat to the peace, rather than its defender, they too may feel free

to "pay any price" to stop us. The likely consequences to two powers claiming the role of policeman is the ruin of both.[2]

The proposition that the exercise of power has some limits which are independent of issues is typical scholarly confusion. Nations act according to their judgment of what is possible and desirable in given circumstances. The concept of an independent principle of restraint unrelated to specific cases is fanciful.

Barnet states a theory of international law which appeals to law-abiding states. But international law is designed also to restrain aggression. The maintenance of international law depends upon the readiness of nations to defend the benefits it confers and to punish transgressors. The proposition that transgressors will be deterred by the good example of their victims is infantile.

As Senator Dodd pointed out to the Senate on February 23, 1965, Britain had faced that question almost thirty years earlier:

> Chamberlain held that a durable agreement could be negotiated with Hitler that would guarantee "peace in our time."
> How I remember those words!
> Churchill held that the appeasement of a compulsive aggressor swiftly whetted his appetite for further expansion and made war more likely. . . .[3]

The argument that resistance to the aggressor brings war is of course fallacious. Only resistance deters the aggressor and the war which he would otherwise wage. Churchill was right. Yet, Richard Barnet continued in that vein:

> If the Vietcong are systematically killing village leaders and the local government is incapable of coping with the problem, then the U. N. should have been invited to investigate and propose solutions. The chances for finding political solutions would have been far greater if the situation

in Vietnam had been viewed as a group of concrete issues in need of resolution rather than as a test of will. At the very least, the remedies provided by law should have been exhausted before the U. S. acted to take the law into its own hands. In neither the Dominican Republic nor Vietnam has the U. S. gained by its haste. . . .

As the most powerful nation in the world, the U. S. creates standards of conduct by its acts. That others disregard international law is undeniable. The important question, however, is not whether the Vietcong or North Vietnam also violated the law, but whether the United States by its acts encourages them and the rest of the world to build a system of legal limits or to throw off the few restraints that remain.[4]

It was a continuing gambit of shallow scholarship to appeal to the United Nations for settlement of Vietnam differences. The game was to condemn the United States for not using the United Nations as an intermediary. As we have noted, the United States had appealed to the United Nations and to every other conceivable source of help. But the Johnson Administration was so solicitous for the good name of the United Nations that it would not expose that body's impotence in open debate in the General Assembly. Or perhaps it was reluctant to publicly pillory the Soviet Union with which it was still pursuing detente. Could Mr. Barnet really be ignorant of these attitudes and actions?

Of course the example of the United States is important to international law. But the implication that the United States has set an example of aggression turns the issue upside down. The United States has in fact undermined international law and fostered aggression by failing to repel instantly and sharply the aggression of North Vietnam.

After the frenetic efforts of the United States to start peace negotiations and the blunt refusal of the enemy even to discuss a settlement, it was remarkable that American writers could still depict the United States as the aggressor. Yet, this was a popular theme of Administration critics. It took some mental and moral gymnastics, but they could do it. Marcus Raskin and

Bernard Fall explained how American belligerence had led it into the pitfall of Vietnam:

> But more important than the arithmetical nuclear superiority, the United States had brandished its nuclear capability with seeming alacrity and skill over the situations in Berlin and Cuba. It appeared that the American leadership was more willing to offer its society as hostage in the nuclear "brinkmanship" game than were the Russians. Second, the United States, under President Kennedy, Secretary of Defense McNamara and General Maxwell Taylor, had adopted the "brushfire"—or counterinsurgency war concept which meant that the American armed forces were now prepared to intervene directly (and not through local proxies) in small wars in local situations of revolution and instability. The new ability intensified the illusion that the United States could solve inherently socio-political, economic, and diplomatic problems in the underdeveloped world by military means. . . .[5]

Lest the reader suppose that the Communists showed any guilt of aggression, Raskin and Fall described their essentially peaceful plans:

> (a) Moscow, while paying lip service to the principle of favoring "liberation wars," was unwilling to forgo its detente with the United States and its growing trade with the West as the price for a guerrilla victory in as marginal an area as Vietnam. (b) Peking, while being most vocal in support of the principle of "liberation wars," was unwilling to confront the United States directly and risk its modest economic recovery for the sake of guerrilla victories in such marginal areas as the Congo and Vietnam; (c) Hanoi, witnessing the gradual disintegration of South Vietnam, was willing to risk a modest support program for the South Vietnamese guerrilla effort on the assumption that American reaction (in view of the admitted ineffectualness of the Saigon regime) would be, as in the case of Laos, in favor of compromise settlement; and (d) the National Liberation Front (NLF) apparently expected to be able to defeat the South Vietnamese government politically and on

the ground before a large-scale American counter-effort could make itself felt. In any case, the relative smallness of the North Vietnamese "input" into the South Vietnamese insurgency up to the time of the massive American escalation of 1965, and the total absence until then in Hanoi and all of North Vietnam of the sophisticated air-defense weapons necessary to withstand a military confrontation with the United States even on a Korean scale, suggest that no one on the Communist side was seriously prepared for a major war over Vietnam. As in the case of Soviet missiles in Cuba, Communist policymakers may well have misread the "signals from Washington."[6]

This is, of course, a fictional account of events. The Communists did not expect to wage war with the United States in order to conquer South Vietnam. They thought that the Johnson advisers would persuade the President to let the Vietcong win without a commitment of U. S. forces to the battle. But neither was the United States planning for war. Both sides increased the reinforcement gradually. Raskin and Fall obscure the vital difference that North Vietnam was the invader and the United States was the defender.

Moreover, this story of a small North Vietnamese input in 1964 is incorrect. North Vietnam organized, directed and supported the entire Vietcong operation. The NLF was a figure-head without power or substance. Infiltration from North Vietnam in 1964 was about 12,500, exceeding U.S. reinforcement of South Vietnam.

Raskin and Fall appealed for a return to moderation and to law. Why they never appealed to Moscow and Hanoi to do so remains a mystery. They wrote:

> Is it still possible for the United States to curb its recent penchant for military solutions to complex foreign policy problems in favor of more conventional tools of international law, negotiation, conciliation, international organizations, and effective multilateral consultation (to replace our present policy of advising our allies at the last minute of about-to-be-accomplished facts)? . . .

The only logical alternative to law, negotiation and conciliation would be for the United States to get on the lonely
treadmill of world-wide empire in which the measure
of politics is raw power, and ever-present and ever-committed military force becomes the arbiter of national
greatness and, eventually, of national survival in a
universe divided, in Camus' terms, into victims or executioners.[7]

This promise that peace-oriented powers can protect themselves against the use of force by Communist aggressors without themselves using force defies common sense. It seems
obvious that negotiation, conciliation, international organizations and consultation cannot stop military aggression.

A cousin of the theme that the United States is an aggressor
is the theme that the United States can't win anyway so there
is no use trying to protect the free nations of Asia. Professor
Hans J. Morgenthau advanced this thesis in the *New York
Times:*

For while China is obviously no match for the United
States in over-all power, China is largely immune to
the specific types of power in which the superiority
of the United States consists—that is, nuclear, air
and naval power. Certainly the United States has the
power to destroy the nuclear installations and the major industrial population centers of China, but this destruction would not defeat China: it would only set her
development back. To be defeated, China has to be conquered.

Physical conquest would require the deployment of millions of American soldiers on the mainland of Asia. No
American military leader has ever advocated a course of
action so fraught with incalculable risks, so uncertain of
outcome, requiring sacrifices so out of proportion to the
interests at stake and the benefits to be expected. President Eisenhower declared on February 10, 1954 that he
"could conceive of no greater tragedy than for the United
States to become involved in all-out war in Indo-China."
General MacArthur in the Congressional hearings concerning his dismissal and in personal conversation with

President Kennedy, emphatically warned against sending American foot soldiers to the Asian mainland to fight China.[8]

Let us say of this power analysis that it is incompetent. When the professor builds his international judgment on such faulty military analysis, he builds a house of cards.

People are not power. As Mao knew, power comes out of the barrel of a gun, and the United States has the big guns. If the Morgenthau thesis of people power had any validity, the Communist regimes in the Soviet Union and Red China could never survive the hostility of their own people.

Professors routinely conjure the spectre of millions of American soldiers bogged down in combat with the Red Chinese Army and people. That could never happen because the United States has no quarrel with the Chinese people. Only their masters are our enemies. We would war with China not to hurt the Chinese people but to free them from slavery. The Professor's thesis operates to persuade the American people that they should never make war against the Red masters. That is the aim of all Communist propaganda also.

The Morgenthau prescription for our Asian policy is this:

In specific terms, accommodation means four things: (1) recognition of the political and cultural predominance of China on the mainland of Asia as a fact of life; (2) liquidation of the peripheral military containment of China; (3) strengthening the uncommitted nations of Asia by non-military means; (4) assessment of Communist governments in Asia in terms not of Communist doctrine but of their relation to the interests and power of the United States.[9]

Of course these conclusions follow logically from the Morgenthau premise of the invincibility of Chinese military power. If it were so, Japan and India and all the lesser powers would have no alternative but to install Communist governments and give fealty to Peking. Why the United States should then give economic aid to Communist satellites is obscure. This seems to be part of the prevailing superstition that we can somehow wean these countries back from the overwhelming Chinese power while the Reds are not looking. Moreover, if Professor Morgenthau has not learned that Communist doctrine defines very accurately the relationship of Communist countries with the United States, he has not been doing his homework.

If you are seeking an honorable solution to our involvement in Vietnam, give thought to the Morgenthau Plan:

> In the light of these principles, the alternative to our present policies in Vietnam would be this: a face-saving agreement which would allow us to disengage ourselves militarily in stages spaced in time; restoration of the status quo of the Geneva Agreement of 1954, with special emphasis on all-Vietnamese elections; cooperation with the Soviet Union in support of a Titoist all-Vietnamese Government, which would be likely to emerge from such elections.
>
> This last point is crucial, for our present policies not only drive Hanoi into the waiting arms of Peking, but also make it very difficult for Moscow to pursue an independent policy. Our interests in Southeast Asia are identical with those of the Soviet Union: to prevent the expansion of the *military* power of China. But while our present policies invite that expansion, so do they make it impossible for the Soviet Union to join us in preventing it. If we were to reconcile ourselves to the establishment of a Titoist government in all of Vietnam, the Soviet Union could successfully compete with China in claiming credit for it and surreptitiously cooperate with us in maintaining it.[10]

There is a fanciful melange! A "face-saving" disengagement must mean coalition government because Hanoi would accept no less. But South Vietnam refuses. How can you save U. S. face while cooperating with the Communists to impose such a surrender on your ally?

Then, restore the 1954 Geneva provisions, including elections. How do you sell that to a Ho Chi Minh? It would mean his undoing. That must be more of the face-saving!

It is comforting also to know that the Sovet Union is on our side in creating "Titoist" governments. Some authorities say the Soviet Union doesn't like such governments, especially in Czechoslovakia.

When professors propose such impractical measures, we can only conclude that their supply of misinformation exceeds their powers of reason.

The "we can't win" syndrome is closely associated with the "we are overextended" complex. If a small country like North Vietnam could stalemate our sea and air forces and half a million ground forces, what would we do with another war of liberation in Berlin, or Korea or Latin America? This worried Ambassador George F. Kennan when he testified before the House Foreign Affairs Subcommittee on the Far East:

> In itself, if you could segregate this Vietnam situation from the repercussions that it radiates in all directions, from the factors of prestige that now become associated with it, in itself I would not think that Vietnam was an area of vital importance to this country. I can well realize that a situation has been created there today where we could not afford simply to get out and to turn it over to the Chinese Communists. But it is my belief that we are seriously overextended in this world, that we are trying to do too much, that we are involved in too many places.[11]

Moreover, the Ambassador considered this extension of our power unnecessary. Like Professor Morgenthau, he seemed to think it would not hurt to have some free countries taken over by communism because the new regimes might be Titoist. The Ambassador said: "I would be the last to generalize about such things or to say that a hands-off policy is everywhere possible and desirable. But there is one thing we might usefully bear in mind. The surest way to invite a strong and effective Communist involvement in a situation of this nature is to involve ourselves heavily, particularly in a military way." This is how erroneous shibboleths are propounded. The Communists did not oppose our forthright commitment in Lebanon in 1958. They opposed our *weak* and *ineffectual* presence in South Vietnam after President Kennedy took office.

The Ambassador continued:

> Where we lay off the road may be open, ostensibly, to Communist intrigue and penetration (it is usually open, no matter what we do) and there may well be takeovers by political forces that make a pretense of Marxist conviction and look to Moscow or Peiping for economic aid and political support. But this is not always so intolerable as we commonly suppose.[12]

What political group in any country has ever *pretended* to Marxist convictions? And why is the Ambassador so complacent about Communist takeovers? He said:

> The less we are in the picture, the less is there any excuse for actual military intervention on the part of the Communist powers and the greater are the chances for rivalry between Moscow and Peiping for political predominance in the region concerned. But in the absence of a Communist military presence, and where this Chinese-Soviet rivalry exists, the local regimes, whether nominally Communist or otherwise, are almost bound to begin to act independently in many ways—to develop, in other words, Titoist tendencies.[13]

That is a theory without support in history. It does not comport with Communist doctrine or practice, nor with the realities of power. We can be sure that the Communist powers would gladly take every country so offered.

Ambassador Kennan thought he had a good policy:

> And this is not always the worst solution, from our standpoint. It is harder for either Moscow or Peiping to interfere extensively with a regime that calls itself Communist than with one that does not. And since we have not engaged our prestige extensively, the situation affords to the Communist powers no such opportunities for political

gains at our expense as those the Chinese and North Vietnamese Communists are now reaping in Vietnam.[14]

These are strange notions to come from a man who has been considered an authority on the Soviet Union and has served as Ambassador to Yugoslavia. Would it really help our prestige if we just allowed our allies to be conquered without help from us —without engaging our prestige extensively? Mr. Kennan is promoting a giveaway program which is of course totally impractical as well as suicidal. Like others who have misjudged the simple realities of power, he is driven to distraction in trying to explain our impotence in Vietnam.

Mr. Kennan never comprehended what was happening in the war. He could see in it only a "massive miscalculation and error of policy, an error for which it is hard to find any parallels in our history." He found U. S. policy "grievously unsound, devoid throughout of a plausible, coherent and realistic object."

These aberrations of the intellectuals illustrate a confusion which pervaded all levels of society. The universities, the news media and the radical Left all seemed engaged in a vast operation to get the United States out of Vietnam.

It was to be expected that the plethora of Communist-front organizations tolerated by our society would be working for the enemy. The bombing of North Vietnam, an operation which seemed to take the whole Communist world by surprise, stirred a worldwide condemnation from every Communist and affiliated news maker. Nor did the clamor subside. From all over the country as well as from foreign lands, cries to stop the bombing were repeated incessantly.

The Communist propaganda machine moved into high gear. Outrageous lies about the purpose and effect of the bombing were given currency. The President was depicted as a murderer of women and children. The United States was accused of genocide against the Vietnamese people, all the while the United States was doing the most accurate and careful bombing of military targets ever known to war. The ratio of civilian casualties was smaller than it had been in World War II. This revolting propaganda spread over the landscape, gaining currency especially on college campuses where scholarship should have exposed its foul character.

The Vietnam war had grown up in the shadow of the American civil rights movement. It was in the early Sixties a remote and relatively minor cloud on the horizon of American concern, while civil rights held center stage. Then the war escalated. American participation increased. It seemed that the war would take center stage.

There was a community of interest in the two movements. Civil rights was a protest movement; so was the anti-war movement. Tactics were similar. Both movements had a hard core of Marxist activists and a great following of sincerely concerned citizens.

In 1966 and 1967, the civil rights propaganda had softened up municipal and state political leaders so as to disarm police response to riotous action. In Newark and Detroit, in Washington and Cleveland, the inner city was set to the torch while police stood by, immobilized by political orders. But those excesses aroused public indignation. The people demanded preservation of public order.

The war protestors had moved into the civil rights movement. Some civil rights leaders like Roy Wilkins opposed linking the two movements. They felt that the civil rights movement should stick to its basic objective of helping black people.

Other civil rights leaders welcomed the anti-war movement as a new vehicle of protest. They condemned the war for its diversion of funds from desirable social service programs. Many of them took up the harsh invective of the Communist line, attacking the United States as a criminal, imperialist power.

On April 4, 1967, Dr. Martin Luther King, Jr., speaking in New York's Riverside Church, made a vitriolic attack on United States participation in the Vietnam war. He had previously spoken against the war in the softer terms of pacifism frequently used by some clergymen, but in this talk he seemed to take his rhetoric straight from the Communist propaganda mills. He condemned the United States as "the greatest purveyor of violence in the world today." He accused it of testing weapons on the people of South Vietnam "just as the Germans tested out new medicine and new tortures in the concentration camps of Europe." He said it was poisoning the water and killing millions of acres of crops in South Vietnam. He thought that U. S. troops "may have killed a million South Vietnamese civilians—mostly children." He deplored the diversion of funds from pressing domestic needs and termed the war "a cruel manipulation of the poor." He called for youth to become conscientious objectors.

Civil rights elders, black and white, deplored the King speech as a disservice to their movement. They felt that the war issue would divide and discredit their own mobilization. Dr. King was obviously tuned in to the young and militant black Marxists who saw the combination of the two movements as a lever to defeat the United States in Vietnam and to destroy American capitalism at home. His speech seemed to be a signal for the devastating riots which overwhelmed Newark and Detroit in July. Under the guise of social protest, the Communist cadres were carrying the war to the citadel of America.

By 1966, Senator Fulbright had broken with President Johnson. He joined the critics who condemned the President for escalating the war. In January 1967 he addressed the Senate on the arrogance of power and gave his prescription for ending the war. He suggested that the United States and South Vietnam must negotiate with North Vietnam and the NLF; that the United States should cease bombing North Vietnam and should pledge eventual withdrawal from Vietnam; that the two sides should negotiate a truce; that an international conference should arrange the reunification of Vietnam; and that, failing negotiations, the United States should withdraw to enclaves and hold indefinitely.

We can see in the perspective of later events how futile were the Fulbright concepts of negotiating peace. But we should be mindful that this futility was plainly visible also in prior events. To suppose that Ho Chi Minh would cooperate in such negotiation was in 1967 a simple refusal to face reality.

The Senator had his enclave to fall back upon, another and equally vapid concept. But in a man so eager to surrender to the Communist aggression, a defective strategy was no doubt comfortable.

Through 1967, as the strength and stability of the South Vietnamese government steadily increased, so did the clamor of the American Left against the war. In April, mass demonstrations were held in New York and in San Francisco. In October, a mass peace march on Washington was converted into an attack on the Pentagon. The Mobilization Committee against the war was having a political effect in the United States which seemed unrelated to progress in Vietnam.

It was true of course that our successes in Vietnam had been achieved with an increasing commitment of manpower and with increasing casualties. Moreover, the Administration strategy had no exit. It merely contemplated continuation of the war as long as the enemy chose to continue his aggression.

Because the President had no positive program for ending the war, his political opponents could logically claim that the war was unwinnable. In time, his own Administration was riddled with that same false conclusion. As Townsend Hoopes, then serving as Under Secretary of Air Force, was later to describe this issue:

> Beyond the question of whether the United States was winning the war stood a more fateful, less quantifiable one: "*Can* we win the war?" Or stated conversely, "Will Moscow and Peking allow North Vietnam's insurgency to be totally defeated?" . . . Would Moscow or Peking stand by and accept a clear-cut American victory in South Vietnam? I thought that, within broad limits, the answer was rather clearly no.[15]

Mr. Hoopes, who was a member of an inner clique bitterly opposed to war policy, recognized the implication of his conclusion. He wrote:

And to move in fact toward serious negotiations and political settlement while the Vietcong remained even a residual military-political power in the South required acceptance of compromise. In this context, compromise could only mean some Communist participation in the government.[16]

As Mr. Hoopes should have known, Ho Chi Minh was not going to negotiate "some" Communist participation in government. He was going to take all, and men like Mr. Hoopes who were committed to surrender would have to surrender unconditionally—with only a face-saving front to deceive the American people.

In these circumstances, talk of negotiation is of course farcical. If you won't fight, you cannot negotiate. You can only accept the dictation of the enemy.

Surely it was whimsical to call such a surrender "compromise." There is no principle of our government by which a bloc can get a share of government without election by the people. The Vietcong could not win such representation in free elections; so Mr. Hoopes proposed to impose it on the people of South Vietnam.

It must have been enormously frustrating to President Johnson to have so many public figures advancing utterly impractical proposals for ending the war. On December 12, 1967, a group of left-wing liberals and Generals Bolte and Ridgway issued a "Bermuda Statement" proposing that the United States should reduce violence in South Vietnam to levels which could be sustained over the long term; stop bombing the North; increase responsibility of the government of South Vietnam for both defense and pacification; and recognize the NLF as "an organized factor in the political life of South Vietnam." This was essentially a re-statement of the Fulbright package of January 1967. On December 20, 1967 fourteen prominent scholars urged the President to "innovate" de-escalation.

The great delusion of these critics was in their assumption that a bombing halt would lead to negotiation and settlement.

After two years of experience with bombing halts, they refused to believe that Ho Chi Minh meant what he said to all such proposals.

Some of the thinking about de-escalation no doubt came from Sir Robert Thompson, one of the British administrators of the Malaya counterinsurgency, who said about this time:

> Now obviously withdrawal means losing, but massive escalation equally means losing. If I may put it very bluntly, it would mean losing stinking. . . . It would mean that the rest of the world would want to have very little to do with you as a people.[17]

The damnable quality of that statement is twofold: first in the false implication that "massive" escalation was required to win; and second, in the lie that the world would condemn victory. The world *loves* a winner. A third damnability is the abhorrent fact that such British arrogance could throw a mental block into American strategic judgment. There was not a man in the whole Johnson Administration who could demolish this nonsensical conclusion that the United States must accept defeat at the hands of North Vietnam.

Political organizations tend to become fiercely defensive. By a progress of deliberate exclusion of hostile ideas in three decades of holding political power, the consensus which ruled both political parties had eliminated the insights and understandings which might have saved it. Lyndon Johnson, with his keen political sense, surely knew that the easy rationalizations being used against him had powerful public appeal. But he was up against a blank wall. No one in his whole entourage could tell him what to do.

The Communist Tet assault was the coup de grace. The President's civilian staff panicked. As Mr. Hoopes told the story:

> Warnke thought Tet showed that our military strategy was "foolish to the point of insanity." Alain Enthoven . . . confided that, "I fell off the boat when the troop level reached 170,000." In various ways, the Under Secretary of

The War for Vietnam269

the Army, David McGiffert, the Assistant Secretary of Defense for Manpower, Alfred Fitt, the Deputy Assistant Secretary for Far Eastern Affairs (ISA) Richard Steadman, and other influential civilians expressed their strong belief that the Administration's Vietnam policy was at a dead end.

One thing was clear to us all: the Tet offensive was the eloquent counterpoint to the effusive optimism of November. It showed conclusively that the U. S. did not in fact control the situation, that it was not in fact winning, that the enemy retained enormous strength and vitality—certainly enough to extinguish the notion of a clear-cut allied victory in the minds of all objective men.[18]

But these were not objective men. The conclusions reached by Mr. Hoopes and company were not at all warranted by the facts. These dilettante warriors could not comprehend that South Vietnam would be immensely strengthened by this Communist assault. What could a President do who depended on such men for war policy?

Mr. Hoopes turned to his own responsibility for planning possible air responses to Tet. He reports:

The Air Staff strongly preferred Alternative 1 [bombing North Vietnam's vital facilities] but Brown and I continued to feel that, while there was little assurance that such a campaign could either force NVN to the conference table, or even significantly reduce its war effort, it was a course embodying excessive risks of confrontation with Russia.[19]

This was the mental attitude which the new Secretary of Defense Clark M. Clifford encountered on all sides as he sought through an ad hoc task force to develop new policy for the President. On one side he had Rostow, Taylor and Wheeler advocating a continuation of the current policy; on the other, he faced a militant group of his own subordinates who were determined to get out of the war at any cost. The task force recommended a minor reinforcement, 20,000 men, to Vietnam but deferred action on further build-up.

On March 14, Senator Robert F. Kennedy and his aide Theodore Sorenson met with Secretary Clifford at the Pentagon to propose a new National Commission on Vietnam Policy to be appointed by the President. Suggested members were to be Edwin Reischauer, Kingman Brewster, Roswell Gilpatrick, Robert Kennedy, Carl Kaysen, General Lauris Norstad, General Matthew Ridgway, Senator Mansfield, and possibly Senators Cooper and Aiken. If the President would accept this proposal, it would then not be necessary for Senator Kennedy to run in the Presidential election.

The very arrogance of the Kennedy proposal reflected the gap in thinking between the President and his critics. Perhaps it reflected also the Kennedy confidence that the President's course was politically untenable.

In public Robert Kennedy was saying:

> There is a question of our moral responsibility. Are we like God in the Old Testament that we can decide in Washington, D.C. what cities, what towns in Vietnam are going to be destroyed? I know that some have said we should intensify the bombing of the North. They should be heard. I do not happen to believe this is the answer to the problem, but I do know that what we have been doing is not the answer . . . that it is immoral and intolerable to continue it.[20]

On March 15, Ambassador Goldberg urged the President to stop bombing North Vietnam, as a means of getting negotiations started.

At the suggestion of Secretary Clifford, the President called former Secretary of State Dean Acheson for advice. After being briefed on current events, Dean Acheson told the President: "With all due respect, Mr. President, the Joint Chiefs of Staff don't know what they are talking about." He said the present course was politically impossible and had to be changed.

On March 25 and 26, the Senior Advisory Group on Vietnam, composed of distinguished leaders in and out of government met at the White House to review Vietnam policy. Although

Generals Bradley and Ridgway and Taylor were in the group, this panel could produce no constructive guidance for the President. Some supported current policy, others wanted change, but there was no alternative offered to endless warfare or surrender.

Surely this must be one of the most amazing scenes in all of history. The greatest power in the world, assembling its elders to chart a course of national policy, had not a single mind capable of escaping the cruel dilemma which fear and incompetence had fastened on the country. "For this reason it was called Babel, because there the Lord confused the speech of all the earth."

The President, overwhelmed by the defection of his chosen advisers, could only accept surrender. He would abandon his policy, but he would also abandon the Presidency. He would halt the bombing, seek negotiations and let his successor try the course of withdrawal which his counselors now favored.

XXIII

TRIAL AND JUDGMENT

WHAT HAS HAPPENED IN VIETNAM OVER THE PAST FIF-
teen years argues not that America has made a simple misjudgment of particular policy, but that the country is gripped by a
deep malaise which affects its capacity to survive. America is
being tried not by any new and insoluble challenges but by the
ordinary experiences of national existence. A republic which
once moved with confidence in a world of greater powers now
quails in fear before the hostility of inferior powers.

I have noted how our policy of recognizing the Soviet Union
was based on assumptions that this association would operate
to change Soviet behavior, and how erroneous that assumption
proved to be. Meanwhile, the false premise has been carved
into a plank of the bipartisan United States foreign policy. It is
assumed that recognition of Red China will be conducive to
international peace. It is *assumed also* that continuing recognition of the Soviet Union is conducive to international peace,
when there is no evidence to support that assumption.

Scholarship and prudence require us to reject these shibboleths and face objectively the question of recognition. We should determine what use of our power and position will really promote the interest of world peace and shape our policy accordingly. The fact that for 38 years the United States has been incapable of performing this simple act of prudence is indicative of our malaise.

We are simply dishonest. We are professing beliefs which will not stand examination. We have escaped from the uncomfortable strictures of reason to indulge in wishful thinking. Gradually, from this basic evasion of truth, we have built a gigantic lie into our whole fabric of policy. Instead of examining forthrightly and fearlessly the requirements of the national interest and shaping policy accordingly, we have sought an expedient and politically easy adjustment to every crisis, conforming in every instance to our dishonest premises. We have erected a panoply of corollary errors related to our false assumptions about Communist political action.

War is the crisis in which erroneous policy is revealed. It is revealed in the consequent disaster. So it has been.

We assumed in World War II that the Soviet Union, through the chance that we had both been attacked by Axis powers, would become a cooperating member of Western civilization. The fatuity of that expectation was revealed in the Soviet conquest of Eastern Europe and of China, while the United States did not even understand what was happening. That failure was intellectual, for the record of Soviet philosophy and purpose was clearly written, the precursor of all that followed. This critical failure of United States policy was the consequence of an incapacity to deal honestly with the facts of history known to us.

At least, we had fought World War II with some efficiency. Our military tradition had not been emasculated by our political effeminacy. We mobilized and applied our power with skill and resourcefulness to defeat the enemy and restore peace. In terms of the effective use of power, the defeat of Germany and Japan in less than four years of war must be counted a substantial achievement.

By 1950, the military tradition had been lost. The insidious dishonesty of political policy had spread its tentacles to cover military policy. In Korea, the military accommodation of political opportunism wasted the national substance in an interminable and witless warfare. This was war by irresolution.

At first, the United States moved with skill and valor to rout the enemy at Inchon. But then, when the Chinese intervened, Washington panicked, as it was to do again in 1968. There was no defeat in the field. After the first shock of the unexpected attack, the United States took the offensive and decimated the Chinese. But that new victory was forbidden in Washington. Possessed now by vague and idle fears, the United States became incapable of prudent action. It could only hold the line of the Thirty-eighth Parallel and hope the enemy would tire of attacking, a vain concept of war to be repeated with even more disastrous consequences in Vietnam a decade later.

In recent months, two of the Korea policymakers have published books giving their perception of that policy. The confessions are revealing.

Dean Acheson, then Secretary of State, with that gracious casuistry for which he has become so justly famed, told the Russell Committee that a distinction should be made between the long-range aims of the United Nations for a unified, democratic Korea and the proper aims of the United Nations Command. "Our objective," he said, "is to stop the attack, end the aggression on that [Korean] Government, restore peace, providing against the renewal of aggression."[1]

Mr. Acheson now says, "MacArthur disagreed with those desired ends, and wished instead to unify Korea by force of arms even though this plan would involve general war with China and, quite possibly, with the Soviet Union as well."[2] But General MacArthur had orders to destroy the North Korean Armed Forces.[3] Who told Mr. Acheson that the unification of Korea would involve general war with China? Did he get this from the Joint Chiefs of Staff, or from the British Ambassador?

At this point, I am concerned about the honesty of his pleading. After the victory at Inchon on September 15, 1950, the U. S.

troops in Korea were not allowed to cross into North Korea until the United Nations restated the U. N. purpose of uniting the country. Mr. Acheson says of the General Assembly resolution of October 7, 1950: "In effect, the resolution revived the dormant United Nations plan of 1947 for what it called, 'a unified, independent and democratic government' of Korea." Mr. Acheson argues, against the clear record of history, that this was merely a general *purpose* not related directly to the United Nations Command objectives in Korea. He misrepresents the case. This declaration of U. N. policy after the victory at Inchon was sought and intended as a declaration of policy to guide the United Nations Command in Korea. That the American Government had that clear understanding of U. N. purpose is shown in the September 27 J.C.S. directive to General MacArthur, to conduct operations north of the Thirty-eighth Parallel. That understanding was further demonstrated in J.C.S. approval of MacArthur's operations, including the march to the Yalu River.

Mr. Acheson wrote: "Opinion at home and abroad would have remained steady and united had the Army under the September 27 plan and directive sealed off the South from further attack until the war should peter out, as it eventually did, even though this would require, as it also did, some hard fighting to prove the strength of the line." Thus does Mr. Acheson garble history with the implication, thrust forward in the welter of lying charges after the Chinese intervention, that the General had entered North Korea without authority from Washington. The British plan to sit behind the Thirty-eighth Parallel after the victory at Inchon had been vetoed by the United Nations, the Joint Chiefs of Staff, the people and the President.

Mr. Acheson knows also that the war did not "peter out." When the United States in 1951 did stop at the Thirty-eighth Parallel, it entered upon two years of bitter fighting and heavy casualties, while the enemy joyfully exploited the initiative which President Truman had surrendered. Messrs. Truman and Acheson never did end the war in Korea, nor even mitigate its ferocity. Only when they were gone from office was a truce arranged. To get that truce, President Eisenhower made it known to Peking that the alternative would be an American offensive into North Korea to destroy the Chinese armies. President Truman and Secretary Acheson could have ended the fighting two years earlier if they had had the perception and wisdom to deal realistically with the enemy that President Eisenhower had.

After the Chinese intervention and a November 30 press conference statement by President Truman which did not rule out the use of atomic weapons, Prime Minister Atlee hurried to Washington for a review of war policy. Secretary Acheson reported:

> The line of Mr. Atlee's argument was that the position of our forces in Korea was so weak and precarious that we must pay for a cease-fire to extricate them. He believed that withdrawal from Korea and Formosa and the Chinese seat in the United Nations for the Communists would not be too high a price. There was nothing, he warned us, more important than retaining the good opinion of Asia. I remarked acidly that the security of the United States was more important.[4]

As talks continued, the Atlee purpose was further revealed:

> Atlee, who apparently liked to operate behind a smoke screen, proceeded to get further off the point. He raised the "difficult and delicate question" of General MacArthur's conduct of the Korean war and the absence of any allied say in what was done. Our two generals (Marshall and Bradley) defended MacArthur and said that a war could not be run by committee. The British had been consulted on matters tending to extend the war, such as the "hot pursuit" of enemy planes into Manchuria and the bombing of airfields there, and their views had been reflected in the action taken. The President added that since all concerned had confided the unified command to the United States we would have to run it as long as that situation continued and we continued to supply so preponderantly the means and the men to carry on the war.[5]

In his perversion of history, Mr. Acheson deals in the shibboleths of the established rhetoric. Those who did not see that
the war would "peter out" if the United States stopped fighting,
those who did not believe that granting sanctuary to Red China
avoided world war, are labeled "primitives." The value of alternative courses of action are not even examined—they are simply dismissed. The important point is that the Acheson foreign
policy proceeded not from any considered judgment of the factors of power and interest but from shallow and untenable
assumptions about the consequences of alternate lines of action. Mr. Acheson had obviously received the truth directly
from Sir Oliver Franks, the British Ambassador.

As Chief of Staff of the United States Army, a member of the
J.C.S. and Chief of the J.C.S. action agency (Army) for the war
in Korea, General J. Lawton Collins was close to the heart of
policymaking. His account of the war therefore makes an important contribution to our understanding of war policy.

On the issue of crossing the Thirty-eighth Parallel, General
Collins wrote:

> Later, on my next visit to Korea in August, this time with
> Admiral Sherman, we discussed with General MacArthur
> the possible follow-up of a successful landing at Inchon.
> We agreed with the General that he should be authorized
> to continue the attack across the Thirty-eighth Parallel to
> destroy the North Korean forces, which otherwise would
> be a recurrent threat to the independence of South Korea.[6]

Of early October, when the United Nations resolution on
Korea had been approved, General Collins wrote:

> There remained no question but that the U. N. General
> Assembly, President Truman, the U. S. Secretaries of State
> and Defense, and the U. S. Joint Chiefs of Staff all had
> approved the crossing of the Thirty-eighth Parallel. Most
> of the questions concerning the wisdom of this decision
> came after the event.[7]

When on November 5 the magnitude of the Chinese intervention became apparent, General McArthur ordered his Air Force to bomb the Korean sides of the Yalu River bridges. A copy of the order transmitted to Washington brought high-level consultation. General Collins wrote:

> Lovett [Deputy Secretary of Defense], doubting that the chances of destroying the bridges warranted the risk of hitting the Soviet city of Antung, at once informed Secretary of State Acheson, who called in Dean Rusk, then Assistant Secretary of State for Far Eastern Affairs. Rusk reminded Acheson that our Government had promised the British that we would take no action that might involve attacks on Manchuria without first consulting them. The United States was then pressing the U. N. Security Council for a resolution calling on the Chinese to cease their intervention in Korea. Rusk felt that this resolution, which was important for continued United Nations support of any future action by the United Nations forces in Korea against the Chinese Communist forces, would be endangered by any accidental bombing of Manchuria. He feared also the possibility of China's invoking the mutual defense treaty with the Soviet Union. Acheson and Lovett concluded that the attack should be held up pending clarification of the situation in Korea.
>
> General Marshall, the Secretary of Defense, concurred in their judgment.[8]

President Truman had the good judgment to qualify his action by saying he would approve the bombing only if there were an immediate and serious threat to the United Nations Command. When had an American Army ever been in greater jeopardy? Yet the J.C.S. ordered General MacArthur to suspend any bombing of the Yalu River bridges and all bombing within five miles of the Manchurian border. It stopped a field commander's action to protect his own forces. It disregarded a specific Presidential authorization of the bombing to humor the irrational fears of the civilian hierarchy.

In the Rusk thesis, you note at once the futility of even seeking a Council resolution against the Red Chinese aggression;

the British veto of U. S. policy (even though the proposed action did *not* contemplate action against Manchuria); and the idle fear that resistance to aggression would invoke a defense pact. Assistant Secretary Rusk was a key blocking back for British policy.

However, General Collins makes clear that the J.C.S. was at this time paralyzed by its own addled conceptions of military policy. It had formed, perhaps from the Berlin blockade, an obsession about the defense of Europe which made the J.C.S. reluctant to defend any other part of the Free World. Thus, the J.C.S. advised the National Security Council on November 9, in General Collins' words:

> After analyzing various considerations that might influence the Chinese to intervene in Korea, the Chiefs stated that in our judgment, the continued involvement of the United States in Korea would be in the interest of Russia and World Communism through its imposition of a heavy drain on our military and economic strength. We still considered Korea strategically unimportant in the context of a possible global war, in which Russia, not China, would be the chief antagonist. We doubted whether China would attempt to drive the United Nations forces from all of Korea without material assistance from Soviet naval and air power. In such event it would be clear that World War III was under way and the United States (and the United Nations) should withdraw from Korea as quickly as possible.[9]

This J.C.S. advice, so typical of the irrelevant, inept analysis which the J.C.S. was to bring to national policymaking in the years ahead, bears some analysis. Here were these military leaders, engaged in war, concerned not about winning that war but about remote and improbable events which might develop in Europe.

In global strategy, how do you get the enemy to fight you in Europe, where you mass your forces, and not in the remote areas where you don't want to fight? Do you sit in Europe and let him take the rest of the world?

Communism is a global though vastly inferior force. If you
refuse to protect an area of the Free World, you give it away.
Where will you draw the line? This question was so basic to the
Truman Doctrine that one would suppose it had been answered.
Apparently the J.C.S. had a very vague comprehension of the
world conflict.

Over all this was the reality of power. The United States had
nuclear weapons and the capacity to deliver them. The Soviet
Union was just beginning its bomb production. The idea that
the Soviet Union or Red China would at this time make war on
the United States was preposterous. Yet, in the thinking of the
Joint Chiefs of Staff, this was the dominant reality. They were
planning retreat before they even saw the shape of the attack
they imagined. Why did they regard Korea as a bleeding operation? It could become so only if they submitted to bleeding.

The fears of the Joint Chiefs of Staff about Soviet intervention in Korea contrast with the calm and objective appraisal of
risk made by field commanders. Admiral C. Turner Joy wrote
of his experiences in the Far East Command: "I know of not a
single military commander of United States forces in the Far
East—Army, Navy or Air Force—who believed the U.S.S.R.
would enter war with the United States because of any action
we might have taken relative to Red China."[10] That kind of
realistic appraisal could not be reached in Washington where
military judgments were warped by political considerations.

We know that Red China attacked our forces in North Korea
only after being assured that its sanctuary in Manchuria would
be allowed by the United States. Without that assurance, there
would have been no attack. How had these military leaders
been persuaded to such sloppy analysis of the power realities?

If I as a Soviet leader knew that the J.C.S. was so fearful of
me, I would certainly put a division or two into Korea just to see
the Americans run. And why wouldn't Soviet leaders know,
with Guy Burgess at the British Embassy in Washington, Don-
ald Maclean on the American desk in London, and Kim Philby
a consultant to the C.I.A.? Why would the Chinese hesitate to
assault a force whose leaders were poised for panic?

This J.C.S. assessment of the situation in Korea is so utterly aberrant to the realities of military power that it in fact constituted an obstacle to the creation of rational national policy. It made the formulation of relevant policy by the civilian leadership virtually impossible.

The truth of the matter is that the J.C.S. itself, as an organizational entity, was incapable of making sound policy. One human mind, charged with the responsibility of resolving conflicting staff differences, can come to a judgment because it must. But four human minds, charged with the same information, can only stall and compromise. The worst of all solutions is likely to become the common denominator.

How could President Truman, who so boldly intervened in Korea when we had only the skimpiest forces there, later be paralyzed with fear when he had his resources mobilized for battle? We can only turn to the conclusion of General MacArthur:

> The conference at Wake Island made me realize that a curious, and sinister, change was taking place in Washington. The defiant, rallying figure that had been Franklin Roosevelt was gone. Instead, there was a tendency toward temporizing rather than fighting it through. The original courageous decision of Harry Truman to meet and defeat communism in Asia was apparently being chipped away by the constant pounding whispers of timidity and cynicism. The President seemed to be swayed by the blandishments of some of the more selfish politicians of the United Nations. He seemed to be in the anomalous position of openly expressing fears of over-calculated risks that he had fearlessly taken only a few months before.[11]

General Collins thought the relief of General MacArthur was precipitated by four events: General MacArthur's visit to Formosa on July 31, which provoked ill-informed press speculation about reinforcing the island; MacArthur's statement to the Veterans of Foreign Wars, released to the press on August 26; MacArthur's offer of March 24 to confer in the field with the opposing commander; and MacArthur's letter to Congressman Joseph Martin, made public on April 5, 1951.

As General Collins noted, the MacArthur visit to Formosa, which was within his command area, and his behavior in that visit, were entirely proper and circumspect. It was the press speculation which nettled President Truman.

General Collins failed to note that the MacArthur message to the Veterans of Foreign Wars was sent subject to Washington clearance, in ample time for veto. It was the ineptitude—or was it the design?—of the Washington staff in withholding this message from the President until two days before the convention, and then exciting the Presidential wrath *after* the Veterans had released the text, which caused the whole imbroglio. The message was a routine statement of MacArthur's well-known views on the war. The General could not have cared less whether General Marshall approved the message or vetoed it.

The MacArthur proposal to the enemy commander for a battlefield truce was designed to exploit the punishment which the U. N. forces were then inflicting on the Chinese forces in order to reap the political fruit of military victory. It was unusual in American practice but a quite common action of Napoleon and his Marshals in their conquest of Europe. It was entirely within the prerogative of a battlefield commander. No doubt General MacArthur was moved by fear that the United States government, which had failed to reap the political fruit of the Inchon victory, would now throw away its new successes (as it did). That is why he moved to make a last effort at a battlefield solution.

The move did upset the President. But why the call for a battlefield truce should upset the negotiations of governments for a solution of conflict is not clear. That was the quick way to get a cease fire, if it proved workable. The call was refused on the spot and became a dead issue. It should not then have impeded any efforts the President had in hand for negotiation with the other side. Two years later, a truce was negotiated at Panmunjom by just such a meeting of military commanders.

It should be noted in this connection that on June 23, 1951, two months after the MacArthur initiative, Soviet Ambassador to the United Nations Jacob Malik suggested in a radio broadcast that commanders in the field should arrange a cease-fire. On June 30, 1951 General Matthew B. Ridgway, who had succeeded General MacArthur, acting on orders from Washington, broadcast an invitation to the opposing commanders to meet for discussion of truce talks on the Danish Hospital Ship Jutlandia in Wonsan Harbor. This initiative led to the meetings at Panmunjon and, after two years of negotiation, to a truce made possible by President Eisenhower's threat of offensive action. All negotiations were conducted by representatives of the opposing military commanders.

The letter to Congressman Martin conformed to MacArthur's lifetime practice of answering queries from Congressmen. He would have given the same answer to any other member of Congress who sought his views. The idea that he should mute or deny honest advice to Congress was simply outside his concepts of the American political system. What the Congressman did with the advice was a matter for the Congressman to decide, not a matter for General MacArthur to dictate.

Representative Martin's use of the MacArthur letter was no doubt indiscreet. But that was his political decision, not MacArthur's.

President Truman's real problem was that his staff assistants read into these events a MacArthur purpose of evasion and rebellion which simply did not exist. In all his communications with Washington, General MacArthur had been entirely frank in stating his position. He said nothing to anyone else which he had not already said to the Washington leadership. The events suggest that the President was manipulated by his councilors into a phobia against General MacArthur which finally exploded with release of the Martin letter. After the event, R. H. S. Crossman, a Labor member of Parliament and party theoretician, was to compliment Prime Minister Atlee for his part in procuring the removal of General MacArthur.

Of his own view on the removal of General MacArthur, General Collins wrote:

I remember saying—as I later testified—that I felt the
President was entitled to have a commander in the field
whose views were more in consonance with the basic policies of his government and who was more responsive to
the will of the President as Commander-in-Chief.[12]

This superficially plausible proposition is in reality deeply
erroneous. President Lincoln would have rejected it out of
hand. Honest Abe just wanted a general who could win the war,
and he searched a long time before he found one. In our government, the idea that a commander must be *simpatico* is likely
to exclude the ablest officers from command, with devastating
consequences to the country. Equally erroneous is the proposition that an officer must sympathize with the political views of
his superiors. Our officers must carry out orders regardless of
personal views, or ask for relief from command. There was no
evidence that General MacArthur ever failed to carry out the
orders he received.

The Collins dictum reflects the state of mind of the Joint
Chiefs of Staff. Instead of presenting honest military views and
then letting the political decision be made in the face of the
realities, military judgments were twisted to conform to the
political premises.

Thus, when the political decision was made to limit the war
to Korea, the military leaders testified that we couldn't bomb
Manchuria anyway. General Collins said:

I firmly believe that . . . when you start bombing, to make
it effective . . . you are involved in the bombing of cities and
all sorts of things, aside from the bombing of strictly military installations such as airfields.[13]

General Vandenberg said:

Air power, and especially the application of strategic air
power, should go to the heart of the industrial centers to
become reasonably efficient. . . . We could destroy or lay
waste to all of Manchuria and the principal cities of China

if we used the full power of the United States Air Force.
. . . If we use less than the full power of the Air Force, in
my opinion it might not and probably would not be conclu-
sive. . . . The attrition . . . would leave us, in my opinion,
naked for several years to come, and therefore I did not
advocate it.[14]

These comments of the military leaders are of course wholly
irrelevant. The issue was this: in order to hold the line of the
Yalu River, which United Nations forces had taken on orders
from Washington, it would be necessary to use *tactical* bombing against enemy forces up to 300 or 400 miles beyond the Yalu
—i.e., on the ground battlefield. The question of strategic bombing of the cities of China was an irrelevancy thrown in to confuse the public.

Generals Collins and Vandenberg must surely have known
that without such tactical bombing in Manchuria, we could not
hold North Korea. This air defense of the United Nations position in North Korea was implicit in the march to the Yalu
directed by the Joint Chiefs of Staff on September 27. It was
implicit in the United Nations resolution of October 7. To suppose that we would take over North Korea, destroy North Korean forces and then retreat as soon as China intervened was
to conceive utterly irresponsible war-making. Yet this was just
what the J.C.S. thought and did! Generals Collins and Vandenberg were bugling to the Russell Committee to cover up indefensible war policy.

When President Truman approved the removal of General
MacArthur, a new dilemma arose. How would the order be
conveyed to him? Obviously it was the duty of Secretary of
Defense George Catlett Marshall to go to Tokyo and deliver the
order. He was the President's cabinet officer in charge of the
war. This was a serious matter.

Secretary Marshall didn't go. He just didn't have the gumption to do what he had voted to do. An attempt was made to
reach Secretary of the Army Pace in Korea; and finally the
message was sent to G.H.Q. General MacArthur learned of his

removal from command when an aide heard a radio news broadcast of the announcement released in Washington.

This was not America speaking. What happened to these military leaders to undermine their judgment and their integrity? I think there were two causes.

After World War II, there arose from the bitter conflict over organization of the Defense Department a new fetish about "civilian control." We had had civilian control from the beginning of the Republic and no one had ever thought twice about it. It was written into a Constitution which required the Commander-in-Chief to be elected by the people and which gave Congress jurisdiction over the military forces. But in the scare tactic used to defeat sensible defense organization, the socialist spectre of the man on horseback had been introduced to American politics. In consequence, military leaders became exceedingly deferential to the civilian bureaucracy, as though its power came from God. The idea of civilian control was corrupted to mean that a civilian bureaucracy would make military decisions. This obsequious subordination of military men to political authority became not a national exercise of judgment but an unthinking ritual. No military leader would think of questioning the wisdom and judgment of a Dean Rusk about bombing the Yalu River bridges to protect an American Army in battle.

The other factor was of course the British control of American policy. While Dean Acheson was Secretary of State, the British sway was virtually absolute—tactful, of course, but absolute. Perhaps someday a historian will find one small deviation of Secretary Acheson from British policy, but none is known today. It was British influence, allied with civilian control of compliant military leadership, which imposed the fatal limitations of sanctuary upon our policy in Korea and in Vietnam.

From Korea to Vietnam, there have been changes—all of them for the worse. Military leadership in the Sixties was even more servile than it had been in the fifties. In Korea, it was possible to establish a battle line across the peninsula to protect our rear areas. In Vietnam our rear areas are continuously open to assault.

British policy dictation has been even more blatant in Vietnam than it was in Korea. British ships use the naval sanctuary at Haiphong which they have induced us to allow, operating a profitable trade with the enemy. Britain, pledged as a member of SEATO to oppose Communist aggression in Southeast Asia, instead aids the Communist aggression against its SEATO allies. Does history reveal a more flagrant breach of faith, or a more pitiful subservience than that of the United States? Our Presidents have been so immobilized by British propaganda that they are incapable of prudent self-defense.

Our illusions about Soviet good intentions and the potential for detente have led us to disarm, so that the enemy, with one-half our industrial power, has outstripped us in nuclear weaponry. Blind zealots in our society cry for further unilateral disarmament. The United States, weighted with false premises and with illusions of peacemaking, is headed straight for oblivion.

At home, in an era of unprecedented wealth and prosperity, our society is distracted about the occurrence of poverty. The ordinary differences of people are magnified into causes and conflict. The society of orderly and responsible people is being ravaged by attacks on the basic premises of its existence.

All these are the products of our dishonesty. The man who refuses to address a problem cannot solve it. He can only hope that somehow he will survive the effects of not solving it. But ours is not that kind of a problem. The effects of not solving it are clear. We have seen them in Russia, in China, in Eastern Europe, in North Korea, in North Vietnam. The question is whether our civilization will survive or free men will be enslaved. We shall not survive failure.

The American turn to appeasement invited the contempt of the Communist enemy. There have been many humiliations of the United States contrived by the Soviet Union and executed by its satellites. One of the most painful and prolonged has been the mistreatment of American prisoners of war.

Korea set the pattern. When the United States traded victory for negotiation as a war objective, it could no longer influence the enemy. We abandoned our prisoners to the merciless exploitation of the barbarians.

A soldier at war risks capture and imprisonment for the duration of the conflict, unless sooner exchanged. But in Korea, the release of prisoners, which should have been a first consideration of the armistice, was deferred to later settlement. We have never had a satisfactory accounting for American prisoners held in North Korea and Red China.

In Vietnam, we have followed the spineless precedent set in Korea. We have shown more concern about world opinion than about the welfare of our men in enemy prison camps. Appeals to the compassion of the barbarians only underscore the depravity of our position.

The conventions of war are designed to meliorate the suffering of war without giving advantage to either side. When the United States suffers an enemy to maltreat American prisoners without swift reprisal, it undermines the humanitarian convention. We must make the consequence of violation so painful that no enemy will choose that course. Why didn't President Johnson require a full exchange of prisoners as a condition for stopping the bombing of North Vietnam? Are we really so contemptible that we are beyond caring for these men who have suffered so much for us?

The reality is this: as long as the United States so obsequiously beseeches the forbearance of the Soviet Government, there can be no justice for our prisoners. Only a complete reversal of past policy can win Communist respect for our country and decent treatment for our men in enemy hands.

If Senator Fulbright and his mellow-tongued apologists for Communist aggression think the difference is small, I would be glad to banish them to Communist countries; but I see no reason why men who cherish freedom should submit to the kind of government these soothsayers are providing in America.

Let us be honest. The Communist system has in one half-century extended its rule over one-third of the world's population. It is functioning today, coordinated by dogma and plan and purpose, to destroy the free societies. By any objective measure its purposes are the same, and its resources are vastly multiplied since Lenin took power in Russia.

The Free World is divided in thought, word and deed. It has no agreement on an assessment of its own danger, on the political course to be followed, nor on the measures required for survival. It has an overwhelming advantage in population and resources and every measure of power except moral purpose. It defends by burying its head in the sand and refusing to recognize the enemy.

The first requirement of statesmanship is to recognize the war we are in. When government, before making any policy at all, commits itself to tell the people the truth about the known purposes, actions and intentions of the Commmunist enemy, the first step toward a sound strategy will have been taken.

When free people understand the threat to their existence they will rise up to meet it. Communism can prevail only if our leaders continue to deceive the people about Communist power and purpose.

When we have so identified the enemy, we can prepare to handle him. He is not a people or a country but a clique of ruthless dictators. His people are our friends. He is their enemy too, and this reality dictates the course of our strategy.

We must form a firm alliance with the Russian and Chinese peoples *against* their dictators. The people must choose freedom, but we can do much to help them.

We can show them that our commitment to freedom is honest and productive. We can extend to them, but not to their rulers, the hand of friendship. We can encourage them to recover their freedom. We can honor and comfort their exiles. We can supply assistance to the freedom underground. We can attack the tyrants in the United Nations, condemn their rule. With such encouragement, the people will throw off the yoke of tyranny. Not even a Communist dictator can hold power for long against the will of his people.

Only the hopelessness of freedom's cause behind the Iron

Curtain, shunned and condemned by free peoples who court the favor of the Communist dictators, has so demeaned the human spirit as to make resistance to tyranny unthinkable.

Winston Churchill's words in *The Gathering Storm* have special significance for the United States today:

> If you do not fight for the right when you can easily win without bloodshed—if you will not fight when your victory will be sure and not too costly, you may come to the moment when you will have to fight with all the odds against you and only a precarious chance of survival. You may have to fight when there is no hope of victory because it is better to perish than to live as slaves.[15]

Churchill's indomitable spirit drew from the British people their finest hour. America could today find in his example the courage to confront and destroy the Communist tyranny, even as he faced up to the Nazi tyranny. Through victory America could open a new age of peace and tranquillity.

The task of defeating the Communist dictators through internal revolution, of restoring freedom in all lands, of banishing war and beating weapons into plowshares is neither big nor difficult.

The formidable task is to change our own thinking, to repossess our truths and our courage, to wipe away the cloud of wishful thinking and to be objective again.

Then we can be honest. That is all there is to civilization. When people lose it, they lose everything. This is the trial which America faces today, in Vietnam and in the world.

Footnotes

★ ★ ★

Chapter 1   THE CURIOUS WAR

1. Douglas Pike, *Viet Cong* (Cambridge, Mass.: M.I.T. Press, 1966), p. viii.

Chapter 5   THE GENEVA SETTLEMENT

1. Douglas Pike, *supra,* p. 52.

Chapter 6   PEACEFUL INTERLUDE

1. Douglas Pike, *supra,* p. 57.

Chapter 9   THE POLICY MAKERS

1. Herman H. Dinsmore, *All the News That Fits* (New Rochelle, N.Y.: Arlington House, 1969), p. 58.

2. Bernard B. Fall, *The Two Vietnams* (New York: Frederick A. Praeger, 1967), p. 442.

Chapter 10   THE KENNEDY POLICY

1. Arthur M. Schlesinger Jr., *A Thousand Days* (Boston: Houghton Mifflin Co., 1965), p. 321.

2. Townsend Hoopes, *The Limits of Intervention* (New York: David McKay Co., 1969), p. 4.

3. Schlesinger, *supra,* p. 163.

4.   George F. Kennan, "American Involvement," in *The Vietnam Reader,* ed. by Marcus E. Raskin and Bernard B. Fall (New York: Random House), p. 28.

5.   Clarence Manion, *The Conservative American* (Victor Publishing Co., 1966), p.17.

Chapter 11   NEUTRALIZING LAOS

1.   Schlesinger, *supra,* p. 163.

2.   Schlesinger, *supra,* p. 332.

3.   *The New York Times,* March 24, 1961.

4.   Schlesinger, *supra,* p. 334.

5.   *The New York Times,* March 29, 1961.

6.   *The New York Times,* June 5, 1961.

7.   Walt W. Rostow, "Guerrilla Warfare in Underdeveloped Areas," in *The Vietnam Reader, supra,* p. 113.

8.   *The New York Times,* July 9, 1961.

9.   Thomas J. Dodd, "The New Isolationism," in *The Vietnam Reader, supra,* p. 168.

10.   Stephen Pan and Daniel Lyons, *Vietnam Crisis* (New York: East Asian Research Institute, 1966), p. 62.

11.   *The World Almanac* (1963), p. 108.

12.   *Ibid.*

13.   *The New York Times,* July 24, 1962.

14.   NBC News, April 4, 1970.

Chapter 12   THE DEFENSE OF SOUTH VIETNAM

1.   Schlesinger, *supra,* pp. 536–537.

2.   Raskin and Fall, *supra,* pp. 109, 111.

3.   Pike, *supra,* p. ix (Preface).

4.   Richard J. Barnet, *supra,* in Raskin and Fall, *supra,* p. 51.

5.   Rostow, *supra,* p. 113.

6.   Thomas J. Dodd, "The New Isolationism," in Raskin and Fall, *supra,* p. 169.

7.   *Ibid.,* p. 174.

8.   Pike, *supra,* p. 140.

Chapter 13   THE BETRAYAL

1. Robert S. McNamara, "Response to Aggression," in Raskin and Fall, *supra,* p. 200.

2. United Press International dispatch, Washington, D.C., May 7, 1961, in *Memphis Commercial Appeal,* May 8, 1961.

3. Pike, *supra,* in Raskin and Fall, *supra,* p. 72.

4. Schlesinger, *supra,* p. 538.

5. Pike, *supra,* p. 66.

6. Pike, *supra,* p. 58.

7. Schlesinger, *supra,* p. 543.

8. Paul Jones, *Intercollegiate Review* (Spring, 1970), p. 125.

9. Marguerite Higgins, "Saigon Summary," cited by Sen. Thomas J. Dodd in the U.S. Senate, Jan. 14, 1964.

10. *The New York Times,* July 3, 1963.

11. *The World Almanac* (1964), p. 116.

12. Marguerite Higgins, *New York Herald Tribune,* Aug. 26, 1963.

13. Pan and Lyons, *supra,* p. 117.

14. Marguerite Higgins, *Our Vietnam Nightmare* (New York: Harper & Row, 1965), p. 186.

15. Pan and Lyons, *supra,* p. 120.

16. Higgins, *supra,* p. 187.

17. Suzanne Labin, *Vietnam: An Eyewitness Account* (Crestwood Books, 1964), p. 34.

18. Labin, *supra,* p. 31.

19. White House statement, "U.S. Policy in Vietnam," in Raskin and Fall, *supra,* p. 128.

20. Higgins, "Saigon Summary," *supra.*

21. McGeorge Bundy, "The Next Steps Toward Peace," in Raskin and Fall, *supra,* pp. 163–164.

22. *The Catholic Virginian,* Aug. 2, 1963.

23. CBS, "Face the Nation," March 8, 1970.

24. Higgins, *Our Vietnam Nightmare, supra,* p. 214.

25. Higgins, *supra,* p. 215.

26. Anthony Bouscaren, *The Last of the Mandarins: Diem of Vietnam* (Duquesne University Press, 1965), p. 2.

Chapter 14   JOHNSON FACES CHAOS

1. McNamara, *supra,* in Raskin and Fall, *supra,* p. 200.

2. Higgins, *Our Vietnam Nightmare, supra,* p. 258.

3. Higgins, *supra,* p. 266.

4. *South Vietnam: U.S.-Communist Confrontation in Southeast Asia, 1961–65,* ed. by Lester A. Sobel et al. (New York: Facts On File, Inc., 1966), p. 111.

5. *Ibid.*

6. *Ibid.,* p. 94.

7. *Ibid.*

8. *Ibid.,* p. 114.

Chapter 15   THE GREAT PEACE GAMBIT

1. Admiral U.S.G. Sharp and General W.C. Westmoreland, *Report on the War in Vietnam* (Washington, D.C.: Government Printing Office, 1969), p. 98.

2. Townsend Hoopes, *The Limits of Intervention* (New York: David McKay Co., 1969), p. 44.

3. *South Vietnam: U.S.-Communist Confrontation in Southeast Asia, 1961–65, supra,* p. 209.

4. *Ibid.,* p. 136.

5. *Ibid.,* p. 212.

6. *Ibid.,* p. 213.

7. Pan and Lyons, *supra,* p. 213.

8. *South Vietnam: U.S.-Communist Confrontation in Southeast Asia, 1961–65, supra,* p. 153.

9. Pan and Lyons, *supra,* p. 202.

10. Pan and Lyons, *supra,* p. 242.

Chapter 16   TURNING THE TIDE

1. Hoopes, *supra,* p. 62.

2.   Pan and Lyons, *supra,* p. 261.

3.   *The Wanderer,* St. Paul, Minn., Nov. 3, 1966.

4.   Pan and Lyons, *supra,* p. 273.

5.   *Ibid.,* p. 274.

6.   *Ibid.*

Chapter 18   THE TET ASSAULT

1.   Gen. Jan Segna, "Russia Plotted the *Pueblo* Attack," *Reader's Digest* (July, 1969), p. 74.

2.   Hoopes, *supra,* p. 59.

3.   Hoopes, *supra,* p. 21.

4.   Edward Gibbon, *The History of the Decline and Fall of the Roman Empire,* ed. by Dr. William Smith (New York: Bigelow, Brown & Co.), Vol. 1, p. 701.

5.   Lyndon B. Johnson, "American Policy in Vietnam," in Ruskin and Fall, *supra,* p. 346.

Chapter 19   THE NIXON POLICY

1.   Richard M. Nixon, "Needed in Vietnam: The Will to Win," *Reader's Digest* (August, 1964).

2.   *Washington Evening Star,* April 5, 1970.

3.   Sir Robert Thompson, *No Exit From Vietnam* (New York: David McKay, 1969), p. 197.

Chapter 20   STRATEGIC APPRAISAL

1.   *U.S.News & World Report,* Oct. 27, 1969.

Chapter 21   THE MILITARY FACTOR

1.   Dwight D. Eisenhower, *Waging Peace* (New York: Doubleday, 1965), p. 610.

2.   Schlesinger, *supra,* p. 337.

3.   Schlesinger, *supra,* p. 338.

4.   Hoopes, *supra,* p. 53.

5.   Maxwell D. Taylor, "Post-Vietnam Role of the Military in Foreign Policy," *Air University Review* (Maxwell A.F.B., Ala.), July-August 1968, Vol. 19, No. 5.

Chapter 22   THE TOWER OF BABEL

1. J. W. Fulbright, "The War in Vietnam," in Raskin and Fall, *supra,* pp. 205–208.

2. Barnet, *supra,* in Raskin and Fall, *supra,* p. 46.

3. Dodd, *supra,* in Raskin and Fall, *supra,* p. 174.

4. Barnet, *supra,* in Raskin and Fall, *supra,* p. 48.

5. Raskin and Fall, *supra,* p. 5.

6. Raskin and Fall, *supra,* p. 211.

7. Raskin and Fall, *supra,* p. 6.

8. Hans J. Morgenthau, "Are We Deluding Ourselves in Vietnam?" in Raskin and Fall, *supra,* p. 32.

9. *Ibid.,* p. 40.

10. *Ibid.,* p. 40.

11. George F. Kennan, "American Involvement," Report of the Subcommittee on the Far East and the Pacific, Committee on Foreign Affairs, House of Representatives, released May 14, 1965. Cited in Raskin and Fall, *supra,* p. 16.

12. *Ibid.*

13. *Ibid.*

14. *Ibid.*

15. Hoopes, *supra,* p. 109.

16. Hoopes, *supra,* p. 125.

17. Cited in Hoopes, *supra,* p. 129.

18. Hoopes, *supra,* p. 146.

19. Hoopes, *supra,* p. 176.

20. Hoopes, *supra,* p. 203.

Chapter 23   TRIAL AND JUDGMENT

1. Dean G. Acheson, *Present at the Creation* (New York: W. W. Norton & Co., 1969), p. 531.

2. *Ibid.,* p. 526.

3. *Ibid.,* p. 452.

4. *Ibid.,* p. 481.

5. *Ibid.,* p. 483.

6. J. Lawton Collins, *War in Peacetime* (New York: Houghton Mifflin Co., 1969), p. 144.

7. *Ibid.,* p. 149.

8. *Ibid.,* p. 200.

9. *Ibid.,* p. 205.

10. Admiral C. Turner Joy, *How Communists Negotiate* (Santa Monica, Calif.: Fidelis Publishers Inc., 1970), p. 177.

11. Douglas MacArthur, *Reminiscences* (New York: McGraw-Hill Book Co., 1964), p. 363.

12. Collins, *supra,* p. 283.

13. Collins, *supra,* p. 290.

14. Collins, *supra,* p. 291.

15. Winston Chruchill, *The Gathering Storm* (New York: Houghton Miflin Co., 1948), p. 348.

4

BAY

OF

BENGAL

ANDAMAN   SEA

ANDAMAN
ISLANDS

NICOBAR
ISLANDS

MYMENSINGH
Sylhet
Kishorganj
DACCA
COMILLA
AGARTALA
CHITTAGONG
Cox's Bazar
Noakhali
Rangamati

MANDALAY
MYINGYAN
Sagaing
Monywa
PROME
HENZADA
RANGOON
BASSEIN
Pegu
BILIN
MOULMEIN
TAVOY
Mergui

AKYAB
Pyinmana
Toungoo

MOUTHS OF THE
IRRAWADDY
GULF OF
MARTABAN

CHIANG MAI
CHIANG RAI
PHITSANULOK
Sukhothai
Uttaradit
KRUNG THEP
BANGKOK
Phet Buri
Prachuap Khiri Khan
Chumphon
SURAT THANI
Nakhon Si Thammarat
PHUKET
Trang
Songkhla

GULF

OF

THAILAND

PHONG SALY
SON LA
KENGTUNG
Luang Prabang
Vientiane
LAOS
VIETNAM

CHANTHABURI
BATTAMBANG
PHNOM
PENH
Kompong Som

CHIEN-SHUI
MENG-TZU
K'AI-YUAN
WEN-SHAN
CHINA

TEN DEGREE
CHANNEL

DUNCAN PASSAGE

SOUTH ANDAMAN I
Port Blair

MIDDLE ANDAMAN I
RITCHIE'S ARCHIPELAGO

LITTLE ANDAMAN I

GREAT NICOBAR I

25°
24°
23°
22°
20°
19°
18°
17°
16°
15°
14°
13°
12°
11°
10°
9°
8°
7°

95°
100°

MALAY PE